THE OLYMPICS CITY

What better time to visit Los Angeles, the sun, sand, surf and cinema center of the world, than the summer of 1984, when you can see California and take in the summer Olympic Games as well. But it's not easy to get around in L.A., even for an experienced traveler, and since the more than 20 Olympic events will be held at 25 different locations, you'll need the clearest, most complete guide possible.

The *Los Angeles Times* Olympics Guide is designed specifically to make your visit fun and hassle-free, whatever your interests, regardless of how much (or little) you plan to spend while you're in L.A. Here, under one cover, is an information-packed Olympic Games handbook—complete with maps, calendar of Olympic events, and list of places to go before and after the games—as well as an essential guide to travel in Southern California at any time of year.

THE
Los Angeles Times
OLYMPICS GUIDE TO L.A.
AND SOUTHERN CALIFORNIA

Super Sports Books from SIGNET

THE
Los Angeles Times
OLYMPICS GUIDE TO L.A.
AND SOUTHERN CALIFORNIA

**By the Editors
of the
*Los Angeles Times***

Introduction by Jack Smith, Columnist

A SIGNET BOOK

NEW AMERICAN LIBRARY

Ø SIGNET TRADEMARK REG. U.S. PAT. OFF. AND FOREIGN COUNTRIES
REGISTERED TRADEMARK—MARCA REGISTRADA
HECHO EN CHICAGO, U.S.A.

SIGNET, SIGNET CLASSIC, MENTOR, PLUME,
MERIDIAN and NAL BOOKS
are published by New American Library, 1633 Broadway,
New York, New York 10019

First Printing, April, 1984

  2 3 4 5 6 7 8 9

PRINTED IN THE UNITED STATES OF AMERICA

Contents

PART 3

The peristyle entrance to the Los Angeles Memorial Coliseum, the site of the 1932 and 1984 Olympiads.

INTRODUCTION

Los Angeles: The Olympics City
by Jack Smith, Columnist

When the Tenth Olympiad was held here in 1932, Los Angeles was thought of by eastern journalists and their readers—when they thought of it at all—as an overgrown Midwestern cow town in a cultural wasteland.

There was some truth in that view. Downtown Los Angeles, its buildings limited to twelve stories in fear of earthquakes, looked much like Milwaukee and Des Moines. One of the earliest and most durable of the many scornful epithets invented for it was "Double Dubuque."

Few Angelenos were natives. They spoke with twangs or drawls that betrayed the states of their origin. Their regional inflections had not yet been amalgamated into "Californian."

The nation was aware of Los Angeles only through the annual Tournament of Roses and the Rose Bowl football game, which are held in Pasadena, and through newspaper accounts of Hollywood scandals.

The cultural event that received the most coverage in the local newspapers was the annual Iowa picnic at Sycamore Grove.

In 1932 Los Angeles was already, by annexation and default, the nation's largest city geographically, sprawling over the coastal plain between the San Gabriel Mountains and the Pacific, and spilling like floodwater into the San Fernando Valley. But much of the land was still in beanfields and truck farms. Wilshire Boulevard passed through the countryside on its way to Santa Monica. A village was constructed on a barren hillside overlooking the stubby city to house the Olympic athletes.

Today, two generations later, visitors who come for the

1

1984 Olympics will find Los Angeles grown to the nation's second most populous city, its vast area settled almost to the bursting point by Americans seeking warmth, dreams, and a change; by immigrants seeking a better life; and by refugees from turmoil and oppression.

Instead of an outpost of the American Midwest, visitors will find what is perhaps the world's most cosmopolitan and polyglot city, a city oriented toward the Pacific and the Far East. Most Olympic competitors and visiting spectators, wherever they come from, will be able to find in Los Angeles an enclave of their countrymen, speaking their language.

Chinatown and Little Tokyo go back further than 1932, though the Japanese were forced to abandon their ground during World War II, and not long after the war the old Chinatown

Queen Anne Cottage at the Los Angeles State and County Arboretum in the San Gabriel Valley. This building is also the setting for television's *Fantasy Island.*

Chinatown, just a few minutes north of the downtown business district. *The Chinese Historical Society*

was razed; but the Japanese came back to reclaim and revitalize Little Tokyo, and the Chinese moved a few blocks away and built a new Chinatown.

Since the Korean War, Korean immigrants have established their turf in Koreatown, making a town within a city, not by building but by the vigorous infiltration and renewal of a decaying central neighborhood. Thus today we find a Protestant Korean congregation worshiping in a former synagogue, with sunlight pouring through a Star of David in a stained-glass window.

And all over Los Angeles you will find Thai and Vietnamese restaurants in storefronts and other humble quarters; the fare is exotic, spicy, and inexpensive.

As your aircraft descends toward Los Angeles International Airport, you may even be impressed by the skyline, which soars up to sixty stories in slender sticks of mirrored glass and steel, though it would hardly cast a shadow in New York.

But you may look in vain for a landmark that gives you a sudden flash of recognition, even though you have seen it only in magazines and movies. Unless your eyes happen to catch our City Hall, the white tower you may have seen in *Dragnet* and other TV shows, you will see no mark that says "Los Angeles," as the Statue of Liberty and the Manhattan skyline say "New York," the Big Ben clock tower says "London," the Eiffel Tower says "Paris."

It is this lack of familiar structures, along with the city's sheer size and its fragmentation by freeways, that disorients and sometimes demoralizes visitors. It was also what inspired another of our epithets—"The Nowhere City."

Finding no monolithic landmarks from the air, however, you will sense that you are looking at a city unlike any other. You will fly in over desert or ocean, suddenly to see below you the seemingly endless carpet of rooftops; the long streets lined with palm trees; the thousands of swimming pools—variously colored green, blue, turquoise—like jewels scattered by some profligate sheikh; freeways curving, looping, soaring, intersecting in knots, and alive with cars. You will look down on miles of seashore, curving around the metropolis from Malibu to Seal Beach, putting an end, finally, to the ocean's greed for land.

If your eyes are sharp, you will detect the *Queen Mary*, sealed for eternity in her berth at Long Beach Harbor, and nearby the enormous geodesic bubble under which, like a pea under a shell, we have entombed the enigmatic billionaire Howard Hughes' mythical white elephant, the Spruce Goose.

If your airliner has approached by land, you will already have passed over Disneyland and spotted the fiberglass Matterhorn, capped by its permanent mantle of plastic snow.

By the time you touch down and are disgorged into the airport, the bewildering labyrinth called LAX, you will already be well indoctrinated into the great transcendental and all-encompassing myth—the myth that Los Angeles is not real.

Perhaps it would be a shame, and pointless, to disillusion you. You will already have seen about all that most visiting journalists will see of Los Angeles before they round up the usual clichés and write their stories.

Among the legacies of billionaires, Hughes' flying boat is a toy compared to the two-thousand-year-old Roman villa built by the oil plutocrat Paul Getty on a wooded hillside above Malibu. It is only a fanciful copy of a villa buried by the eruption of Vesuvius in A.D. 79, but it looks magnificent in its setting, and Getty stocked it with classical sculpture and left money enough that it need never beg.

Gradually, as you explore Los Angeles, and of course its suburbs—whatever their municipal names may be, they are a part of the metropolis, sharing its insults, breathing its air—you will discover that the line blurs between illusion and reality.

It will vanish altogether if you drive into the Hollywood Hills, just a short way up the coiling streets above the Boulevard. For here you will find the houses that Nathanael West decried in *The Day of the Locust*, a novel that portrays Los Angeles as surreal, a nowhere place of false fronts and hopeless dreams.

They are still there: bungalows disguised as Spanish castles, Swiss chalets, Tudor houses, Chinese pagodas, Islamic mosques, all fabricated of two-by-fours and plaster, like movie sets. These dwellings were not dropped on the landscape by some mischievous dirigible; they were built by artists and craftsmen who worked in the studios and for whom the construction of illusions was all in the day's work. Today they are lived in by a new generation of tenants who believe in make believe and have their own set of myths and dreams.

The nabobs of the film industry and the merchants and tycoons who came here from the frigid Midwest to retire in Hancock Park or Beverly Hills were no less afflicted by romantic fancies than the craftsmen; their mansions of brick and stone were/are more expensive and more pretentious versions of the miniature castles and tombs to be found above the Boulevard.

Everywhere in Los Angeles visitors can find signs of this impulse to make believe, this playfulness. In a place where tradition has little force, where everything is optional and the sun shines almost always, people will play.

This freedom, though, has attracted and nourished not only playful artificers but also generations of distinguished architects. In recent years, design critics have discovered Los Angeles, and have called it among the most interesting cities, architecturally, in the world.

The visitor interested in the works of Wright, Schindler, Neutra, the brothers Greene, and other architects of international repute can find their houses here among the Spanish balconies and Moroccan minarets. The city itself is a virtual museum of commercial buildings in the Art Deco and Art Moderne vogue of the twenties and thirties.

You will have heard it said that Los Angeles has no decent restaurants. In fact, as you may learn elsewhere in this book, it has hundreds of excellent restaurants, serving an internationally diversified cuisine, and they don't make hamburgers better anywhere else in the world.

Of course, some of the clichés and complaints are true. Unless you drive or can be driven, transportation is frustrating, if not impossible. If there are two places you want to see, don't count on being able to walk from one to the other, and don't count on finding a taxi, except, perhaps, in front of your hotel.

Some days the air is less than pure; some days it is dreadful. But many days, especially in winter or after a rain, are clear and lovely, and it's true—you *can* see Catalina.

You have to live here to enjoy living here. If you've come for the Olympic Games, but want to find out why people live in Los Angeles, you'd better stay over for a year.

Once you learn to drive them, the freeways are a wonderful place to get your head together; and the Februaries are grand.

Cautionary Note

The Olympics events of 1984 will not only bring many visitors to Southern California, but may also cause some changes in hours, telephone numbers, and location for certain establishments. Add this to the vastness of the area and the complexity of the many communities of which it is composed, and the reader is cautioned to always double check by telephone before embarking on an outing for dinner or a performance.

A single telephone call in advance can confirm the information contained in this guide, or if there has been a change, save one needless trouble. And, remember, details as to the best route for travel need to be double checked when traveling in the world's most extensive city.

The New Los Angeles Telephone Area Code

As of January 7, 1984, the traditional Los Angeles 213 area code has been divided, with 818 added, and 213 to continue. But don't worry, Pacific Bell and General Telephone are doing it in an orderly manner. It works as follows:

For these communities, 818 has become their new area code: San Fernando Valley, La Canada, Burbank, Glendale, Covina, Monrovia, El Monte, Pasadena, Alhambra, and part of Monterey Park and other northern Los Angeles County areas.

Downtown Los Angeles, Beverly Hills, Malibu, West Los Angeles, and the southern part of Los Angeles County will retain 213.

While the 818 prefix may be used beginning January 7, 1984, *it is not necessary to use it* for the first nine months of operation.

Beginning in October 1984, if you forget to use 818 where it is appropriate, you will automatically be told to redial and which prefix to use.

The cost of calls from the 213 to the 818 area or vice versa, or of outside calls into these two areas, *will not change*.

PART 1

How to Get Around in Los Angeles
by Kenneth Reich, Olympics Correspondent

Not only athletes, but spectators, will have their ingenuity tested if they are to perform in Southern California—the athletes to win gold medals, the spectators to position themselves to see them win.

Other summer Olympic cities have had events scattered hither and yon, but it is safe to say that no Games in Olympics history will have quite the scattered quality of the Los Angeles Games. From one end of the 1984 Olympics to the other lie two hundred miles of mostly urbanized Southern California—from Santa Barbara on the north, where athletes competing in the rowing and canoeing events will live, to Fairbanks Ranch near San Diego on the south, where an endurance equestrian event will be held. And the Games extend nearly sixty miles inland, to San Bernardino County's Prado Recreational Area, where the shooting ranges have been constructed.

There is even considerable range climatically among the twenty-five different cities and five distinct unincorporated areas where Olympic events or training will take place. It is not at all uncommon during July and August for the temperature to be in the low 70s in Santa Monica, where the marathon runs will start, while at the same time, forty miles away, it is in the high 90s at the Santa Anita racetrack in Arcadia, where most of the equestrian events will be held. Smog levels also vary widely within the Los Angeles metropolitan area, although Olympic planners have carefully situated most of the events and training in locales close to the Pacific, where smog is usually not a major factor.

Traveling around to see the 1984 Olympics is going to be a challenge, especially if one holds tickets to a variety of events. Those interested in seeing just fencing can, perhaps, find a hotel within walking distance of the Long Beach Convention Center, where all the matches will take place. But those who have tickets for track and field in central Los Angeles, water polo in Malibu, wrestling in Anaheim in Orange County, cycling in Carson, and canoeing at Lake Casitas in Ventura County—to name one mix—are likely to find themselves on the freeways for long periods day after day, and not always in public or charter buses either. They will need, at least on some occasions, to drive or be driven in rented cars, taxicabs, or private autos.

Los Angeles at the best of times is confusing as well as entertaining. Even longtime residents often know their way well only in limited areas, and are acquainted with only some of the 750 miles of freeways, not to mention thousands of miles of major surface streets. During the Olympics, if precautions of traffic planners are taken into account, there will, at the very least, be added problems.

Good news: There will be a special Olympic bus service. The board of the Southern California Rapid Transit District will be operating an $11.8 million system of 475 buses rolling on special lines to take up to 300,000 spectators each day during the sixteen-day Olympic period to and from events at one-way fares of $2, $4, or $6.

The lines will not go everywhere and they will not always be of great frequency. They will be at least moderately expensive. The fare plan, for example, calls for a $2 one-way charge between downtown Los Angeles and the Coliseum, just four miles away, where opening and closing ceremonies and eight days of track-and-field competition will be held. This means it would cost a family of four $16 a day to make the trip both ways. If they come from park-and-ride facilities in the suburbs, the family round-trip charge will be $48.

Boxing and swimming events will be held close to the Coliseum too, in what is as much of an Olympic complex as Los Angeles will have. So if someone is lucky enough to be staying in the downtown area and be holding tickets to the Coliseum-area events, he or she might find walking to be a desirable alternative.

Charter buses from outlying areas may not be a cost-saving answer; most companies have already posted rate increases for the Olympic period.

More good news: Adequate parking will be available at most of the outlying Olympic avenues, and the scattered nature of the sites means that there won't be heavy traffic involved in getting to all of them. So, in these cases, driving oneself becomes much more feasible; the car-rental companies have announced extensive plans for increasing the size of their fleets (and, like the charter bus companies, increasing the rates charged during the Games).

Good advice: Taking the bus will be by far the best motorized option for arriving at the Coliseum area. All of these sites will have severe traffic and parking problems. At the Coliseum, for example, the Los Angeles Olympic Organizing Committee has leased all the public parking spaces for use by buses and dignitaries. Those who make their way on their own through expected traffic jams to the vicinity will apparently have to park in the backyards and driveways of local residents, perhaps at great expense and in unguarded spaces. In addition, a whole set of new one-way or bus-only streets are being set up in the areas of greatest traffic problems, so the usual maps of pre-Olympics periods won't be of much use.

"Uncertain"—that is probably the best word to describe the prospects for satisfactory travel to Olympic events. Scenic variety—that is probably the best benefit in travel to sites scattered from the ocean to the inland mountains. The most sensible course will be to start early, be prepared for some delays and expense, and trust to a gradual ironing out of the kinks in traffic and transportation systems as the Games proceed. Visitors should plot the events for which they have tickets on a map, then try to locate themselves in accessible hotels or other accommodations. Residents may have a marginal advantage in knowing the city, but even for them the Olympics period is likely to pose real tests of endurance.

What Happens When I Arrive?

Los Angeles International Airport (LAX)

LAX was one of the world's most overcrowded and frustrating airports, but its remodeling, which coincides with the 1984 Olympics Year, has achieved a minor miracle. In the past, all arrivals and departures were on the same level. Now, arrivals are on the lower level and departures on the upper level. This and other improvements, including construction of international computer terminal facilities and the expansion by individual airlines, have greatly eased congestion and made LAX a positive experience.

In addition to taxi service, there are numerous bus services offered for arriving and departing passengers. For information regarding these services call (213) 646-5252 for general information and (213)-AIRPORT for recorded information.

Upon arrival one can find a bus dispatcher's kiosk outside each terminal. There are frequent departures to all major areas and centrally located hotels. Rates are generally about 20 to 30 percent of taxi fares. If one's destination is one of the hotel drop-offs or a nearby area, the bus service could be advantageous.

Taxis are available at dispatcher's stations. Be sure to confirm the route and estimated fare before departure with the dispatcher's assistance. From LAX to downtown or to West Los Angeles (Beverly Hills and Hollywood) takes about thirty minutes or a little more, and surface routes are sometimes faster and cheaper than freeway routes.

The most frequently asked LAX question is, How do I get from one terminal to another? Take the airport tram, the "A" shuttle bus, which makes frequent stops outside all terminals.

Following is a map of LAX and its access routes. Major passenger services are listed below and keyed to the map.

LAX ROADWAY ACCESS

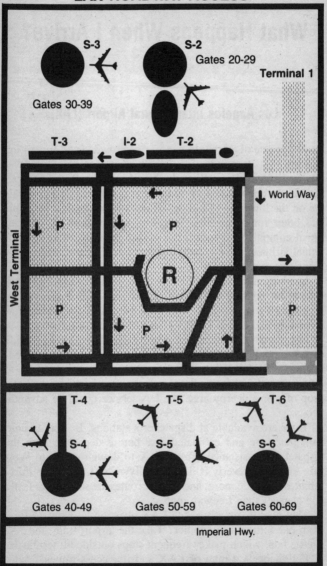

See pages 14-15 for map legend.

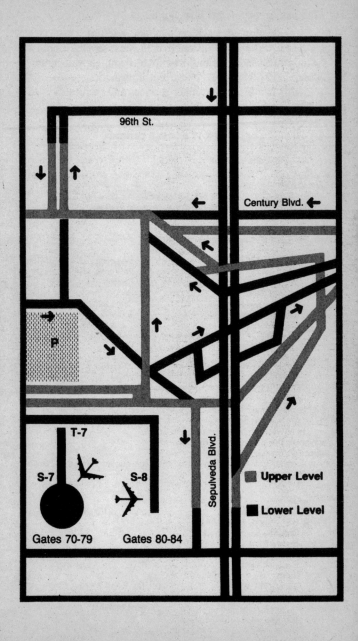

Note: As relocation of some airlines and addition of service by new air carriers are anticipated over the next several months, the list of airlines and locations may not be completely accurate. Telephone (213) 646-5252 for current information.

Following is a list of passenger services and facilities keyed to the LAX map.

LAX ROADWAY ACCESS LEGEND

Passenger Services and Facilities:

I. Airline Terminals   Note: These locations are subject to change and should be confirmed at (213) 646-5252.

Terminal 1: PSA, Air California, Southwest, MUSE Air, US Air.

Terminal 2: Pan Am, Northwest, CAAC, LTU, Avianca, Hawaiian Express, Capitol, Air Canada.

Terminal 3: TWA, Eastern, Pacific Express.

West Terminal (most international carriers):

Aerolíneas Argentinas	Mexicana
Aeroméxico	Philippine
Air France	Qantas
Air New Zealand	SAS
British Airways	Singapore
British Caledonian	TACA
China Airlines	Transamerica
CP Air	TWA
Japan Air Lines	UTA
KLM	Varig
Korean Air Lines	Western
LACSA	World
Lufthansa	

Terminal 4: American, Mojave, Dash Air, Wings West, Sun Aire, Airspur, Desert Sun, Western Pacific.

Terminal 5: Western, Air Resorts, Pacific Coast.

Terminal 6: Delta, Continental, Republic, Frontier.

Terminal 7: United, Finnair, Imperial.

At the Imperial Terminal at 6661 West Imperial Highway: World Airways, Pacific East, Regent Air.

II.   Facilities

1. Airport Security	Telephone: (213) 646-6254
2. Barbershop, 7 A.M.–7 P.M.	S-6
3. Christian Science Reading Room, 7 A.M.–7 P.M.	S-7
4. Cocktail Lounges, 6 A.M.–2 A.M. daily	S-2, S-3, S-4, S-5, S-6, S-7, S-8, R
5. Bars 7 A.M.–11 P.M. daily	1-2, S8, T-6, T-7
6. Currency Exchange	1-2, S-2, S-3, S-4, T-5, S-6, and West Terminal

7. Duty-free Shops	S-2, S-3, S-4, S-5, T-2, and West Terminal
(All purchases must be made one hour before departure on non-stop international flights.)	
8. Host International Restaurant; at center of airport	R
9. Newsstands	S-2, S-3, S-4, S-5, S-6, S-7, S-8, and West Terminal
and 24-hour service in	S-2, T-6
10. Lost and Found	Check airline or call (213) 646-4268
11. Medical, First Aid	Telephone: (213) 646-6254
12. Observation Deck, 9 A.M.–5 P.M. daily at Host International Restaurant	R
13. Parking	P
14. Police Department	Telephone: (213) 646-2256
15. Traffic Radio, 7 A.M.–11 P.M., daily	(530 am dial)
16. Travelers Aid 7 A.M.–10 P.M. Monday–Friday 9 A.M.–9 P.M. weekends	T-2, T-3, T-4, T-5, T-6, T-7
17. USO Desk afternoons/evenings	S-4 Telephone: (213) 642-0188
18. Visitors and Convention Bureau	R (213) 215-0606
19. Wheelchairs	Check airline

Greater Los Angeles Area Map

To cope with the seemingly endless stretch of freeways and urban/suburban sprawl of the Los Angeles Basin, the visitor needs to grasp a few basic facts.

Los Angeles is not a city in the traditional sense. There is a growing downtown with a burgeoning skyline and redevelopment, but ultimately greater Los Angeles is a collection of many separate communities, each with its own life-style and business center. H. L. Mencken called it "Double Dubuque," and indeed the Iowa Day picnic is a popular event. But many of Los Angeles' "Double Dubuques" have matured into progressive and lively communities. Pasadena, Santa Monica, Long Beach, and Anaheim (to name a few)—each seems light-years from the other. And, indeed, a resident of Santa Monica might visit San Francisco or New York more often than Pasadena or Anaheim.

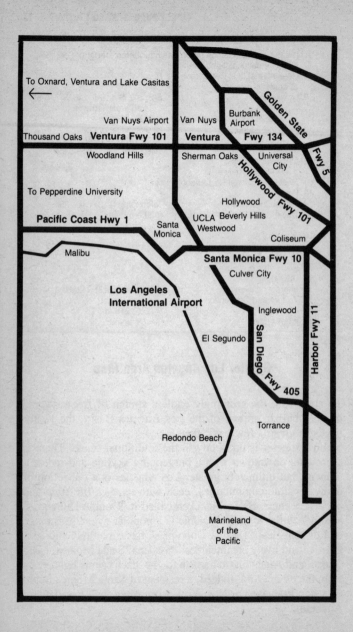

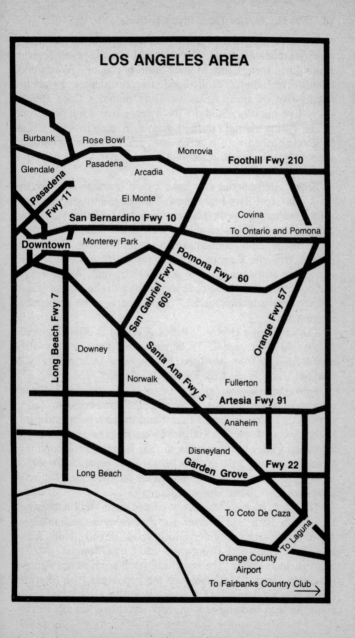

In fact, during normal traffic, the freeways bring these communities relatively close. The primary barrier is psychological. From downtown, Santa Monica is thirty minutes; Westwood, twenty-five minutes; Hollywood, twenty minutes; Pasadena, twenty-five minutes; Anaheim, forty minutes; Long Beach, thirty-five minutes; Studio City, twenty-five minutes. If one elects, during the right traffic hours, a drive "across town" can be accomplished with relative ease, and a unique community with its own heritage, restaurants, and life-style can be found at the other end.

Every international city has its own characteristic driving style: Mexico City's high-speed, bumper-to-bumper precision drill; Manhattan's pocket billiard, pot-hole destruction derby; and Paris' waterbug scramble. The Southern California driver? Professional, cold-blooded, and no room for error. As long as no one errs, the flow of traffic is rapid. If an accident does occur, the freeways come to a screeching halt. As one radio station traffic commentator reported from his helicopter watch shortly after a fender-bender, "There seems to be perceptible movement."

The California Highway Patrol (CHIPS) is efficient, courteous, and professional. To be respected, they strike swiftly and seemingly from nowhere. For highway information, you can call CHIPS, not Erik Estrada, (213) 626-7231.

Surrounding and dividing the greater Los Angeles Basin are a series of mountain ranges. North of the San Fernando Valley is the Los Padres National Forest and the San Fernando pass; to the northeast, the San Gabriel Mountains rise above the San Fernando Valley and Pasadena; the San Bernardino Mountains, to the north and east of San Bernardino, separate the basin from Palm Springs; to the southeast are the Cleveland National Forest and the Santa Monica Mountains.

The Santa Monica Mountains extend from Malibu eastward to Griffith Park and Chavez Ravine (Dodger Stadium) and separate West Los Angeles (Hollywood, Beverly Hills, Century City, Westwood, Brentwood, and Santa Monica) from the San Fernando Valley. The two major north-south passes through the Santa Monica Mountains are the Sepulveda Pass (the San Diego Freeway) and the Cahuenga Pass (the Hollywood Freeway). Several twisting canyon roads also traverse these mountains and form the stylish residential areas of Coldwater Canyon, Beverly Glen, Laurel Canyon, Beachwood Canyon, and others. Riding the crest of the Santa Monica Mountains from the Hollywood Freeway to beyond the San Diego Freeway is Mulholland Drive. On a clear day or night, this is the perfect way to see, from a bird's-eye view, much of Los Angeles.

This basin, ringed by five-thousand-foot-high (and more) mountain peaks (Mt. San Gorgonio near Palm Springs is over ten thousand feet, and Mt. Wilson overlooking Pasadena is over five thousand feet), faces southwest onto the ocean. The Santa Monica Mountains' seaward extension is the Santa Barbara Channel Islands. To the south, the high plateau of the Palos Verdes Peninsula overlooks the city, and its seaward point, Point Vicente, looks out twenty-plus miles to Catalina Island. And, one can proceed south to the beach communities of Balboa, Newport, and Laguna; to the north, from Malibu on to Ventura and Santa Barbara.

A magnificent and diverse physical setting, there is one curse, however. The basin, ringed as it is by mountains, acts as a natural trap for air pollution. Only high winds or stormy weather can ease the smog. And when this happens, the view is breathtaking. After a storm or a high wind, it's not uncommon to see, from Mulholland Drive or from a vantage point on the coast, the snow-capped peaks of the San Gabriel or San Bernardino mountains, some fifty miles away.

Rules of the Road

In Los Angeles, the car's the thing, and if you have one or have rented one, be sure to become familiar with Los Angeles streets and freeways. (This is the key to "happy" motoring in and around the large basin.) A detailed and thorough street map will become your best friend, so be sure to study it carefully and learn to depend on it.

If you're driving in or out of Los Angeles on an excursion, or simply trying to get across "the basin," which is the world's *largest* city, the Automobile Club of Southern California could be an invaluable service. Emergency roadside service and vast and detailed amounts of information are available to *members*.

A telephone call [general information (213) 741-4070] to this *AAA* affiliate will quickly inform you regarding travel and weather information and services available. There are many regional offices scattered throughout Southern California, with the main office a stately California Spanish-style building just a few minutes from downtown Los Angeles and from the Los Angeles Coliseum at 2601 South Figueroa (corner of Adams and Figueroa).

It should be carefully noted that rush-hour traffic into and out of Los Angeles is very much a part of the city; learning to accept this fact will ease some of the pain for there is no getting around it: between the hours of 7:00 and 9:00 A.M. and 3:30 and 6:00 P.M., you will be "stuck" if you happen to be in the wrong place. The most important advice is to avoid most freeways between those hours. Taking surface streets may seem long and boring, but in the long run, they will likely take *less time* than going via the freeway. (Of course, traveling long distances—i.e., from Orange County to Los Angeles—will give you no other option: then, it's freeway or nothing.)

To determine special surface street routes or the few freeways that are "safe" at rush hour, get advice from at least two, not one, Angelenos. As in the case of medical or legal advice, Los Angeles traffic is so complex you'll need a second opinion.

Most Los Angeles' radio stations broadcast regular traffic bulletins during rush hours; this is not only a *necessary* service for all drivers, but entertaining as well. With all those radio listeners in their automobiles, it's no accident that Los Angeles is the *radio capital* of the world. There are stations specializing in all forms of rock, country, nostalgia, and classical music, plus talk radio and more. A quick spin down the dial while on the freeway will be rewarding!

Transportation

Now, some things you'll need to know, from *rental cars* to *limousine services*.

RENTAL CARS

Ajax Rent A Car
(800) 262-1776

Locations in and around Los Angeles, including Airport, Miracle Mile (Mid-Wilshire), and downtown (Los Angeles Convention Center)

**AMC Dealership
Rent-A-Jeep
Walker Brothers**
Olympic and Western, Los Angeles
(213) 733-0112

Specializes in Jeeps only

Avis Rent A Car
(800) 331-1212 (nationwide)
(800) 331-2112 (international)

Various locations throughout Southern California

Bob Leech's Autorental
4810 W. Imperial Highway
Inglewood 90304
(213) 673-2727

Locations in Los Angeles (near Airport) and San Francisco

Budget Rent A Car
(800) 527-0700

Locations throughout Southern California. A special Mercedes rental lot located at Third and La Cienega

Dollar Rent-A-Car
(800) 262-1520

Locations throughout Southern California

Hertz Rent A Car
(800) 654-3131

Locations throughout Southern California

MPG Car Rental
1001 South Figueroa
Los Angeles 90015
(213) 746-2421
(800) 228-2277 (nationwide)

Locations throughout Southern California

Martin Cadillacs
(213) 820-3611

Cadillacs-only rental lot

National Car Rentals
(800) 328-4567

Major Los Angeles locations: Airport, Los Angeles Hilton Hotel, Beverly Hilton Hotel, Downtown Los Angeles, and the Long Beach Airport

Rent-A-Wreck
12333 Pico Boulevard
West Los Angeles
(213) 478-0676

Specializes in renting very used cars ("wrecks") and less desirable models. But dependable cars and good prices

Rolls-Royce Rental
8752 Sunset Boulevard
West Hollywood
(213) 659-5055

Specializes in renting Rolls-Royces

Southwest Leasing and Rental
12312 W. Olympic Boulevard
West Los Angeles
(213) 820-9000

Specializes in leasing, but renting is available at its West Coast locations: Los Angeles, Anaheim, San Diego, San Francisco, Bakersfield, Phoenix, Denver, and Newport Beach

Thrifty Rent A Car
(800) 331-4200

Locations throughout Los Angeles

Ugly Duckling Rent-A-Car
7415 Santa Monica Boulevard
West Hollywood
(213) 874-0975

2929 S. Figueroa Avenue
Los Angeles
(213) 749-4901

As the name implies, not the perfect, pristine models of the national car rentals, but serviceable and functional cars

PUBLIC TRANSPORTATION

RTD Center
ARCO Center
505 South Flower Street; Downtown Los Angeles;
(213) 626-4455

The RTD Center is available to assist bus patrons with information on bus lines, and purchase of bus passes. There are regional RTD Centers located in the South Bay, the San Gabriel Valley, and other areas. There are over 200 routes and more than 2,400 buses available to serve the Southland. The regular bus fare is 50 cents (exact change only), with transfers costing 20 cents. Senior citizens and handicapped patrons pay only 20 cents. There are also express bus lines. Visitors should call the RTD Center for that specific information, as well as for special information on RTD service during the Olympics.

TAXI AND CAB SERVICE

If you're from New York, London, or a more traditional city, you might be accustomed to hailing a cab from curbside, or queueing up at a taxi stand. Not in Los Angeles. You'll have to call in advance. There are many more square miles than taxis. Taxis are relatively rare except at major hotels. So, be prepared to plan ahead.

Also, be sure to *specify the route* to be taken in advance of departure. A roundabout joy ride on the freeways could be expensive and unnecessarily long, and you'll never know the difference. Be sure to have the dispatcher at the airport, or the telephone dispatcher, or your hotel doorman specify the route with the driver and give a dollar estimate.

Cab Companies

Celebrity Cab Company
(213) 278-2500 - Westside of Los Angeles
(213) 988-8515 - Valley
(213) 934-6700 - Mid-Wilshire

Service throughout Los Angeles

Checker Cab
(213) 624-2227 - Greater Los Angeles and Glendale
(213) 481-1234 - Greater Los Angeles
(213) 843-8500 - Burbank and San Fernando Valley
(213) 258-3231 - Pasadena

Twenty-four-hour service, delivery service, reservations, and company accounts

Independent Cab Company
(213) 385-TAXI
(213) 659-TAXI

Services include package and messenger delivery

United Independent Taxi
(213) 653-5050
(213) 995-4343 - Valley and Santa Monica

Twenty-four-hour service, air-conditioning in all cars, messenger and package-delivery services, reservations, major credit cards accepted

LIMOUSINES

A Limousine Service Ltd.
(213) 240-5460

Cadillac and Lincoln Stretch; Cessnas, LearJet, and Westwind Jet services; Bell Ranger Jet Helicopter service. Twenty-four-hour service; major credit cards accepted

Classic Fleet Limousine Service
(213) 971-3788
(213) 277-7895

Cadillac and Lincoln Stretch, including bar, color TV, and sun roof. Twenty-four-hour service and major credit cards accepted

The Limousine Experience
(213) 277-4446
(213) 598-0165
(714) 995-8959

Service throughout all of Southern California. Air charter and limousine service. Limos include color TV, bar, stereo, tinted windows, and uniformed chauffeurs. Services available through Ticketron; major credit cards accepted

Music Express
(213) 845-1502

Cadillacs, Lincolns, and buses, including TV, bar, and phone. Twenty-four-hour service and major credit cards accepted

Palm Springs—Los Angeles Limousine Service
(213) 459-1923 - Los Angeles
(213) 202-8325 - Culver City
(916) 327-8816 - Palm Springs

Twelve—fifteen passenger stretch limos for charter drives to and from Los Angeles—Palm Springs

Rolls-Royce Limousines
(213) 462-3136

Chauffeur-driven, different models available

Shangrila Limousine Service
(213) 273-6791 - Los Angeles and Beverly Hills
(714) 953-6500 - Anaheim, Newport Beach, Santa Ana

Cadillac Stretch models; twenty-four-hour service

Starlite Limousine Service
(213) 990-1060

Cadillac Stretch, including color TV, bar, sun roof, pullman seats, cassette stereo, and plush interior. Twenty-four-hour service; major credit cards accepted

TRAIN SERVICE TO AND FROM LOS ANGELES

Amtrak
Union Station
800 North Alameda
Los Angeles (Downtown)
(213) 624-0171

Two different trains service the Southland, both traveling to and from Los Angeles:
Line #1: Begins in Los Angeles and goes north to Glendale, Oxnard, and Santa Barbara on to San Francisco.
Line #2: Begins in Los Angeles and goes south to Fullerton, Anaheim, Santa Ana, San Juan Capistrano (*or* San Clemente), Oceanside, Del Mar, and San Diego.

The northbound service includes one train daily along the beautiful California coastline and coast range mountains, and two daily services through the San Joaquin Valley to San Francisco.

The southbound route to San Diego isn't quite as lovely, but there are seven trains daily and it's an enjoyable and efficient way to get to San Diego and intermediate communities.

Also, there is Amtrak service to other major Western cities, including Seattle, Phoenix, Denver, Albuquerque, and service to Chicago. All trains depart from historic and beautiful Union Station, which was built in the late 1930s.

REGIONAL AIRPORTS

The regional airports are particularly effective for short laps to Palm Springs, San Diego, Las Vegas, and other nearby locations; plus not-so-near Western cities such as Seattle, Portland, and Phoenix; and others as far away as Dallas and Chicago. The Ontario Airport offers a wide range of transcontinental service to New York and other cities by way of American, United, and Republic airlines.

Burbank Airport
2627 Hollywood Way
(213) 840-8847

Ontario International Airport
Holt and Vineyard
(714) 983-8282

Long Beach Airport
4100 Donald Douglas Drive
(213) 421-8293

John Wayne/Orange County Airport
18741 Airport Way
(714) 834-2400

OTHER OPTIONS

Independent Car

Having an automobile is the easiest, most convenient, and probably most economical method of travel within the city of Los Angeles. One of the city's charms is its variety of locations and sights; this can also be its detriment: getting to and from those myriad places can be costly, time-consuming, and annoying. A private automobile would certainly alleviate many of these annoyances.

Of course, cabs and limos are available options, as already discussed, but they are costly and not always easily available (phone calls and reservations must be made—sometimes well in advance). Public transportation is economical but time-consuming.

If a car is in order, then be sure to stock up on good maps that cover the areas you will be traveling. Once you know *precisely* how to arrive at the destination, much of the anxiety is alleviated.

And, keep in mind, for all the ills of the automobile and freeways to be suffered in Los Angeles, it's only a short drive to get beyond the urban and suburban boundaries. A relatively short drive can put you on a sprawling beach, in a National Forest, in a lovely resort community, or visiting a California mission.

The Southern California passion for motoring and fierce allegiance to the automobile isn't just a local deviation, like fruit flies or earthquakes. It's just the natural way to explore this diverse and sprawling landscape.

Where to Stay:
A Guide to Hotels

All great cities have a tradition of fine hotels, and for many travelers, a city is remembered and imagined by the images of those places of hospitality, social life and dining, and their architecture and decor: the Hotel de Crillon in Paris, the Savoy or the Connaught in London, or the Plaza in the heart of Manhattan.

Like Greta Garbo sweeping in out of the lobby of *Grand Hotel*, visitors and locals alike cluster around their own grand hotels. And, in Los Angeles, these aren't Hollywood sets, but Hollywood itself—well, only a few like the **Beverly Hills Hotel** and the **Hotel Bel Air**. Diversity, as in all other ways of life in Southern California, is the hallmark of hotel life. There are the grand ladies from the 1920s, the **Ambassador** and the **Biltmore**; and the modern giants, the **Westin Bonaventure** and the **Century Plaza**. But there are also the unusual and outlying places, which can be a source of unexpected pleasure and discovery: the **Queen Mary Hotel** in Long Beach, or one of the small hotels on Catalina. Slightly farther away, the **Hotel del Coronado** in San Diego and, to the north, the **Santa Barbara Biltmore** are well worth the trip. And, closer to town, **L'Ermitage** and **Le Parc** offer intimate surroundings.

And if you want to warm yourself in front of a fireplace in the same surroundings as did Laurence Olivier and Vivien Leigh, Doug Fairbanks and Mary Pickford, Winston Churchill, the Kennedys, and more, try the **San Ysidro Ranch** near Santa Barbara.

Whatever your preference and sense of adventure, following is a guide to hotels covering a wide spectrum of price, locale, and ambience.

The Beverly Wilshire Hotel in Beverly Hills, where Rodeo Drive meets Wilshire Blvd.

Major, First-rate Hotels

Ambassador Hotel
3400 Wilshire Boulevard; Mid-Wilshire; (213) 387-7011;
(800) 241-0182 (nationwide); (800) 252-0385 (California)

An exquisite city within a city, the Ambassador Hotel sits on
160 acres of land in the prime section of Los Angeles. Built
in 1921, the hotel offers 500 deluxe rooms, a health club,
restaurants, shops, cocktail lounges, and a travel agency.

Beverly Hills Hotel
9641 Sunset Boulevard; Beverly Hills; (213) 276-2251

The crème de la crème of hotels in the city, the Beverly Hills
Hotel (also known as the "Pink Palace") sits on twelve acres
of lush landscaping in Beverly Hills. It is a bona fide California
landmark, with its main building and adjacent separate bungalows. There is a pool for sunning (or star-gazing), tennis
courts, restaurants, and of course, the Polo Lounge.

Beverly Hilton Hotel
9876 Wilshire Boulevard; Beverly Hills; (213) 274-7777

The Beverly Hilton is a large hotel complex that includes 600
deluxe rooms, restaurants, coffee shops, cocktail lounges, and
shops. There is also a theater-ticket desk, limo service, and a
pool.

Beverly Sunset Hotel
8775 Sunset Boulevard; West Hollywood; (213) 652-0030

Recently renovated, this sixty-room hotel is small and quaint
and overlooks Sunset Boulevard and the Los Angeles Basin.
There are a pool and restaurants.

Beverly Wilshire Hotel
9500 Wilshire Boulevard; Beverly Hills; (213) 275-4282

A beautiful, regal hotel that sits right in the middle of Beverly
Hills, the Beverly Wilshire offers deluxe rooms and suites in

a European atmosphere. There is a garden swimming pool, sauna, several restaurants, and limo service to the airport.

The Biltmore Hotel
515 S. Olive Street; Downtown Los Angeles;
(213) 624-1011; (800) 421-0156 (nationwide);
(800) 252-0175 (California)

This hotel, located in the heart of downtown near Pershing Square, has just been completely renovated. It is a deluxe hotel whose interior features award-winning European architecture. There are plenty of restaurants and shops to keep the patron happy, plus full health-club facilities.

Century Plaza Hotel
2025 Avenue of the Stars; Century City; (213) 277-2000;
(800) 228-3000

A stylish and deluxe hotel complex, the Century Plaza is right in the heart of Century City, where shopping, theater, movie houses, restaurants, and cocktail lounges abound. Each room in the hotel has a refrigerator, a lanai, and a beautiful view.

Hyatt Regency Hotel
711 S. Hope Street; Downtown Los Angeles; (213) 683-1234;
(800) 228-9000

The Hyatt Regency is an integral part of the Broadway Plaza shopping area, which houses thirty-five fine shops and restaurants. Each of the hotel's 500 rooms has a wall of windows that allows a beautiful city view.

Hyatt Wilshire Hotel
3515 Wilshire Boulevard; Mid-Wilshire; (213) 381-7411;
(800) 228-9000

There are 397 rooms in this newly renovated hotel. The twelve-story building also offers a lounge, a disco, and a concert pianist who creates ambience in the lobby.

Los Angeles Hilton Hotel
930 Wilshire Boulevard; Downtown Los Angeles;
(213) 629-4321

A large (1,200 rooms) and serviceable hotel, the Los Angeles Hilton also offers a restaurant, a lounge, a twenty-four-hour coffee shop, and a pool.

Miramar Sheraton Hotel
101 Wilshire Boulevard; Santa Monica; (213) 394-3731

A beautiful, deluxe, but intimate hotel, the Miramar Sheraton is situated directly across the street from Santa Monica Beach and Pacific Palisades Park. The 276 rooms are accompanied by two restaurants and a lounge.

The New Otani Hotel and Garden
120 S. Los Angeles Street; Downtown Los Angeles; (213) 629-1200; (800) 421-8795

This hotel is a beautiful Japanese garden, complete with running stream and waterfalls. Each of the 446 rooms has a refrigerator and an alarm clock. The hotel also houses some fine restaurants (A Thousand Cranes, Commodore Perry's, and Genji Bar).

Sheraton Grande Hotel
333 South Figueroa Street; Downtown Los Angeles; (213) 617-1133

The hallmark of this new hotel (opened summer of 1983) is traditional and elegant service. There are floor butlers, in the style of a grand European hotel, to serve all 470 rooms. The lobby is gracious and warm behind the modern facade. Dining services include The Ravel for a gourmet dinner, and it has the formal Back Porch for breakfast, lunch, and dinner.

Sunset Marquis Hotel
1200 Alta Loma Road; West Hollywood; (213) 657-1333; (800) 421-4380 (U.S.); (800) 858-7125 (Canada)

This is a small, intimate, but deluxe hotel. The three-story, 115-room hotel offers nightly entertainment, a Jacuzzi, complimentary breakfast, and a beautiful garden area.

Westin Bonaventure Hotel
404 South Figueroa Street; Fifth and Figueroa; Downtown
Los Angeles; (213) 624-1000; (800) 228-3000

One of the city's most strikingly different hotels, this thirty-
five-story circular structure with mirrored glass was designed
by John Portman and boasts 1,474 rooms, pool, five-level
shopping gallery, and lots of restaurants, bars, and lounges.
Ponds and waterfalls, plus the outdoor elevators, add to the
hotel's ambience.

Westwood Marquis Hotel
930 Hilgard Avenue; Westwood; (213) 208-8765

This is a deluxe hotel that offers elegance and style in the
public areas and in each of the different 225 suites. Tea is
served every afternoon in the Westwood Lounge, and there is
also a pool and sauna. The hotel is conveniently located next
door to Westwood Village.

Expensive but Intimate

Hotel Bel Air
701 Stone Canyon Road; Westwood; (213) 472-1211

This is a charming, romantic, secluded hotel that also boasts
beautiful rooms, deluxe service, ultimate privacy, and beautiful
grounds, complete with a creek and swans. There is also a
pool for the guests' enjoyment.

Beverly Comstock Hotel
10300 Wilshire Boulevard; Beverly Hills; (213) 275-5575

This fifty-room hotel has only suites. It's a small hotel with
nice appointments.

Beverly Rodeo Hotel
360 N. Rodeo Drive; Beverly Hills; (213) 273-0300

This is a small but lavish hotel, right in the heart of Beverly
Hills' famous Rodeo Drive. Each of the one hundred rooms

s its own elegant, Old World unit. There is also a sundeck
nd a very nice outdoor restaurant called Café Rodeo.

L'Ermitage Hotel
9291 Burton Way; Beverly Hills; (213) 278-3344

One of the city's nicest and most elegant hotels, L'Ermitage
has Old World charm and sophistication. Each of the 117 suites
offers a sunken living room with fireplace, wet bar, and private
balcony. There is the Café Russe, a fine dining establishment
that is open only to the hotel's guests. A complimentary Continental breakfast is served each day. A rooftop garden, swimming pool, whirlpool, spa, and private solaria are available,
as is limo service.

Marina del Rey Hotel
13534 Bali Way; Marina del Rey; (213) 822-1010; (800)
421-8145

This deluxe waterfront hotel, which is completely surrounded
by water, sits on the Marina's main channel. It is close to
shopping and restaurants. Don the Beachcomber's Restaurant
is located here.

Marina International Hotel and Villas
4200 Admiralty Way; Marina del Rey; (213) 822-1010;
(800) 421-8145

Known for its luxury decor, it features such rooms as "The
African Queen," "The King Tut Hut," and "The Old Hollywood." The hotel is conveniently located directly across from
an inland beach.

Marina-Pacifica Hotel and Apartments
1697 Pacific Avenue; Venice; (213) 399-7770;
(800) 421-8151

This quaint hotel is Los Angeles' only beachfront hotel. Located right on Venice beach, it features rooms with fireplaces
and kitchens. It has an indoor-outdoor café. There are 92 rooms;
one-bedroom apartments are available.

Le Parc Hotel
733 North West Knoll; West Hollywood; (213) 855-8888;
(800) 421-4666

A charming European-style hotel housed in a modern low-rise
building in a quiet residential area near Farmers Market, the
Beverly Center, and the Los Angeles County Art Museum.
Guests enjoy their own private eaterie, Café Le Parc, reserved
exclusively for them. Each of the 154 suites includes a living
room with a fireplace, a kitchenette, and a private balcony.
There is a rooftop garden, lighted tennis courts, heated pool,
spa, sauna, and exercise rooms.

UNUSUAL

Chateau Marmont Hotel
8221 Sunset Boulevard; Hollywood; (213) 656-1010

Located among the billboards of Sunset Boulevard, this French
Normandy castle is a secluded hideaway convenient to Hollywood hot spots. All kinds of accommodations are available,
including fully equipped cottages, bungalows, and a penthouse.

Hollywood Roosevelt
7000 Hollywood Boulevard; Hollywood; (213) 469-2442;
(800) 421-0767

Across the street from the famous Chinese Theater and the
tallest building in the heart of Hollywood, the hotel never lets
you forget where you are. It has a magnificent lobby, ornate
fountains, an Olympic-size pool, and the Tropicana bar.

Los Angeles Athletic Club
431 West 7th Street; Los Angeles; (213) 625-2211

Located in Los Angeles' financial district and minutes from
the Convention Center, the Athletic Club offers deluxe accommodations, complete athletic facilities, including gym, pool,
track, racquetball, Jacuzzi.

Marina City Club Resort
4333 Admiralty Way; Marina del Rey; (213) 822-0611;
(800) 421-0000

hirty acres, right on the water, include complete recreational
acilities, nightly entertainment, three restaurants, and of course
xcellent lodgings. Just seven minutes from LAX.

Queen Mary Hotel
ier J; Long Beach; (213) 435-3511

he noble *Queen Mary*, formerly a 50,000 ton luxury liner,
ow resides in the Long Beach Harbor. It has been successfully
nade over to a hotel with 387 rooms, including a small number
f grand suites. Dining facilities include the Promenade Café
nd Restaurant, the elegant Sir Winston's, and for a cocktail
he Art Deco Lounge, looking over the bow.

There are nostalgia exhibits, courteous staff, and numerous
hops and facilities on board, and the Spruce Goose (Howard
Iughes' Flying Boat) is alongside in its own exhibition dome,
nd an English-style village of shops, London Towne, on shore.

MODERATE, SUBURBAN

Breakers Motel
1501 Ocean Avenue; Santa Monica; (213) 451-4811

There are thirty-four rooms in this two-story motel, and they
are all large, luxurious, and well-maintained. This European-
style motel is also only a minute away from the beach.

Hacienda Hotel
525 N. Sepulveda Boulevard; El Segundo; (213) 615-0015;
(800) 421-5900 (nationwide); (800) 262-1314 (California)

The 660 rooms in this hotel are well-maintained. Its convenient
location to the Los Angeles Airport is a plus, as are the free
our advice, free transportation to two nearby shopping malls,
wenty-four-hour limo service, Jacuzzi, pools, and twenty-four-
hour room service.

Hotel Carmel
01 Broadway; Santa Monica; (213) 451-2469

This building was built in the 1920s and has lost none of its
harm. It's close to the beach, to the shopping mall, and to

theaters. There are 110 rooms and they all have color TV. Free parking is also provided.

The Huntley Hotel
1111 Second Street; Santa Monica; (213) 394-5454

Huntley Hotel is one block away from the Santa Monica Beach; it sits on a quiet street and overlooks the ocean. Home-cooked meals are served for breakfast and lunch. The seventeen-story building houses 210 rooms. The hotel is also convenient to shopping, restaurants, and leisure activities.

Mission Hills Inn (Best Western)
10621 Sepulveda Boulevard; Mission Hills (San Fernando Valley); (213) 891-1771

This is a warm and intimate Southern California hotel. The 120 spacious rooms surround a large pool with flower gardens and palm trees. It is also close to Magic Mountain and the San Fernando Mission. There is an adjoining restaurant and lounge. Free parking and room service are provided.

Pacific Shore
1819 Ocean Avenue; Santa Monica; (213) 451-8711;
(800) 854-2933 (nationwide); (800) 532-3733 (California)

This hotel is a half-block away from Santa Monica Beach. The 172 rooms are attractive and the guests are able to use the pool, sauna, therapy pool, Jacuzzi. There is also a gift shop and a cocktail lounge, as well as an Ajax Rent A Car at the guests' disposal.

Ramada Inn
6333 Bristol Parkway; Culver City; (213) 670-3200;
(800) 228-2828

The Ramada Inn is a well-known nationwide chain and there will be no surprises at this one: 260 rooms are located in this modern high-rise, which is convenient to the airport (free airport transportation every half-hour) and shopping. Room service, cocktail lounge, and a pool are additional amenities.

Sheraton Universal
3838 Lankerseim Boulevard; North Hollywood;
(213) 980-1212

This large, twenty-three-story hotel is a place to see the stars, visit the newly renovated Universal Amphitheater, and tour nearby Universal Studios. There are two restaurants, a rooftop pool, sauna, spa, and exercise room.

Sportsmen's Lodge Hotel
12825 Ventura Boulevard; Studio City; (213) 769-4700

Beautiful gardens and waterfalls, pools stocked with trout, an English country-style atmosphere abounds. The rooms are large, the pool is Olympic-size. The restaurant provides European cuisine. Room service is available. Studio suites with private patios are available.

The Valley Hilton
15433 Ventura Boulevard; Sherman Oaks; (213) 981-5400

Part of the Hilton chain, this hotel is located conveniently at the 405 (San Diego) and the 101 (Ventura) freeways. The 210 rooms include plush executive suites and banquet rooms accommodating up to 500 people.

Near Olympic Villages

USC

Alexandria Hotel
501 S. Spring Street; (213) 626-7484; (800) 421-8815

A restored turn-of-the-century charmer, this landmark hotel has attractive accommodations at reasonable rates. Located in the heart of the financial district, close to the Convention Center and City Hall, the hotel has 500 rooms and offers room service.

Best Western in Town
925 S. Figueroa Street; (213) 628-2222; (800) 421-6222

This is a three-story hotel located one and one half blocks from the Convention Center and right down the street from the famous twenty-four-hour Pantry Café restaurant. Offerings include room service, pool, facilities for the handicapped; parking is free.

Figueroa Hotel
939 S. Figueroa; (213) 627-8971

This 280-room hotel was built in a charming Spanish style directly across the street from the historic Variety Arts Theater. There is a twenty-four-hour coffee shop on the premises, a pool, and a Jacuzzi. Parking is free; airport service is available every hour.

Holiday Inn Convention Center
1020 S. Figueroa Street; (213) 748-1291; (800) 238-8000

Many athletic teams stay at this newly renovated hotel next door to the Convention Center. It offers the lovely Courtyard Restaurant, a pool, a laundry room, and complimentary garage parking.

Mayflower Hotel
535 S. Grand Avenue; (213) 624-1331; (800) 421-8851

Located in the center of downtown, this 350-room hotel offers room service, valet laundry, and a multilingual staff.

Olympian Hotel
1903 West Olympic Boulevard; (213) 385-7141

This medium-priced hotel has an aviary full of tropical birds right in the center of the lobby. It offers a swimming pool and free downtown shuttle bus service.

Sheraton Town House
2961 Wilshire; (213) 382-7171; (800) 325-3535

Built in the 1920s, this is one of the Sheraton chain's finest establishments. Howard Hughes slept and lived here. It has a country-estate setting with marble fireplaces, tennis courts, swimming in the Olympic-size pool, two restaurants, a coffee shop, and garden room for fine dining. It's right across from Bullock's Wilshire. There are 300 rooms.

University Hilton
3540 S. Figueroa Street; (213) 748-4141

Ideal for doing business at USC, the Coliseum, or the Sports Arena, this 241-room hotel is equipped to handle banquets, meetings, and conventions. It also offers the Trojan Horse Restaurant plus a coffee shop and lounge. Courtesy shuttle to both LAX and Amtrak train station is available.

Westwood

Best Western Royal Palace Hotel
2528 S. Sepulveda Blvd.; West LA; (213) 477-9066

A small thirty-two-room hotel right off the 405 Freeway. A pool and sauna are available, as well as free parking.

Century Wilshire
10776 Wilshire; West LA; (213) 474-4506

A European-style hotel offering mostly suites, many with kitchenettes. It's near UCLA and Westwood. Amenities include pool, laundry, and room service.

Holiday Inn—Brentwood Bel Air
170 N. Church Lane; West LA; (213) 476-6411

This seventeen-story round hotel is near UCLA and right off the 405 Freeway. There is a van shuttle to UCLA and free parking. There are outdoor kennels for animals.

The New Bel Air Sands
11461 Sunset Blvd.; (213) 476-6571; (800) 421-6649

Recently renovated, you'll find a Bahaman atmosphere in the decor. A putting green, tennis courts, and a cocktail lounge with live entertainment are available to guests.

Near Olympic Sites

Airporter Inn Hotel
18800 MacArthur Blvd.; Irvine; (714) 752-8777

Opposite the John Wayne Airport, this deluxe hotel has a heated pool, dining room, suites, private pools, cocktails, and entertainment.

Disneyland Hotel
1150 West Cerritos Avenue; Anaheim; (714) 778-6600

Connected to Disneyland by monorail, this 1,000-room hotel is a sixty-acre resort. Three pools, ten tennis courts, fourteen restaurants, and entertainment are available. Accommodations are either in tropical villages or perched in the spacious towers. Reservations are necessary year-round.

Grand Hotel
7 Freedman Way; Anaheim; (714) 772-7777

This hotel is adjacent to Disneyland and offers a free shuttle to the park. There are boutiques and a gift shop on the premises. Dinner theater, dining room, coffee shop, pool are available. No pets allowed.

Huntington-Sheraton Hotel
1401 South Oak Knoll Ave.; Pasadena; (213) 792-0266

This rambling mission-revival hotel is the only remaining resort hotel in Pasadena. Once run by railroad magnate Henry Huntington, it is now operated by the Sheraton chain.

Long Beach Hyatt House
6400 East Pacific Coast Highway; Long Beach;
(213) 434-8451; (800) 228-9000

A new section of this deluxe hotel offers first-floor rooms with beautiful garden views. In addition, there is a coffee shop, restaurant, and lounge.

Industry Hills Sheraton Park Resort
1 Industry Hills Parkway; City of Industry (San Gabriel
Valley); (213) 965-0861; (800) 325-3535

There are 300 deluxe rooms and suites on 650 acres containing
seventeen tennis courts, two eighteen-hole golf courses, meeting rooms, conference centers, and complete spa facilities.

Hilton at the Park
1855 South Harbor Blvd.; Anaheim; (714) 750-1811

Private balconies overlook the man-made Matterhorn at Disneyland and the Santa Ana Mountains. There is a heated pool,
restaurant, and coffee shop. Suites are available.

Pasadena Hilton Hotel
150 South Los Robles Ave.; Pasadena; (213) 577-1000

This is a European-flavor full-service hotel that is convenient
to the center of Pasadena. The 264 rooms sit amid lovely
landscaping. Skylights, a gourmet restaurant, is located in the
penthouse of the hotel.

Portofino Inn
260 Portofino Way; Redondo Beach; (213) 379-8481

Located on a man-made finger of land near King Harbor, this
inn is a complete resort. It has attractive rooms, many with
kitchenettes. There is a heated pool, room service, laundry
facilities, and meeting rooms.

Queensway Bay Hilton
700 Queensway Drive; Long Beach; (213) 435-7676

This deluxe hotel has its own marina with moorings for over
one hundred boats. Many of the rooms have a marina view.
Adolph's Restaurant, located in the hotel, is one of the area's
most popular. There is also nightly entertainment.

Ojai Valley Inn and Country Club
Country Club Drive; Ojai; (805) 646-5511

There are 115 rooms in this deluxe hotel set on magnificent grounds. There is a golf course (site of an annual tournament), tennis courts, and riding stables. Three meals a day are included.

The Registry Hotel
18800 MacArthur Blvd.; Irvine; (714) 752-8777

Close to John Wayne Airport, Disneyland, and the Pacific Ocean, this 300-room hotel offers a swimming pool, tennis courts, and Jacuzzi. The Grand Portage dining room offers dinner and dancing nightly. Complimentary limousine service is available from the John Wayne Airport.

Shangri-la Hotel
1301 Ocean Avenue; Malibu; (213) 394-2791

Streamlined, modern, yet quaint and charming, with ocean views from every room. Available amenities include laundry facilities, room service, restaurants; meeting rooms are surrounded by garden patios. There is free parking.

The Westin South Coast Plaza
666 Anton Blvd.; Costa Mesa; (714) 540-2500

Set across the street from South Coast Plaza, with its 200 stores, this 400-room hotel provides a variety of sports facilities. Volleyball, shuffleboard, putting green, swimming pool, tennis courts are all available. Alfredo's Restaurant adds to the charm. In addition, there are three bars and live entertainment nightly.

Willow Tree Lodge
1015 South Harbor Blvd.; Fullerton; (714) 871-5430

This sixty-one-room motor lodge has a heated pool. Family units are available.

NEAR THE AIRPORT

Amfac Hotel Los Angeles
8601 Lincoln Blvd.; (213) 670-8111; (800) 277-4700

Located in a quiet residential area perfect for jogging, tennis, and golf, this hotel provides excellent dining in the Bistro Restaurant and 754 fine deluxe rooms. Airport transportation is available.

Hyatt Hotel—LAX
6225 W. Century Blvd.; (213) 670-9000; (800) 228-9000

This elegant, twelve-story hotel is close to LAX, Hollywood Park, and Marina del Rey. The 600 rooms are elegantly furnished. There are large meeting rooms and banquet space available.

The Los Angeles Marriott
5855 West Century Blvd.; (213) 641-5700; (800) 228-9290

There are over 1,000 rooms in this truly luxurious hotel featuring a heated pool with a swim-up bar, three lounges, three restaurants, and several conference rooms. Free parking is available.

Pacifica Hotel
6161 Centinela Ave.; (213) 649-1776

Three miles north of the airport and near Marina del Rey, this Spanish-American-style hotel offers convenience and fine dining. There are tennis courts, saunas, therapy pools, a health spa, and nightly entertainment.

Sheraton Plaza La Reina
6101 West Century Blvd.; (213) 642-1111

This fifteen-story hotel offers the perfect setting for business. There are ninety-six meeting rooms, with in-house audiovisual equipment. Groups of up to 1,000 can be accommodated. There is Landry's for steak, lobster, and sushi, and Le Gourmet for modern elegance. Forty-eight of the 810 rooms were especially designed for the handicapped.

Skyways Airport Hotel
9250 Airport Blvd.; (213) 670-2900

This semimodern, ninety-three-room hotel is within seconds of the airport. It offers free limo service to and from LAX. There is room service and free parking.

OUTLYING AREAS

Atwater Hotel
P.O. Box 797; Avalon (Catalina Island); (213) 599-1010

Avalon's largest hotel, the Atwater, with over 200 rooms, is family-oriented and is only a half-block from the beach.

Marriott's Santa Barbara-Biltmore
1260 Channel Drive; Santa Barbara; (805) 969-2261

Hotel rooms as well as cottages are offered in this traditional yet elegant hotel. Across the street is a private beach and there are two pools as well. Complimentary bicycles are provided; golf and tennis can be arranged. There are 169 rooms and 11 cottages.

Canyon Hotel Racquet and Golf Resort
2850 South Palm Canyon Drive; Palm Springs; (619) 323-5656

This luxurious resort offers three swimming pools, an eighteen-hole private golf course, horseback riding, tennis, and a sauna. There is a restaurant and cocktail lounges with live entertainment. All suites come with kitchen and wet bar.

Hotel Catalina
129 Whittley Ave.; Avalon (Catalina Island); (213) 510-0027

This charming old-style inn has both rooms and cottages. It is only a half-block from the beach. There is a spa, a sun patio, and a free movie theater as well.

Hotel del Coronado
1500 Orange Avenue; Coronado (San Diego); (619) 435-6611

This famous Victorian-style hotel set on thirty-three acres is a choice vacation spot, offering several elegant restaurants, two swimming pools, seven tennis courts, a golf course, and lavish accommodations.The oceanfront rooms have spacious balconies and fantastic views. Celebrities and statesmen stay here.

Hermosa Hotel and Cottages
131 Metropolis St.; Avalon (Catalina Island);
(213) 510-1010

This inexpensive but charming hotel has cottages and rooms, some with kitchens. There are about 100 rooms in all.

La Mancha Resort
444 N. Avenida Caballeros; Palm Springs; (619) 323-1775

A very private, deluxe resort with thirty-three villas, half of which have their own swimming pools. They have fully equipped kitchens, fireplaces, widescreen TVs with tape players. A nine-hole golf course, gym, sauna, and tennis courts are also on the premises. There is gourmet dining at the club.

Santa Barbara Miramar Hotel-Resort
1555 S. Jameson Lane; Santa Barbara; (805) 969-2203

Set in subtropical gardens near the Pacific, this tranquil hotel has two swimming pools, tennis courts, a private beach, and a terraced dining room. There are 195 units, 35 with kitchens.

The San Ysidro Guest Ranch
900 San Ysidro Lane; Montecito (Santa Barbara);
(805) 969-5046

Dating from 1893 as a guest ranch and once owned by Ronald Colman, the San Ysidro (Saint Isidore, the patron saint of farmers and plowers) has a very special sense of seclusion and peace. Its thirty-eight cottages (many with hot tubs, but no television) are nestled at the base of the Santa Ynez Mountains, five minutes by car from the beaches. There is riding (and hiking) on its 550 acres of mountainside trails, and pool and tennis facilities overlooking the California coast. The superb restaurant and its romantic downstairs bar are both the Plow

& Angel (named in honor of Saint Isidore). Expensive, but a brief visit will leave no doubt why the rich and famous are among the San Ysidro's devoted following.

Sundance Villas
378 Cabrillo Rd.; Palm Springs; (619) 325-3888

This resort has beautifully decorated suites with fireplaces, wet bars, kitchens, and private patios. Each villa has a private pool or Jacuzzi. Tennis courts are available.

Vacation Village
1404 W. Vacation Rd.; San Diego; (619) 274-4630;
(800) 854-2900

Set on forty-three acres amid tropical freshwater lagoons, 449 rooms have patios or lanais as well as the usual amenities. There are eight tennis courts, a mile of beach, five swimming pools, and three restaurants, including a Don the Beachcomber.

How to Work While Visiting: Business and Personal Services

For some, coming to Los Angeles during the Olympic year will be a combination of business and pleasure. For those who have to work, a brief listing of services follows. For additional listings, one should consult local Yellow Pages and local newspapers. Remember, Los Angeles is a collection of communities and each usually has its own Yellow Pages and newspaper.

COMMUNICATIONS

AT&T Company
Long-distance communications
(800) 222-0300

**ITT United States
Transmission Systems**
Business telecommunications
(800) 526-3000

MCI Telecommunications
Long-distance communications
(213) 642-4623

Sprint Telephone Service
(213) 515-5353

Western Union
Mailgrams, telegrams,
cablegrams, singing telegrams,
or charge-card money orders
(213) 687-9750 (Central Los
Angeles)

SECRETARIAL SERVICES

Apple One
3323 Wilshire Boulevard
Los Angeles
(213) 383-8710

Jane Arden Agency
3540 Wilshire Boulevard
Los Angeles
(213) 386-8250

Employers Overload
1737 N. Ivar
Los Angeles
(213) 464-4191

Kelly Services
Various locations, from Los
Angeles to Long Beach
For Los Angeles:
3600 Wilshire Boulevard
(213) 381-7951

London Temporary Services
3250 Wilshire Boulevard
Los Angeles
(213) 386-0711

**Manpower Temporary
Services**
Locations in Los Angeles and
Orange counties
(213) 452-5896

Office Overload
Offices in Los Angeles,
San Gabriel, Burbank,
and Airport areas
For Los Angeles:
3435 Wilshire Boulevard
(213) 385-5726

Park Avenue Temps
Locations in Beverly Hills,
Mid-Wilshire, and Glendale
For Beverly Hills:
8500 Wilshire Boulevard
Beverly Hills
(213) 855-1515

Remedy Temporary Services
Offices in Downey, Torrance,
West Covina, and Long Beach
For Long Beach:
3613 Long Beach Boulevard
(213) 595-4931

Stivers Temporary Personnel
Offices in Los Angeles,
Westwood, Pasadena, and
Sherman Oaks
For Westwood:
10889 Wilshire Boulevard
(213) 208-5656

Unicorn Personnel Agency
8447 Wilshire Boulevard
Beverly Hills
(213) 655-5403

Western Temporary Services
Offices in Burbank, Thousand
Oaks, Anaheim, Long Beach,
Los Angeles, Rosemead, South
Gate, Tustin, and Westchester
For Anaheim:
866 S. Brookhurst
(714) 776-0380

Word Processing Temporaries
5455 Wilshire Boulevard
Suite 1504
Los Angeles
(213) 934-8211

MESSENGER SERVICE

BC Messenger Service
328 N. Highland Avenue
Hollywood
(213) 462-2000

Air Couriers International
451 W. Century Boulevard
Los Angeles
(213) 614-0890

Air Express International
Pick-up and delivery
(213) 776-0860; (714) 972-1685

Federal Express
Pick-up and information
(213) 776-4111

Rocket Messenger
Service, twenty-four hours
(213) 469-7155

United Parcel Service
Information
(213) 626-1441

PHOTOCOPIERS

A-! Quick Printing
106 Wilshire Boulevard
(213) 932-1857

Big Red Q Quickprint
823 Wilshire Boulevard
Santa Monica
(213) 829-4188
Century City, (213) 277-9796
Downtown, (213) 254-3935
Glendale, (213) 241-8937

Charlie Chan Printing
110 W. Sunset Boulevard
Hollywood
(213) 464-7228
961 Wilshire Boulevard
Los Angeles
(213) 380-6121

Copy Center
6147 Wilshire Boulevard
Los Angeles
(213) 655-7880

Postal Instant Press (PIP)
Locations throughout the
Southland
For information, contact
corporate headquarters,
(213) 653-8750

Tam's Stationers
3303 S. Hoover
Los Angeles
(213) 746-1500
Branch offices in Costa Mesa,
Long Beach, Los Angeles,
Northridge, Pasadena, San
Diego, and Torrance

Money Exchange

American Foreign Exchange
350 S. Figueroa Street
(World Trade Center)
(213) 626-0255

Associated Foreign Exchange
9365 Wilshire Boulevard
Beverly Hills
(213) 274-7610

Deak-Perera
677 S. Figueroa Street
Los Angeles
(213) 624-4221

Airport (S-2)
(213) 646-7716

Grace Foreign Exchange
3807 Wilshire Boulevard
Los Angeles
(213) 389-2700

New York Foreign Currency Exchange
300 E. 1st Street
Los Angeles
(213) 623-2046

Office Supplies

Alexander's
1531 Cahuenga Boulevard
Hollywood
(213) 464-1151

Apex Stationers and Printers
8666 W. Pico Boulevard
Los Angeles
(213) 655-0920

Empire Stationers
5711 Sepulveda Blvd.
Van Nuys
(213) 782-7502

**The Great American
Stationery Company**
8411 W. 3rd Street
Los Angeles
(213) 655-3515

Office Supplies Unlimited
11625 W. Pico Boulevard
West Los Angeles
(213) 879-0577

Pen and Paper Supplies
8960 Santa Monica Boulevard
West Hollywood
(213) 652-2232

Royal Office Supplies
603 N. La Brea Avenue
Los Angeles
(213) 930-1770

Westwood Stationers
10940 Santa Monica Boulevard
West Los Angeles
(213) 477-3942

PART 2

The Olympic Sites:
An Introduction

The 1984 Olympic Games will be held at sites spread across the greater Los Angeles area, from Lake Casitas, eighty-four miles to the north, to Fairbanks Country Club, 110 miles to the south. Most of the sites, however, will be at distances much closer to downtown.

Many of the sites will offer opportunities for exploring places of interest and discovering restaurants and recreational areas, and much scenic beauty as well.

Following is a list of Olympic event sites, including comments on the distance of each site from downtown; and an Olympic calendar. Also included are an Olympic Events Sites map, traffic-plan maps for Coliseum Area and for UCLA Complex, and a marathon route map.

Archery: Eldorado Park in Long Beach, Site 1; 24 miles from downtown, 23 miles from USC, 32 miles from UCLA.

Baseball: Dodger Stadium in Chavez Ravine, Site 2; 1 mile from downtown, 3 miles from USC, 15 miles from UCLA.

Basketball and Handball Finals: The Forum in Inglewood, Site 3; 9 miles from downtown, 10 miles from USC, 13 miles from UCLA.

Boxing: The Memorial Sports Arena at the Coliseum, Site 4; 2 miles from downtown, 0.5 miles from USC, 16 miles from UCLA.

Canoeing and Rowing: Lake Casitas in the Ojai Valley, Ventura County, Sites 5 and 14; 84 miles from downtown, 85 miles from USC, 70 miles from UCLA.

Cycling: California State University, Dominguez Hills, Carson, Site 6; 17 miles from downtown, 16 miles from USC, 22 miles from UCLA.

Gersten Pavilion at Loyola Marymount University, the site of the weight lifting events, just north of the Los Angeles International Airport.

Equestrian: Santa Anita Park in Arcadia, the San Gabriel Valley, Site 7; 18 miles from downtown, 19 miles from USC, 30 miles from UCLA. Also Site 7a at Fairbanks Country Club in San Diego County; 110 miles from downtown, 118 miles from UCLA.

Fencing: Long Beach Convention Center, Site 8; 23 miles from downtown, 22 miles from USC, 32 miles from UCLA.

Gymnastics: Pauley Pavilion, UCLA in Westwood, Site 9; 14 miles from downtown, 16 miles from USC.

Handball: Titan Gymnasium, California State University, Fullerton, in Orange County, Site 10; 27 miles from downtown, 28 miles from USC, 40 miles from UCLA.

Finals at the Forum, Inglewood, Site 3; 9 miles from downtown, 10 miles from USC, 13 miles from UCLA.

Hockey: East Los Angeles College, Monterey Park, Site 11; 17 miles from downtown, 16 miles from USC, 31 miles from UCLA.

Judo: Eagle's Nest Arena, California State University, Los Angeles, Site 12; 7 miles from downtown, 9 miles from USC, 21 miles from UCLA.

Modern Pentathlon: Coto de Caza in Orange County, in the Saddleback Mountains, Site 13; 56 miles from downtown, 55 miles from USC, 70 miles from UCLA.

Shooting: Prado Recreation Park in Chino, San Bernardino County, Site 15; 48 miles from downtown, 50 miles from USC, 62 miles from UCLA.

Soccer: The Rose Bowl in Pasadena, Site 16; 11 miles from downtown, 12 miles from USC, 26 miles from UCLA.

Swimming, Synchronized Swimming, and Diving: Univer-

The Anaheim Convention Center in Orange County, the site of the wrestling events.

sity of Southern California, Site 17; 2 miles from downtown, 16 miles from UCLA.

Water Polo: Pepperdine University in Malibu, Site 18; 30 miles from downtown, 32 miles from USC, 16 miles from UCLA.

Tennis: UCLA in Westwood, Site 19; 14 miles from downtown, 16 miles from USC.

Track and Field: The Los Angeles Memorial Coliseum, Site 20; 2 miles from downtown, 0.5 mile from USC, 16 miles from UCLA.

Volleyball: The Long Beach Arena, Site 21; 25 miles from downtown, 23 miles from USC, 32 miles from UCLA.

Weight Lifting: Gersten Pavilion, Loyola Marymount University near LAX Airport, Site 22; 18 miles from downtown, 17 miles from USC, 8 miles from UCLA.

Wrestling: The Anaheim Convention Center in Orange County, Site 23; 27 miles from downtown, 25 miles from USC, 33 miles from UCLA.

Yachting: The Long Beach Marina, Site 24; 26 miles from downtown, 24 miles from USC, 33 miles from UCLA.

Olympics Events Calendar

Locations are indicated by the site number on the calendar; see map of Olympic events sites.

Event	July 28 Sat	29 Sun	30 M	31 Tu	Aug 1 W	2 Th	3 F	4 Sat	5 Sun	6 M	7 Tu	8 W	9 Th	10 F	11 Sat	12 Sun
Opening Ceremonies	20															
Archery												1	1	1	1	
Baseball				2	2	2	2	2	2	2	2					
Basketball		3	3	3	3	3	3	3	3	3	3	3	3			
Boxing		4	4	4	4	4	4	4	4	4	4	4		4		
Canoeing									5	5	5	5	5	5		
Cycling		6	6	6	6	6	6		6							
Diving									17	17	17	17	17	17	17	17
Equestrian		7	7		7a	7a	7a/7	7	7		7	7	7	7		7
Fencing					8	8	8	8	8		8	8	8	8	8	
Gymnastics		9	9	9	9	9	9	9	9			9	9	9		
Handball				10	10	10	10	10	10	10	10	10	10	3	3	
Hockey		11	11	11	11	11	11	11	11	11	11	11	11	11	11	
Judo									12	12	12	12	12	12	12	12
Modern Pentathlon		13	13	13	13											
Rowing			14	14	14	14	14	14	14							
Shooting		15	15	15	15	15	15									
Soccer		16	16	16	16	16	16		16	16		16		16	16	
Swimming		17	17	17		17	17	17								
Synchronized Swimming										17			17			
Tennis									19	19	19	19	19	19	19	
Track & Field							20	20	20	20		20	20	20	20	20
Volleyball		21	21	21	21	21	21	21	21	21	21	21	21	21	21	
Water Polo					18	18	18		18	18		18	18			
Weight Lifting		22	22	22	22	22		22	22	22	22	22				
Wrestling			23	23	23	23	23			23	23	23	23	23		
Yachting				24	24	24	24		24	24	24					
Closing Ceremonies																20

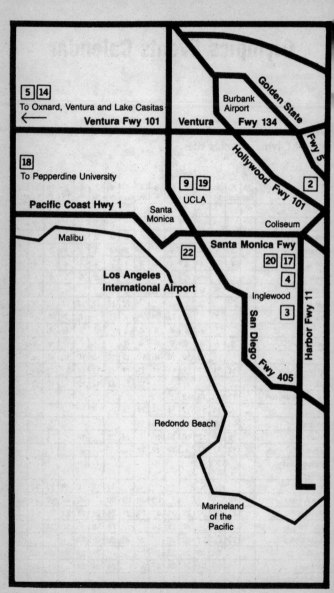

See page 58 for map legend.

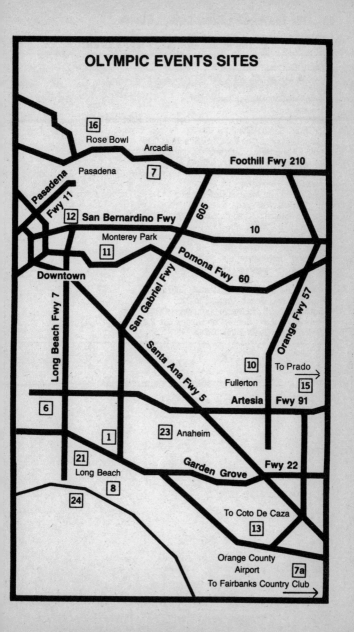

OLYMPIC EVENTS SITES MAP LEGEND

Archery, Eldorado Park, Site 1
Baseball, Dodger Stadium, Site 2
Basketball, The Forum, Site 3
Boxing, Memorial Sports Arena, Site 4
Canoeing, Lake Casitas, Site 5
Cycling, California State University, Dominguez Hills, Site 6
Equestrian, Santa Anita Park, Site 7
    and Fairbanks Country Club, Site 7a
Fencing, Long Beach Convention Center, Site 8
Gymnastics, Pauley Pavilion, UCLA, Site 9
Handball, California State University, Fullerton, Site 10
    and The Forum, Site 3
Hockey, East Los Angeles College, Site 11
Judo, Eagle's Nest Arena, Site 12
Modern Pentathlon, Coto de Caza, Site 13
Rowing, Lake Casitas, Site 14
Shooting, Prado Recreation Park, Chino, Site 15
Soccer, Rose Bowl, Site 16
Swimming, University of Southern California, Site 17
Water Polo, Pepperdine University, Site 18
Tennis, UCLA, Site 19
Track and Field, Memorial Coliseum, Site 20
Volleyball, Long Beach Arena, Site 21
Weight Lifting, Loyola Marymount University, Site 22
Wrestling, Anaheim Convention Center, Site 23
Yachting, Long Beach Marina, Site 24

TRAFFIC PLAN FOR COLISEUM AREA

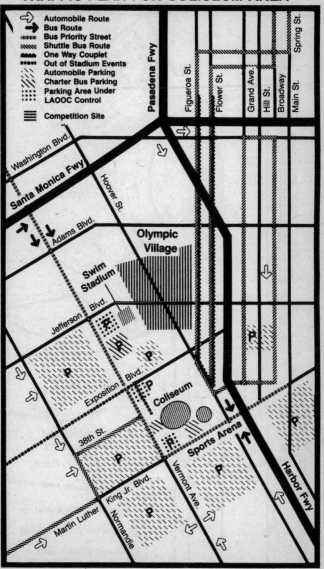

TRAFFIC PLAN FOR UCLA COMPLEX

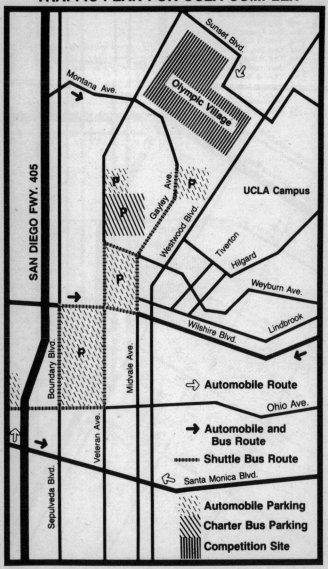

MEN'S AND WOMEN'S MARATHON ROUTES

Men's and Women's Marathon Routes

Women's Marathon, Sunday, August 5, 8:00–11:30 A.M.
Men's Marathon, Sunday, August 12, 5:30–8:15 P.M.

These two classic Olympic Events will begin at Santa Monica City College and proceed north and east to Bundy Drive and San Vicente. At San Vicente Boulevard, the runners will pro-

Theatre Sans Fils of Montreal, Quebec, will perform Tolkien's *The Hobbit* with forty-eight larger-than-life-sized puppets.

The Korean National Dance Company will perform eight national dances at the Arts Festival, marking their third Olympic appearance.

ceed west, along one of the most popular Southern California runner's courses, to the ocean. San Vicente is picturesque and tree-lined, and Ocean Avenue, at the bluffs overlooking the ocean, offers a spectacular view of the curving, mountainous Santa Monica to Malibu coastline.

The Men's Marathon, run in the late afternoon, will provide the spectator with a beautiful Pacific sunset. The portion of the marathon run along Ocean Avenue will provide spectators and performers alike with a dramatic combination of athletics and scenic beauty.

The Olympic Arts Festival

The Olympics and arts? Why do athletes and the arts go together? The ancients combined the two from the very beginning, nearly three thousand years ago. In 1906, Baron Pierre de Coubertin, the founder of the modern Olympic Games, initiated a revival of the arts in conjunction with the Games. Five competitions: architecture, sculpture, painting, music, and literature were proposed.

Beginning in 1912 at Stockholm, the arts competitions failed to live up to the athletic competitions and suffered from many difficulties. Nevertheless, the arts competitions survived and were sometimes staged in spectacular style. At the 1932 Los Angeles Games, there were over 1,100 works of art submitted by artists from thirty-two countries, and by 1948 the original five categories for arts competitions had grown to thirteen.

However, because of the difficulties and the primary focus on athletics, the arts competition, with awarding of prizes and the concept of winners, was dropped in favor of an exhibition and festival concept.

The arts festival has taken varying shapes during succeeding Olympic celebrations. Montreal, in 1976, and Moscow, in 1980, were primarily national, with Mexico City in 1968 and Munich in 1972 international in scope. The 1984 Games in Los Angeles will present one of the most diverse and spectacular arts festivals.

Beginning June 1, 1984, and continuing until the Olympic closing ceremonies on August 12, it will be, perhaps, the most significant, as well as the largest, arts festival ever held in North America. It will recognize America's contribution to the arts; Southern California's diverse and creative arts community and its ethnic and cultural richness; and the beauty and scope of the arts worldwide.

There will be approximately sixty performing companies from sixteen countries (over six continents), twenty art exhibitions, and some three hundred performances. All this will take place over a ten-week period at forty-three sites, including Santa Barbara and Newport Beach sites.

The 1984 Olympic Festival will comprise five major categories: dance, theater, music, visual arts, and film. Among the twenty-five dance companies will be Les Ballets Africains, the Korean National Dance Company, Bella Lewitzsky from the West Coast, the Royal Winnipeg Ballet, Sankai Juku and Kodo from Japan, and the Joffrey Ballet.

Theater will include Shakespeare presented in three languages (French, Italian, and English). The Chengdu Acrobatic Troupe from the People's Republic of China will make their first American appearance.

Music will feature a Hollywood Bowl Los Angeles Philharmonic concert conducted by Michael Tilson Thomas on July 27, the night before the Games begin. The Royal Opera of Covent Garden will present *Turandot*, *Peter Grimes*, and *The Magic Flute*. And there will be chamber music (the Guarnieri and Sequoia quartets), and folk, blues, jazz, and contemporary.

The visual arts will be highlighted by a major exhibition of French Impressionism, *A Day in the Country*, staged by the Los Angeles County Museum of Art, the Louvre, and the Chicago Art Institute. Many other exhibitions will be displayed (twenty in all) including *The Automobile and Culture* at the new Museum of Contemporary Art.

Film will be represented by Filmex, the largest public film festival in the world, and by an animated film presentation by the Academy of Motion Picture Arts and Sciences, *The Olympiad in Animation*.

For further information on the 1984 Olympics Arts Festival one may call (213) 305-8444. Ticket brochures are being distributed, with tickets going on sale in January 1984. Tickets for the Arts Festival events will be reasonably priced, thanks to a very significant grant by the Times Mirror Corporation.

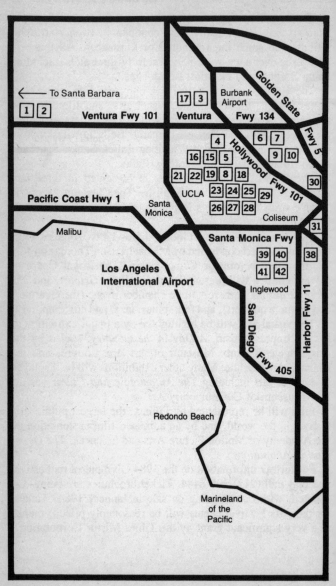

To Santa Barbara
1 2
Ventura Fwy 101
17 3 Ventura
Burbank Airport
Fwy 134
Golden State
Fwy 5

4
6 7
16 15 5
9 10
21 22 19 8 18
30
UCLA
23 24 25 29
26 27 28
Coliseum
31

Pacific Coast Hwy 1
Santa Monica

Malibu

Santa Monica Fwy
39 40
41 42
38

Los Angeles International Airport

Inglewood

San Diego Fwy 405

Harbor Fwy 11

Redondo Beach

Marineland of the Pacific

See pages 68-69 for map legend.

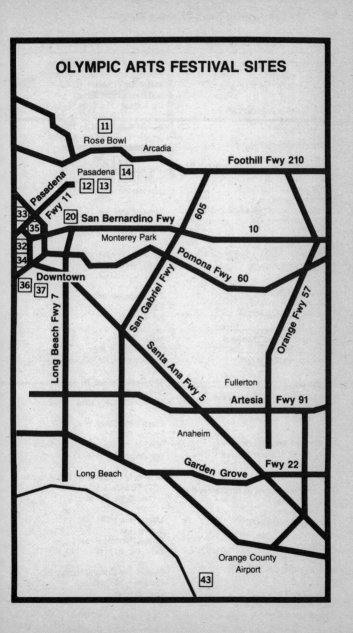

THE OLYMPIC ARTS FESTIVAL MAP LEGEND

Santa Barbara Museum of Art 1
1130 State Street
Santa Barbara, CA 93101

The University Art Museum 2
University of California
Santa Barbara
Santa Barbara, CA 93106

Social & Public Arts Resource Center 3
The Great Wall of Los Angeles
The Tujunga Wash Flood
Control Channel
Coldwater Canyon & Oxnard Blvd.
North Hollywood, CA

Room for Theatre 4
4327 Laurel Grove Avenue
Studio City, CA 91604

Hollywood Bowl 5
2301 North Highland
Los Angeles, CA 90028

John Anson Ford Theatre 6
2580 Cahuenga Blvd. East
Los Angeles, CA 90078

The Planetarium 7
The Griffith Park Observatory
2800 East Observatory Road
Los Angeles, CA 90027

American Film Institute 8
2021 North Western Avenue
Los Angeles, CA 90027

Los Angeles Municipal Art Gallery 9
Barnsdall Park
4804 Hollywood Blvd.
Los Angeles, CA 90027

Victory Theatre 10
4424 Santa Monica Blvd.
Los Angeles, CA 90029

Rose Bowl 11
1001 Rose Bowl Drive
Pasadena, CA 91103

**Pasadena Center Conference
Building and Pasadena Civic
Auditorium/Theatre 12**
300 East Green Street
Pasadena, CA 91101

Pacific Asia Museum 13
46 North Los Robles Avenue
Pasadena, CA 91101

The Huntington Library 14
1151 Oxford Road
San Marino, CA 91108

The Groundlings Theatre 15
1912½ Hillcrest Road
Los Angeles, CA 90068

Odyssey Theatre 16
7810 Hillside
Los Angeles, CA

Television Center 17
846 North Cahuenga Blvd.
Hollywood, CA

Matrix Theatre 18
7657 Melrose Avenue
Los Angeles, CA 90046

The Cast Theatre 19
804 El Centro Avenue
Hollywood, CA 90038

Plaza de la Raza 20
Lincoln Park
3540 North Mission Road
Los Angeles, CA 90031

University of California Los Angeles 21
405 Hilgard
Los Angeles, CA 90024

Macgowan Hall
Royce Hall
Royce Rehearsal Hall
Schoenberg Hall

Museum of Cultural History 22
University of California
Los Angeles
405 Hilgard
Los Angeles, CA 90024

Academy of Motion Pictures Arts &
Sciences 23
Samuel Goldwyn Theatre
8949 Wilshire Blvd.
Los Angeles, CA 90211

Pan Pacific Park 24
7600 Beverly Blvd.
Los Angeles, CA

Los Angeles Institute of Contemporary
Art 25
2020 South Robertson Blvd.
Los Angeles, CA 90034

Beverly Hills High School 26
255 South Lasky Drive
Beverly Hills, CA 90212

Craft and Folk Art Museum 27
5814 Wilshire Blvd.
Los Angeles, CA 90017

Los Angeles County Museum of Art 28
5905 Wilshire Blvd.
Los Angeles, CA 90014

Los Angeles Actors' Theatre 29
1089 North Oxford Avenue
Los Angeles, CA 90029

Dorothy Chandler Pavilion 30
Los Angeles Music Center
1st and Grand Avenue
Los Angeles, CA 90012

Mark Taper Forum 31
Los Angeles Music Center
1st and Grand Avenue
Los Angeles, CA 90012

Central Library/City of Los Angeles 32
630 West 5th Street
Los Angeles, CA 90071

City Hall Rotunda 33
200 North Spring Street
Los Angeles, CA 90012

Japanese-American Cultural and
Community Center 34
244 South San Pedro Street
Los Angeles, CA 90012

Temporary Contemporary 35
Museum of Contemporary Art
152 North Central Ave.
Los Angeles, CA 90013

Arco Center for the Visual Arts 36
Arco Towers
505 South Flower Street
Los Angeles, CA 90071

Ensemble Studio Theatre 37
839 South Grand Avenue
Los Angeles, CA 90017

Shrine Auditorium 38
3228 Royal Street
Los Angeles, CA 90007

Fisher Gallery 39
University of Southern California
823 Exposition Blvd.
Los Angeles, CA 90089

Los Angeles Memorial Coliseum 40
Exposition Park
Los Angeles, CA

California Museum of Afro American
History and Culture 41
700 State Drive
Los Angeles, CA 90012

Los Angeles County Museum of
Natural History 42
900 Exposition Blvd.
Los Angeles, CA 90007

Newport Harbor Art Museum 43
850 San Clemente Drive
Newport Beach, CA 92660

What to Do
Before and After an Event

Following is a guide to dining, recreation, and places of special interest in and around the prime major areas where most of the Olympic events will be held.

For each of the areas there are listings in five categories: Inexpensive Eating Establishments; Major Restaurants; Park Areas; Special Attractions; and Major Cultural Points of Interest.

Before visiting one of the places listed, be sure to call in advance to check hours, location, and other details. Because of the Olympic year, house rules may change, and in any case, you will want advice on travel time and the best route.

Metropolitan Los Angeles

The heart of downtown Los Angeles, bounded on the east by the Harbor Freeway and on the north and south by the San Bernardino and Santa Ana freeways, is studded with new, gleaming office towers and hotels. And within this new downtown skyline and maze of high-rise modern buildings, some of the traditional is being preserved and restored, and new street-level areas with a human scale are being created.

The Oviatt Building (an Art Deco masterpiece), the Biltmore, the Fine Arts Building, and others have been restored. And others remain, such as the Los Angeles Central Public Library with the ARCO Tower rising above it.

Chinatown and Little Tokyo are flourishing nearby areas, perfect for sightseeing, with many small restaurants and shops. Newly created pedestrian spaces, the ARCO Plaza and the

The Security Pacific Plaza is a delightful park area beneath the fifty-five-story Security Pacific National Bank Headquarters tower built in 1974. A large Alexander Calder red stabile is located here amidst the flowers and trees, a perfect spot for a sunny midday stroll in the heart of the downtown business and financial district.

Security Pacific Plaza, are a superb achievement of walkways, mini-park areas with sculpture, and shopping plazas.

The old canards about downtown Los Angeles no longer hold. There is a great deal of old and new, and one can and should do much of it without a car.

Nearby-to-downtown Olympic sites are one of the two Olympic villages at the University of Southern California, the adjacent Coliseum and Sports Arena, and Dodger Stadium in Chavez Ravine. Events to be held at these sites include track and field, swimming, boxing, and baseball. The Press Center will be located at Los Angeles Convention Center at Figueroa Street and Pico Boulevard.

INEXPENSIVE EATING ESTABLISHMENTS

Anna Maria Ristorante
1356 South La Brea Avenue; Mid-Wilshire; (213) 935-2089, (213) 659-6497
Tuesday–Friday, 11 A.M.–10 P.M.; Saturday and Sunday, 4–10:30 P.M. Closed Monday

A heated patio makes Anna Maria's a pleasant place for Neapolitan cuisine. Menu includes generous portions of pasta, chicken, veal, fresh seafood (when available), and pizza. Wine and beer. Credit cards.

Atomic Cafe
422 East First Street; Little Tokyo; (213) 628-6433
Seven days, 4 P.M.–4 A.M.

Chinese, Japanese, and American food served to the strains of punk rock and new wave music. A different experience. Cash only.

Betty's (Los Feliz Golf Course Coffee Shop)
3207 Los Feliz Boulevard; Los Feliz; (213) 669-9289
Monday–Friday, 7 A.M.–3:30 P.M.; Saturday and Sunday, 8 A.M.–3:30 P.M.

A charming coffee shop adjacent to the Griffith Park driving range. Fine hamburgers, sandwiches, and malts.

Cassell's Hamburgers
3300 West Sixth Street; Mid-Wilshire; (213) 480-8668
Monday–Saturday, 10 A.M.–3 P.M.

Don't be put off by the plain interior: this restaurant has first-rate hamburgers char-boiled, one-or two-thirds pound of freshly ground USDA prime steak, plus a full salad bar (with home-

made mayonnaise, ketchup, mustard, and dressings), and grilled
sandwiches (for those who can't cope with all that meat). Cash
only.

Chinese Friends
984 North Broadway; Chinatown; (213) 626-1837
Sunday–Thursday, 11:30 A.M.–9:30 P.M.; Friday and Saturday,
until 10:30 P.M.

Hot and spicy Hunan meat dishes, seafood, and noodles (at
lunch). Visa, MasterCard. No reservations.

Clifton's Silver Spoon Cafeteria
515 West Seventh Street; Downtown; (213) 485-1726
Monday–Friday, 7 A.M.–3:30 P.M.

At last, a cafeteria with style. Clifton's serves an eclectic array
of international dishes. A Soup Kitchen in the basement features soups and salads. Personal checks or cash accepted. (Clifton's may be open seven days a week, three meals a day, so
call ahead.)

El Cholo Mexican Café
1121 South Western Avenue; Los Angeles; (213) 734-2773
Monday–Thursday, 11 A.M.–10 P.M.; Friday and Saturday,
11 A.M.–11 P.M.; Sunday 11 A.M.–9 P.M.

Other locations in La Habra, Orange, and Newport Beach.
Rolled tacos, tostada compuestas, oversized margaritas, and
low prices. The covered outdoor patio is ideal for summer
dining. Credit cards. Reservations suggested.

El Tepeyac Café (Manuel's)
812 North Evergreen Avenue; East Los Angeles;
(213) 268-1960
Sunday–Thursday, 7 A.M.–9:45 P.M.; Friday and Saturday,
7 A.M.–11 P.M. (Closed Tuesday)

Informal dining with large portions at very low prices. Try
"garbage burrito." Cash only. No reservations.

Gorky's
536 East Eighth Street; Downtown; (213) 627-4060
Open twenty-four hours

In the middle of dark downtown, a little oasis of high-tech lighting and cafeteria-style Russian food. Live music some evenings. Cash only. No reservations.

Kam Wah Restaurant
747 North Hill Street; Chinatown; (213) 680-0640
Seven days, 11 A.M.–9:30 P.M.

Like many Chinese restaurants, Kam Wah puts its energy into food, not atmosphere. Cantonese food is the fare here, with offerings of such home-style dishes as steamed spareribs and pork hash. Fresh seafood, when available. Beer and wine. Visa, MasterCard. Reservations not required.

Langer's Delicatessen
704 South Alvarado Street; Los Angeles; (213) 483-8050
Sunday–Thursday, 6:30 A.M.–1 A.M.; Friday and Saturday, 6:30 A.M.–3 A.M.

A Jewish deli where the food is good and the service is quick. Try it at off-peak hours; Langer's is always busy. Visa, MasterCard. Reservations for large parties.

Les Frères Taix
1911 Sunset Boulevard; Echo Park; (213) 484-1265
Open seven days. Monday–Saturday, 11 A.M.–3 P.M.; 5–10 P.M.; Sunday, 1–9 P.M. (dinner only)

Les Frères Taix offers simple but complete French meals, with a fine wine list and excellent service. Menu lists six permanent entrees plus two daily specialties. Full bar. Visa, MasterCard. Reservations advised.

The Original Pantry Café
877 South Figueroa Street; Downtown; (213) 972-9279
Open twenty-four hours every day

A landmark café (there is no key to the front door) that offers American steaks, chops, and pot roasts. A huge bowl of iced vegetables and all the sourdough you can eat accompany the main course. The most expensive item on the menu is a four-teen-ounce tenderloin at $7.95. Breakfasts are especially boun-teous. Be patient: there's always a line. Cash only.

Philippe's Original Sandwich Shop
1001 North Alameda Street; Downtown; (213) 628-3781
Seven days, 6 A.M.–10 P.M.

"Home of the French Dip Sandwich," Philippe's has been around since 1908, serving its specialty, plus cole slaw, salads, chili, soups, and 10¢ cups of coffee. Wine and beer. Cash only.

Tommy's World Famous Hamburgers
2575 Beverly Boulevard; Los Angeles; (213) 389-9060
Open twenty-four hours

Other locations in San Fernando, Sepulveda, Tujunga, Eagle Rock, and Van Nuys.
Home of the double-chili-cheeseburger. Watch the burger "ar-tisans" slap your meal together faster than you can pour ketch-up.

Vickman's Restaurant and Bakery
1228 East Eighth Street; Downtown; (213) 622-3852
Monday–Friday, 3 A.M.–3 P.M.; Saturday, 3 A.M.–1 P.M.

Vickman's is noted for eggs and omelets; if you go at lunch, you'll find more basic staples on its menu, such as soups, sandwiches, and salads. Delicious fresh-baked goods.

MAJOR RESTAURANTS

Bernard's (The Biltmore Hotel)
515 South Olive Street; Downtown; (213) 624-0183
Monday–Friday, 11:30 A.M.–2 P.M. for lunch; Monday–Sat-urday, 6–10 P.M. for dinner.

Inside the renovated Biltmore Hotel. The menu features mostly seafood. The wine list is well chosen and the ambience refined. Full bar. Credit cards. Reservations required.

The Cove
3191 West Seventh Street; Mid-Wilshire; (213) 388-0361
Monday–Friday, 11:30 A.M.–11 P.M.;
Saturday, 4:30 P.M.–midnight; Sunday, 4:30–10 P.M.

German specialties are served here, accompanied by violins
and accordions. All major credit cards. Bar. Reservations recommended.

Diamond Seafood Restaurant
724 North Hill Street, #131 Food Center; Chinatown;
(213) 617-0666 or 617-0668
Seven days, 11:30 A.M.–11 P.M.

Fresh seafood; big tanks of live fish and lobsters greet you at
the door. Beer and wine. Credit cards. Reservations for large
parties only.

François
555 South Flower Street; ARCO Plaza "C" Level;
Downtown; (213) 680-2727
Monday–Friday, 11:30 A.M.–2 P.M.; 6–10 P.M.; Saturday,
5:30–10 P.M.

Freshly prepared French food carefully served in a dignified
setting. A convenient choice for dinner before an event at the
nearby Music Center. Full bar. Reservations required.

Horikawa
111 South San Pedro Street; Little Tokyo; (213) 680-9355
3800 South Plaza Drive; Santa Ana; (714) 557-2531
Monday–Friday, 11:30 A.M.–2 P.M.; 5:30–10:30 P.M.;
Saturday, 5–11 P.M.; Sunday, 5–10 P.M.

A long sushi bar plus a dining room and teppan steak service;
traditional sukiyaki and shabu shabu are tasty. Full bar. Credit
cards.

Lawry's California Center
570 West Avenue 26; Los Angeles; (213) 224-6850
Daily, 11 A.M.–3 P.M.; Tuesday–Saturday, 5–10 P.M.;
Sunday, 4–9 P.M.

Informal semi-Mexican dishes served during the day. At night, a romantic setting for barbecued steak, fish, chicken, at a fixed price that's reasonable. Sunday lunch and nightly dinners feature Mariachi singers. Full bar open at 3, serving Mexican hors d'oeuvres. Reservations for parties of six or more. Credit cards accepted at dinner only. During the day, there are guided tours of the California Center, where Lawry's salt is manufactured.

Miriwa
750 North Hill Street; Chinatown; (213) 687-3088
Seven days, 10:30 A.M.–2:30 P.M.; 5–9:30 P.M.

For a fancy dim sum brunch, Miriwa may be the best place in Chinatown. Dinner is more formal, with Cantonese entrees. Full bar. Credit cards.

Pacific Dining Car
1310 West Sixth Street; Downtown; (213) 483-6000
Open twenty-four hours

Good for a hearty breakfast or for a full meal before the Music Center. Beef is the specialty and there is a full and fairly priced wine list. Full bar. Credit cards. Reservations suggested.

Rex II Ristorante
617 South Olive Street; Downtown; (213) 627-2300
Monday–Friday, noon–2 P.M.; Monday–Saturday, 7–10 P.M.

Located in the refurbished Art Deco Oviatt Building, with its Lalique glass and marble, Rex specializes in light meals. A small dance floor and Italian coffee bar complete the mood. Full bar. Credit cards. Reservations required.

A Thousand Cranes Japanese Restaurant
New Otani Hotel; 120 South Los Angeles Street; Little Tokyo; (213) 629-1200
Seven days, 11:30 A.M.–2 P.M., 6–10 P.M.; Monday–Friday, 7 A.M.–10 A.M.

Traditional Japanese cuisine, served in an elegant room facing a rooftop garden. There also is a sushi bar and tempura. Saturday and Sunday there's a traditional Japanese buffet-style brunch. Credit cards. Reservations required.

The Tower
1150 South Olive Street (Transamerica Center); Downtown;
(213) 746-1554 or 746-1825
Monday–Friday, 11:30 A.M.–3 P.M.; Monday–Thursday,
6–9:30 P.M.; Friday and Saturday, 6–10:30 P.M.; bar open
until 2 A.M.

Classic French food served atop the Transamerica Center, where
full glass windows afford a spectacular view of Los Angeles.
Credit cards. Reservations preferred.

The Windsor
3198 West Seventh Street; Mid-Wilshire; (213) 382-1261
Monday–Friday, 11:30 A.M.–2 P.M.; Monday–Saturday,
4:30 P.M.–midnight

Continental fare in a luxurious setting. The desserts are ex-
ceptional. Spacious, elegant bar. Credit cards. Reservations
preferred.

PARK AREAS

El Pueblo de Los Angeles State Historic Park (Olvera Street)
Between Sunset Boulevard and Main Street, the Plaza and
Los Angeles Street; Downtown; (213) 628-1274

This area—the Plaza, Olvera Street, and adjacent historic
buildings—is the founding site of the city of Los Angeles.
Olvera Street offers sidewalk craftwork, food concessions, and
glassblowing (a must-see for children). Call for free guided
tours.

Exposition Park
Figueroa Street at Exposition Boulevard; Los Angeles;
(213) 744-7400

The Los Angeles Sports Arena, Coliseum, and a rose garden
plus two major museums: the California State Museum of Science and Industry and the Los Angeles County Museum of
Natural History. There will be a special Olympics exhibition
during the Games.

Griffith Park
Visitors Center: 4730 Crystal Springs Drive; Los Angeles;
(213) 665-5188

The largest municipal park in the country. The park contains
the Los Angeles Zoo, Travel Town (open-air museum of transportation), Live Steamers (small steam locomotives that run
every Sunday), Train Ride (runs daily), Pony Ride, two separate areas of tennis courts, a soccer field, fifty-two miles of
bridle, a swimming pool, hiking trails and bike paths, a baseball
diamond, merry-go-round, four public golf courses, and a bird
sanctuary. Of special note is the Observatory and Planetarium,
which features a laser rock show.

Lafayette Park
2800 Wilshire Boulevard; Mid-Wilshire; (213) 387-2707

One of Los Angeles' oldest, Lafayette Park has tennis courts,
a picnic area, and recreation and senior citizens' centers.

MacArthur Park
Wilshire Boulevard, between Alvarado and Park View
streets; Los Angeles; (213) 387-1023

Recommended for daytime use. A lake, paddle boats, snack
bars, children's playground area. It contains over eighty species
of rare plants and trees.

Pershing Square
Fifth and Hill streets; 448 South Hill; Downtown;
(213) 627-5117

Named for General John J. Pershing, this is a concrete park
with minimal landscaping. In the heart of downtown, a respite
for weary shoppers.

SPECIAL ATTRACTIONS

ARCO Plaza
505 South Flower; Downtown; (213) 625-2132

ARCO Plaza, located between the Atlantic Richfield Tower and Bank of America Tower in downtown Los Angeles, offers seven acres of subterranean shopping and dining. Also located in ARCO Plaza is the Los Angeles Visitors Information Center and the Southern California Rapid Transit District (RTD) Center. The ARCO Center for Visual Art is a nonprofit gallery sponsored by Atlantic Richfield Company as a public service Check individual stores for days and hours.

New Chinatown
On Broadway, between Ord, Alameda, Bernard, and Yale streets; Downtown

New Chinatown offers a multitude of restaurants (from humble to expensive), gift shops, bakeries, jewelry stores. Stop and make a wish at the wishing well.

Grand Central Public Market
317 South Broadway; Downtown; (213) 624-2378
Monday–Saturday, 9 A.M.–6 P.M.

An indoor agora of fifty-two stalls, with every type of meat, fruit, and vegetable. Established 1917. A feast for eye and palate.

Little Tokyo
Between San Pedro, First and Third streets, and Alameda Avenue; Downtown; (213) 620-0570

Restaurants, specialty stores, Oriental goods, the New Otani Hotel and Japanese Village Plaza mall. Tours Tuesday and Wednesday, 10 A.M. and 2 P.M.

Los Angeles Mall
Main between First and north of Temple streets; Downtown

After touring City Hall, stroll through the multilevel underground mall. Bookstores, clothing stores, bakeries, and restaurants (fast-food and sit-down).

MAJOR CULTURAL POINTS OF INTEREST

Children's Museum
310 North Main Street (Los Angeles Mall, street level);
Downtown; (213) 687-8800
Wednesday–Thursday, 2:30–5 P.M.; Saturday and Sunday,
10 A.M.–5 P.M. (Hours extended during vacations)

A museum designed specifically for children, with touchable exhibits. Regularly scheduled classes and workshops.

Cirrus Gallery
542 South Alameda Street; Downtown; (213) 680-3473
Tuesday–Saturday, 11 A.M.–5 P.M.

Contemporary art. At the same address is Cirrus Editions, publisher of fine-art prints by Southern California artists. One of many fine galleries downtown worth visiting.

City Hall
200 North Spring Street; Downtown; (213) 485-4423

City Hall, designed by Austin, Parkindon, Martin and Whittlesey, is a mixture of Greek, Roman, and Renaissance architecture, and a landmark made famous through use in many television shows. An observation deck is located on the twenty-seventh floor and a forty-five-minute guided tour offers a brief history of Los Angeles and California. Tours by reservation only.

Exposition Park Museums
Figueroa Street at Exposition Boulevard; Los Angeles;
(213) 744-7400

California State Museum of Science and Industry
Finally, a museum that promotes touching. A great place for children, who can go up to exhibits and push buttons and pull levers to learn about math and engines and electricity.

Hall of Health
Explains the human body, including the five senses, the reproduction system, and the nervous system.

The Dental Exhibition Hall
Located next door to the Hall of Health; explains the basics of
the science of dentistry.

The Space Museum
This is a branch of the Museum of Science and Industry. In
it, you'll find missiles and other space equipment on loan from
NASA.

Los Angeles County Museum of Natural History
900 Exposition Boulevard; (213) 744-3411
Permanent displays include minerals and gems, reptile and
mammal fossils (the dinosaurs are intriguing), insects, marine
and bird life. Also a bookstore, gift shop, and cafeteria.

Japanese American Cultural and Community Center
244 South San Pedro; Little Tokyo; (213) 628-2725

The gallery changes exhibitions regularly and the schedule of
classes offers courses in Japanese culture. Next door is the
James Irvine Garden—a moment of meditation and refresh-
ment.

Los Angeles Central Library
630 West Fifth Street; Downtown; (213) 626-7461
Monday, Wednesday and Friday 10 A.M.–5:30 P.M.; Tuesday
and Thursday, noon–8 P.M.

Designed in 1925 by Bertram Goodhue and Carleton Winslow,
a city and national monument. Go for the books but also soak
up the Byzantine, Egyptian, Roman, and other exotic styles
that comprise this building's architecture.

Los Angeles Conservancy
849 South Broadway, Suite M22; Downtown;
(213) 623-CITY

A nonprofit historic preservation organization. Walking tours,
bus tours, and film programs of the architectural sites in the
area are regularly offered.

Los Angeles Times.
202 West First Street; Downtown; (213) 972-5000
Tours: Monday–Friday, 11:15 A.M. and 3:00 P.M.

The original building was designed in 1935 by Gordon Kaufman; its steel and glass corporate addition (by Pereira) was erected in 1974. The free tour lets you see the making of the paper from editorial to print shop.

Los Angeles Zoo
533 Zoo Drive; Griffith Park; (213) 666-4090
Seven days, 10 A.M.–6 P.M. (summer); 10 A.M.–5 P.M. (spring, fall, winter)

The two thousand animals in this zoo are grouped according to continent. Natural habitats simulated wherever possible. The Children's Zoo allows cubs to mingle with the human small fry. The Animal Nursery, a big attraction, lets you see the newest kids on the block.

University of Southern California
Between Jefferson and Exposition boulevards, Figueroa Street and Vermont Avenue; Los Angeles; (213) 744-2311

USC is the oldest major, independent, coeducational, nonsectarian university on the West Coast. It was founded in 1880 and has a student population of over 27,000. The campus' 152 acres are home to 191 buildings. Located across the street from Exposition Park.

Westwood

Nestled beneath the sweeping tree-lined curves of Sunset Boulevard, complete with its Bel Air mansions, is the UCLA campus and Westwood Village. A lively villagelike atmosphere pervades the local shopping area, which includes many restaurants, shops, and movie theaters within walking distance of the UCLA campus.

Just minutes away by car are the Bel Air Hotel, the Beverly Hills Hotel, and the stylish shopping areas of Rodeo Drive and

The UCLA campus in Westwood, site of one of the two Olympic villages. (The other is at the University of Southern California adjacent to the Coliseum.)

Melrose, and easy access for sightseeing into the hillside residential areas of Beverly Hills, Bel Air, and Brentwood.

A slightly farther drive, but only fifteen minutes by the San
Diego Freeway (south) and the Santa Monica Freeway (west)
or twenty minutes by surface streets (Sunset Boulevard and
San Vicente Boulevard), is Santa Monica. There one can find
the last survivor of the amusement piers from the 1930s—the
storm-battered but still-charming Santa Monica Pier. The
promenade area along the palisades overlooking the ocean is
ideal for a picturesque stroll, a Sunday brunch at one of the
many cafés, and a breathtaking sunset. The beaches are wide
and the view picturesque. Main Street (Santa Monica) is a chic
and zesty shopping and dining area. And several English pubs
and sushi bars are to be found throughout the Santa Monica
area.

Nearby Olympic sites and events are: one of the two Olympic villages (the other is at arch rival, the University of Southern
California), tennis at UCLA, and gymnastics to be held in
Pauley Pavilion. The latter is the home of the UCLA basketball
team and ten national championship banners hang from its
rafters. It is revered by sports lovers as "the house that Wooden
built."

The two rivals, UCLA and USC, are justly the sites for the
Olympic villages. Both have produced many Olympians
throughout their history: Rafer Johnson (UCLA) and Mel Pat-
ton (USC) among a list running into the hundreds. These two
schools have not only produced more Olympians than any other
American university, but they also are numbers one and two
among all universities in national championships. Of the two,
which is number one? You'll have to ask a Bruin or Trojan—
the question is too hot for cold type.

INEXPENSIVE EATING ESTABLISHMENTS

The Apple Pan
10801 West Pico Boulevard; West Los Angeles;
(213) 475-3585
Tuesday–Thursday, 11 A.M.–midnight; Friday and Saturday,
11 A.M.–1 A.M.

No atmosphere, but delicious hickory burgers and fresh-baked apple pie. If it's too busy, order to go and eat your meal in neighboring Rancho Park. Cash only. No reservations. No liquor.

Barney's Beanery
8447 Santa Monica Boulevard; West Hollywood;
(213) 654-2287
Seven days, 6 A.M.–2 A.M.

An extensive menu of chili-with-whatever, plus pool tables, video games, and a fully stocked bar featuring beers from around the world. Cash only. No reservations.

Bicycle Shop Café
12217 Wilshire Boulevard; West Los Angeles;
(213) 826-7831
Sunday–Thursday, 11 A.M.–midnight; Friday and Saturday, 11 A.M.–1 A.M.

A light, eclectic menu featuring crepes, salads, and omelets. The Bicycle Shop also offers trendy furnishings and "beautiful people." Visa, MasterCard. Reservations for large parties.

Café Casino
Gayley Center; 1135 Gayley Avenue; Westwood;
(213) 208-1010
Sunday–Thursday, 7 A.M.–10 P.M.; Friday and Saturday, 7 A.M.–midnight.

Other locations in Beverly Hills and Santa Monica. French food and chic decor. Cafeteria-style service. A good place to meet friends for a cappuccino and pastry. Visa, MasterCard. No reservations.

Chung King
11538 West Pico Boulevard; West Los Angeles;
(213) 477-4917
Seven days, 5 P.M.–10 P.M.

A hole-in-the-wall that serves good, spicy Szechwan Chinese food. Beer and wine. Cash only. No reservations.

Damiano's Mr. Pizza
10761 West Pico Boulevard; West Los Angeles;
(213) 475-6751
Monday–Thursday, 11:30 A.M.–11:30 P.M.; Friday, 11:30 A.M.
–2 A.M.; Saturday, noon–2 A.M.; Sunday, noon–midnight.

Other locations in Beverly Hills and West Hollywood. Short
on atmosphere but fairly long on tasty food. Antipasto is notable, definitely to be shared, and so is the pizza. Visa. Reservations recommended on weekends. Full bar at Pico location;
beer and wine at others.

Danny's Teriyaki Oki Dogs
7450 Santa Monica Boulevard; West Hollywood;
(213) 876-6273
Seven days, twenty-four hours.

A ruddy hot-dog stand in the middle of West Hollywood offering such unusual creations as the Oki Dog: two wieners on
a tortilla with pastrami, chili, and cheese.

Duke's at the Tropicana
8585 Santa Monica Boulevard; West Hollywood;
(213) 652-9411
Monday–Friday, 8 A.M.–9 P.M.; Saturday and Sunday,
7 A.M.–4 P.M.

A small, unobtrusive coffee shop, but a haven for stars and
nonstars, at long communal tables. Noisy and always crowded,
but the food compensates. Cash only. No reservations.

Gardens of Taxco
1113 North Harper Avenue; West Hollywood;
(213) 654-1746
Tuesday–Thursday and Sunday, 4:30 P.M.–11 P.M.; Friday and
Saturday, 4:30 P.M.–midnight.

Fine Mexican restaurant. Visa, MasterCard, American Express. Reservations for four or more. Beer and wine.

Islands

10948 West Pico Boulevard; West Los Angeles;
(213) 474-1144
Monday–Thursday, 11:30 A.M.–11 P.M.; Friday and Saturday,
11:30 A.M.–11:30 P.M.; Sunday, 11:30 A.M.–10 P.M.

Clean, wooden booths, messy hamburgers, and the house specialty, a huge basket of fresh-sliced Island fries. One free refill
on your soft drink. Visa, MasterCard, American Express. No
reservations. Full bar.

Junior's

2379 Westwood Boulevard; West Los Angeles;
(213) 475-5771
Seven days, 7 A.M.–1 A.M.

A deli-restaurant-coffeeshop-bakery; something for everyone.
Visa, MasterCard. Reservations required for six or more. Beer
and wine.

La Barbera's

11813 Wilshire Boulevard; West Los Angeles;
(213) 478-0123
Seven days, 11 A.M.–1:30 A.M.

Large portions and above-average pizza; a popular spot for
students. The low prices help. Cash only. No reservations.
Cocktails.

Mario's

1001 Broxton Avenue; Westwood; (213) 208-7077
Monday–Thursday, 11:30 A.M.–11:30 P.M.; Friday, 11:30 A.M.–
12:30 A.M.; Saturday, 4 P.M.–12:30 A.M.;
Sunday, 4–11:30 P.M.

Neapolitan cuisine and economic prices have made Mario's a
continuing favorite of students in and around Westwood. Major
credit cards. Reservations recommended. Beer, wine.

Monte Carlo's Pinocchio Westwood
1084 Glendon Avenue; Westwood; (213) 208-4663
Monday–Thursday, 11 A.M.–9 P.M.; Friday and Saturday,
11 A.M.–10:30 P.M. Other locations in Burbank and Santa Monica.

Make your selection at the deli counter; both hot and cold
choices are available. Sparse decor, but tasty food. Cash only.
No reservations. Beer, wine. Validated parking.

O-Sho Sushi
10914 West Pico Boulevard; West Los Angeles;
(213) 475-3226
Sunday–Thursday, 11:30 A.M.–2 P.M., 5–10 P.M.; Friday and
Saturday, 5–11 P.M.

A full sushi bar and exemplary teriyaki. Visa, MasterCard.
Reservations not required. Full bar.

Pancho's Family Café
12244 West Pico Boulevard; West Los Angeles;
(213) 820-9948
Seven days, 10 A.M.–2 A.M.

The restaurant is shaped like a hat. Though the decor is bland,
the waitresses are friendly, the chicken mole is good, and the
prices are extra low. Sit at the bar and you can watch Pancho
make menudo. Cash only. No reservations. Beer.

MAJOR RESTAURANTS

Adriano's Ristorante
2930 Beverly Glen Circle; Beverly Glen; (213) 475-9807
Tuesday–Thursday, 11:30 A.M.–2:30 P.M., 6–10 P.M.; Friday
and Saturday, until 11; closed Monday

Unusual dishes dot the menu at Adriano's, and the setting on
top of Beverly Glen canyon enhances the charm. Visa,
MasterCard, American Express. Reservations required. Full
bar.

Le Bistro
246 North Canon Drive; Beverly Hills; (213) 273-5633
Monday–Friday, noon–midnight; Saturday, 6 P.M.–midnight

Le Bistro Garden
176 North Canon Drive; Beverly Hills; (213) 550-3900
Monday–Saturday, 11:30 A.M.–midnight

Le Bistro and its formal counterpart, Le Bistro Garden, serve French/Continental with extravagance. Major credit cards. Reservations required. Full bar.

Café Four Oaks
2181 North Beverly Glen; Beverly Glen; (213) 474-9317
Tuesday–Saturday, 6:30 P.M.–midnight; Sunday brunch, 10:30 A.M.–2:30 P.M.

An old house that has been converted into an enticing Continental restaurant; menu changes every three months. Cash only. Reservations required except at brunch. Beer, wine.

Gatsby's
11500 San Vicente Boulevard; West Los Angeles; (213) 820-1476
Monday–Friday, 11:30 A.M.–3 P.M.; Monday–Saturday, 5:30–11:30 P.M.

Opulent setting and traditional Continental menu. Show-business owners have attracted the right celebrities as clientele. Major credit cards. Reservations recommended. Full bar.

Ma Maison
8368 Melrose Avenue; West Hollywood; (213) 655-1991
Monday–Saturday, noon–2:30 P.M., 6:30–10 P.M.

Very chic, this is French cuisine in a relaxed California setting. World-renowned. Major credit cards. Reservations required. Cocktails.

Madame Wu's Garden
2201 Wilshire Boulevard; Santa Monica; (213) 828-5656
Sunday–Thursday, 11:30 A.M.–10 P.M.; Friday, 11:30 A.M.–11 P.M.; Saturday, 5–11 P.M.

Typical Cantonese and Mandarin cuisine, but there is nothing typical about owner Sylvia Wu, whose presence makes the dining experience worthwhile. Major credit cards. Reservations recommended. Full bar.

Mangia
10543 West Pico Boulevard; West Los Angeles;
(213) 470-1952
Monday–Thursday, 11:30 A.M.–9:30 P.M.; Friday and Saturday; 11:30 A.M.–10:30 P.M.

Mangia tried to be *the* deli in the area, offering fine cold pastas, but the public wouldn't allow it. It's now a full-fledged restaurant, serving homemade pastas, soups, antipastos. Visa, MasterCard, American Express. Reservations required. Beer, wine.

Mr. Chow L.A.
344 North Camden Drive; Beverly Hills; (213) 278-9911
Seven days, 6:30 P.M.–midnight; Monday–Friday lunch, noon–2:30 P.M.

A sleek, fashionable Chinese restaurant with Peking cuisine to match. Major credit cards. Reservations required. Full bar.

Trader Vic's
9876 Wilshire Boulevard; Beverly Hills; (213) 274-7777
Sunday–Thursday, 4:30 P.M.–12:30 A.M.; Friday and Saturday, 4:30 P.M.–1 A.M.

The ultimate in Polynesian-Chinese food: a romantic tropical setting, attentive service, and fresh, delightful, somewhat exotic food. Major credit cards. Reservations required. Full bar.

Valentino
3115 Pico Boulevard; Santa Monica; (213) 829-4313
Monday–Friday, noon–3 P.M.; Monday–Saturday,
5:30–11:30 P.M.

A favorite for many, Valentino combines a romantic decor, varied Northern Italian menu (it changes every few months), and excellent service. Major credit cards. Reservations required. Full bar.

Verdi Ristorante di Musica
1519 Wilshire Boulevard; Santa Monica; (213) 393-0706
Tuesday–Sunday, from 5:30 P.M. (flexible close).

Where else can you go for tasty Tuscan cuisine *and* opera or musical comedy? Visa, MasterCard, American Express. Reservations required. Full bar from which you can order pasta, hors d'oeuvres, and desserts and watch the show.

Yamato Restaurant
2025 Avenue of the Stars (Century Plaza Hotel); Century City; (213) 277-1840
Monday–Friday, 11:30 A.M.–2:30 P.M., 5–11:30 P.M.;
Saturday, 5–11:30 P.M.; Sunday, 4:30–11 P.M.

Serenity, fresh food, and polite service are the Yamato watchwords; sushi bar, teppan grill, tatami room, and a main dining room. Major credit cards. Reservations required. Full bar.

PARK AREAS

General park information for Beverly Hills is (213) 550-4864

Beverly Hills Electric Fountain
Intersection of Wilshire and Santa Monica boulevards;
Beverly Hills

Cactus Garden
North of big Santa Monica Boulevard, between Camden and Bedford drives; Beverly Hills

These two go hand-in-hand; a walk leads from one directly to the other. The Electric Fountain was erected in 1931 and designed by Ralph Flewelling (who designed the Beverly Hills Post Office), sculpted by Merrel Gage. The Cactus Garden features cacti and succulents from several continents.

Greystone Park
501 North Doheny Road; Beverly Hills; (213) 550-4769

Edward Doheny built this opulent mansion for his family in 1923. (The roof, gray slate, is where the name comes from.) Vacant now, but the grounds are operated as a park. Outdoor concerts are held during the summer months. The parking lot at the top of the drive sits on a reservoir and overlooks the city of Los Angeles in a breathtaking view.

UCLA Campus
405 Hilgard Avenue; Westwood; (213) 825-4321

Franklin Murphy Sculpture Gardens
Noguchi and Matisse are two of the twentieth-century sculptors whose works are displayed in this four-and-one-half-acre garden.

Mathias Botanical Gardens
This is an eight-and-one-half-acre canyon, located on the southeast corner of the campus (near Hilgard and Le Conte avenues).

Will Rogers State Historic Park
14253 Sunset Boulevard; Pacific Palisades; (213) 454-8212
Call for hours.

The former home of the cowboy-humorist, this 187-acre park houses Rogers memorabilia, a visitor center that shows a ten-minute film on his life, and a polo field where matches are held every Saturday and Sunday during the summer. The park also has picnic areas and several hiking trails.

SPECIAL ATTRACTIONS

Canyon Roads to Mulholland Drive
Enter on Laurel Canyon Drive, Coldwater Canyon Drive, or Beverly Glen Boulevard

Strictly a fair-weather activity (it's crowded, slippery, and dangerous during the rainy season), these roads wind up and around and connect at the top, Mulholland Drive. The drives up take you past homes (some beautiful, some plain) and lush greenery.

Main Street to Santa Monica Pier Walk
Santa Monica

Main Street, especially on a warm day, is a delight to the senses. Touristy galleries, boutiques, pastry shops, outdoor cafés, bars,

line this street, which is one block from Santa Monica beach.
Cut over from Main Street for a walk along the shore and you'll
soon end up at the pier, a weathered, though prominent attraction
in the area since the early 1900s.

Century City
Between Olympic and Santa Monica boulevards, Century Park
East and West

Once the backlot of Twentieth Century-Fox Studios, it is now a
booming center all its own. The area hosts a full shopping mall
(Century City Square), a legitimate theater (Shubert), two movie
houses, myriad restaurants (take-out and sit-down), live entertainment, bars, and boutiques. Bustling by day, it is practically
deserted at night save for the entertainments.

Rodeo Drive
Between Santa Monica and Olympic boulevards; Beverly Hills

What can be said about Rodeo Drive that isn't already known by
anyone concerned with fashion, celebrities, or wealth? This is
the place to shop if you have the time to browse and the money
to spend.

Self-Realization Fellowship Lake Shrine
117190 Sunset Boulevard; Pacific Palisades; (213) 454-4114.
Tuesday–Saturday, 9 A.M.–5 P.M.; Sunday, 12:30–5 P.M.

Ponds, lakes, waterfalls, windmills, and gazebos transform this
former movie set into an open-air temple where those of any faith
are invited to come for a walk or bit of meditation.

Venice Beach
Modeled after the other Venice, this city was once a festive beach
town, canals included. It has changed drastically, but the festivity
is still alive. Catch Ocean Front Walk on a Sunday afternoon and
you'll see skaters, cyclists, craftspeople selling their wares, street
entertainers.

Westwood Village
Between Wilshire Boulevard and Le Conte, Gayley and
Glendon avenues; Westwood

An area jumping with students (from preteens to college-aged), who come to the Village for movies, arcades, food, drink, shopping, and flirting. Jammed Friday and Saturday nights.

MAJOR CULTURAL POINTS OF INTEREST

Craft and Folk Art Museum
5814 Wilshire Boulevard; (between Fairfax and La Brea); (213) 937-5544

Contemporary and ethnic folk art; also crafts and books for sale. The Egg and the Eye Restaurant, on the upper level, serves more than fifty types of omelets.

Fowler Museum
9215 Wilshire Boulevard; Beverly Hills; (213) 278-8010
Monday–Saturday, 1–5 P.M.

European and American decorative arts.

Los Angeles County Museum of Art
5905 Wilshire Boulevard; Mid-Wilshire; (213) 937-2590
Tuesday–Friday, 10 A.M.–5 P.M.; Saturday and Sunday, 10 A.M.–6 P.M.

This complex houses three wings: The Ahmanson Gallery (the Museum's permanent collection), The Hammer Gallery (temporary collections), and the Leo S. Bing Theater. There is a museum gift shop, concession stands, walkways. On the same grounds are the La Brea Tar Pits and the George C. Page Museum of La Brea Discoveries.

Mormon Temple
10777 Santa Monica Boulevard; West Los Angeles; (213) 474-1549
Visitor Information Center, 9 A.M.–9:30 P.M., seven days.

Outside of its home base in Salt Lake City, Utah, this towered edifice is the largest temple of the Church of Jesus Christ of Latter-day Saints. The temple itself is open only to members of the Church, but the Visitor Center is open to the general public. A local landmark.

Santa Monica Heritage Square Museum
2612 Main Street; Santa Monica; (213) 392-8537
Thursday–Saturday, 11 A.M.–4 P.M.; Sunday, noon–4 P.M.

Two nineteenth-century homes, almost leveled, happily saved and restored. The Roy Jones home, designed by Sumner P. Hunt, houses local archives and artifacts, with each room depicting a different American period. The second home is now The Chronicle Restaurant.

Airport and Inglewood Area

Only twenty minutes north of LAX Airport is Marina del Rey with its many waterside restaurants and Fisherman's Village. Nearby is funky Venice with one of the most bizarre boardwalks in the world. Shops and outdoor cafés abound, as do joggers, cyclists, roller skaters, and roller disco performers. Also street musicians, bodybuilders, and bikinis on the beach and on skates.

The beach scene continues south of LAX as well in Manhattan and Redondo beach communities twenty to thirty minutes from the airport—clubs, waterholes, shops, and lots of beach volleyball, and more bikinis and bodybuilders.

The nearby Olympic events and sites are: basketball in the Forum, the home of the Los Angeles Lakers. They have a few championship banners of their own plus a couple of former UCLA Bruins: Kareem Abdul Jabbar and Jamal Wilkes. And weight lifting at Loyola Marymount University, fifteen minutes north of LAX on the slopes looking northward over the Marina Canal and Marina del Rey.

INEXPENSIVE EATING ESTABLISHMENTS

Baja Cantina
311 Washington Street; Marina del Rey; (213) 821-2250
Monday–Saturday, 11:30 A.M.–11 P.M.;
Sunday, 10:30 A.M.–11 P.M.

Wooden booths and ubiquitous plants and flowers provide an intimate and romantic setting. The food's not bad, either.

The Forum in Inglewood, site of Olympic Handball and Basketball, is also the home for the Los Angeles Lakers.

Benihana of Tokyo
14160 Panay Way; Marina del Rey; (213) 821-0888
Monday–Friday, 11:30 A.M.–2:30 P.M. for lunch,
5:30–10:30 P.M. for dinner; Sunday, 5–11 P.M. for dinner.

Adept Japanese chefs wielding flashing knives provide tableside entertainment with every meal. A national chain with Los Angeles locations. All major credit cards. Full bar. Reservations recommended.

Bruno's Restaurant
3838 Centinela Avenue; Mar Vista; (213) 397-5703
Sunday–Thursday, 11 A.M.–11 P.M.; Friday and Saturday,
11 A.M.–midnight.

A warm and comfortable restaurant filled to the gills with knick-knacks, art, and lots of furniture. The menu offers standard Italian fare plus specialties. Full bar. Visa, MasterCard, American Express.

Casa Escobar
14160 Palawan Way; Marina del Rey; (213) 822-2199

Monday–Friday, 11:30 A.M.–2 A.M.; Saturday and Sunday, 10 A.M.–2 A.M.

A nice menu with Mexican favorites and an outdoor patio.

Cliff House Restaurant
6805 Vista del Mar Lane; Playa del Rey; (213) 823-1530
Seven days, 8 A.M.–10 P.M.

A block away from Playa del Rey beach, this restaurant offers an eclectic menu of seafood, omelets, vegetable plates, and salads. Beer and wine. Cash or personal check only. Reservations for large parties only.

Charley Brown's
4445 Admiralty Way; Marina del Rey; (213) 823-4534
Monday–Friday, 11 A.M.–3 P.M.; Monday–Thursday, 5–10 P.M.; Friday and Saturday, 5–11 P.M.; Sunday, 9:30 A.M.–3 P.M., 4:30–10 P.M.

Eight other Southland locations; check individual restaurants for days and times.

Meats and fresh fish broiled on an open grill. Friendly, efficient waitresses and a magnificent view of the Marina from full glass windows. Full bar. Visa, MasterCard, American Express. Reservations suggested.

Johnnie's Patio Restaurant
4017 South Sepulveda Boulevard; Culver City; (213) 397-6654
Seven days, 10 A.M.–3:30 A.M.

Transport yourself back to the Fifties with a meal at Johnnie's Patio Restaurant. Have his specialty: pastrami dip on a French roll: Play some music on the tabletop jukes and enjoy. Beer served. Cash only. No reservations.

Marie Callender Pie Shops
7415 La Tijera Boulevard; Los Angeles; (213) 670-1183
Sunday–Thursday, 11 A.M.–10 P.M.; Friday and Saturdays, 11 A.M.–11 P.M.

One of the largest and best-regarded chain coffee shops in the city, Marie Callender's forte is fresh-baked pies; burgers are thick and juicy; good cornbread, too. No liquor. Cash or personal check. No reservations.

Peilin Chinese Restaurant
10706 Jefferson Boulevard; Culver City; (213) 870-3183
Sunday–Thursday, 11:30 A.M.–9:45 P.M.; Friday and Saturday, 11:30 A.M.–10 P.M.

An unassuming Mandarin and Szechwan restaurant with such specialties as Mongolian beef. Beer and wine. All credit cards. Reservations required on weekends.

Stern's on the Hill
8415 Pershing Drive; Playa del Rey; (213) 822-4448

Stern's Restaurant
12658 West Washington Boulevard; Los Angeles;
(213) 306-7947
Seven days, 7 A.M.–11 P.M.; bar open until 2 A.M.

Simply delicious ribs, chicken, fish, and steak, barbecued over hickory coals. Full bar. American Express, Visa, MasterCard. Reservations accepted but not required.

Szechwan Restaurant, Marina del Rey
2905 Washington Boulevard; Marina del Rey; (213) 821-6256
Monday–Saturday, 11:30 A.M.–3 P.M., 5–10 P.M.

Mandarin and Szechwan cuisine. A full bar and all orders can be packed for take-out. All credit cards. Reservations recommended on weekends.

MAJOR RESTAURANTS

Castagnola's Lobster House
4211 Admiralty Way; Marina del Rey; (213) 823-5339
Monday–Friday, 11:30 A.M.–11 P.M.; Saturday,
4 P.M.–midnight; Sunday, 10 A.M.–10 P.M.; bar until 2 A.M.

The highest volume outlet of the 48-restaurant Hungry Tiger chain. Lobster, naturally, is the specialty here, but Castagnola's also offers other fresh seafoods and steaks in congenial surroundings. Visa, MasterCard, American Express. Reservations advised.

Fiasco
4451 Admiralty Way; Marina del Rey; (213) 823-6395
Monday–Friday, 11:30 A.M.–2 P.M.; Saturday and Sunday brunch, 10 A.M.–2:30 P.M.; seven days, 5:30–10 P.M.

An uncluttered menu, featuring steaks, seafood, and veal. A beautiful view of the Marina. Full bar. All credit cards. Reservations necessary on weekends.

Le Gourmet
6101 West Century Boulevard (Sheraton Plaza La Reina Hotel); Airport Area; (213) 642-4840
Monday–Saturday, 6–11 P.M.

A nouvelle-cuisine menu with refreshingly different entrees: quail with pureed plums, chicken and vegetable mousse. Elegant dining. All major credit cards. Reservations required.

Gulliver's Restaurant
13181 Mindanao Way; Marina del Rey; (213) 821-8866
Monday–Friday, 11:30 A.M.–3 P.M., 5:30–10 P.M.; Saturday, 5–11 P.M.; Sunday, 4–11 P.M.

A full roast-beef dinner plus Long Island duck, rack of lamb, lobster tail, and other perennial favorites. Served by cheerful and efficient "wenches" in large, homey rooms. Full bar. Visa, MasterCard. Reservations preferred.

Peking Restaurant
234 West Manchester Boulevard; Inglewood;
(213) 678-6993
Seven days, 11:30 A.M.–10 P.M.

Mandarin, Cantonese, and Szechwan cuisine appear on Peking's menu, with a buffet lunch featured Monday through Friday. Sunday champagne brunch. Three-minute drive from the Forum. Full bar. All major credit cards. Reservations suggested.

T.J. Peppercorn's
6225 West Century Boulevard (Hyatt Hotel); Airport Area; (213) 670-9000
Monday–Friday, 11:30 A.M.–2:30 P.M.; daily, 6–10:30 P.M.; open until 11 P.M. Friday and Saturday.

A warm and comfortable interior, Peppercorn's offers a salad bar and a dessert bar with interesting things like lamb, duckling, and seafood in between.

The Warehouse
4499 Admiralty Way; Marina del Rey; (213) 823-5451
Monday–Friday, 11:30 A.M.–2:30 P.M.; Monday–Thursday, 5–10 P.M.; Friday and Saturday, 5–11 P.M.;
brunch, 11 A.M.–2:30 P.M. Saturday, 9:30 A.M.–2:30 P.M. Sunday. Other locations in Newport Beach, Redondo Beach (Beachbum Burt's), and West Covina.

Youthful steak house with a conscience. A nice bar and lilting harp music. Full bar. Visa, MasterCard, American Express. Reservations for parties of eight or more.

PARK AREAS

Burton Chace Park
End of Mindanao Way; Marina del Rey

A lovely park area, perfect for picnics, boat watching, fishing, kite flying, or relaxing with a loved one.

SPECIAL ATTRACTIONS

Fisherman's Village
13723 Fiji Way; Marina del Rey; (213) 823-5411

A charming, brick-paved village with lots of small, quaint shops, restaurants (eat-in or take-out), and pastry shops. It lines one side of the Marina, where sail and other pleasure craft perform their daily parade.

Hollywood Park
1050 South Prairie Avenue; Inglewood; (213) 419-1500

This beautifully landscaped, major-league racetrack offers thoroughbred racing April through July, harness racing August through December. A children's play area is especially helpful.

MAJOR CULTURAL POINTS OF INTEREST

The Forum
Manchester Boulevard and Prairie Avenue; Inglewood; (213) 674-6000

The Forum is an architectural wonder of columns and cantilevered ceiling. The facility seats 17,000 plus, sponsors the Lakers basketball from September through May, and Kings hockey in the winter. In between, it hosts rock concerts, ice shows, the circus, tennis matches, rodeos. The Forum is the 1984 Olympics basketball site.

Marina del Rey
On Via Marina

Built in 1960, the Marina houses over 10,000 private pleasure craft, which makes it the largest man-made small-boat harbor in the world.

Long Beach and South Bay

Long Beach is undergoing a renaissance of new building, waterfront development, and restoration. The harsh steel constructions and odors of oil refineries and waterfront industry are still apparent, but much has been accomplished to make the area attractive and full of surprises.

The Long Beach Convention Center is the focal point for downtown development and an increase in major hotel facilities. Next to the Convention Center is Seaport Village and Marina, a new complex of shops and restaurants. This faces, on the opposite side of the harbor, the major visitor attraction operated by Wrather Port Properties—the *Spruce Goose* and

The *Queen Mary*, with its neighbor, the Howard Hughes Flying Boat, which rests inside the dome alongside. The *Queen* is now a hotel, and together with the *Spruce Goose* forms a major tourist attraction drawing more than 3 million visitors annually.

the *Queen Mary*. The world's largest luxury liner and airplane side-by-side make for a unique and completely enjoyable visit.

A few minutes to the north are the special hideaways of San Pedro and the Los Angeles Harbor, and the elegant homes and rugged coastline of Palos Verdes, Rolling Hills, and Point Vicente.

To the south, in less than thirty minutes, one can reach Newport Beach and Balboa Island, both high-rolling oceanside resorts for boaters and anyone with a zest for going out.

Departures to Catalina by ferry [Catalina Cruises can be reached at (213) 514-3838] are five minutes from downtown for the two-hour ride to Avalon, and by plane from the local airport. In Avalon, one can find many small restaurants, hotels, and shops. No cars permitted from the mainland. The vast portion of the island is protected wilderness ideal for hiking and camping, and there are real buffalo! In fact, for arrival by plane at the small airport atop a flat-topped mountain peak in the center of the island (and a thirty-minute drive from Avalon), the special of the day is always Buffalo Burgers and chili at the airport café. It is delicious, and knowledgeable Angelenos occasionally will fly from Santa Monica or Long Beach airports for a treat. The entire trip, including lunch, can be made by plane in considerably less than two hours and there is no waiting for a table!

For Long Beach, the Olympic events and sites are: cycling at California State University, Dominguez Hills; fencing at the Long Beach Convention Center; volleyball at the Long Beach Arena; yachting in the Long Beach marina; and archery in Eldorado Park.

INEXPENSIVE EATING ESTABLISHMENTS

Acapulco y Los Arcos
733 East Broadway; Long Beach; (213) 435-2487
Seven days, 11 A.M.–10 P.M.; open until 11 P.M. Friday and Saturday

Acapulco y Los Arcos is a chain of nearly forty Mexican restaurants nationwide, but you don't feel it; the food, service, and atmosphere are fresh and fun. Twenty-one flavors of margaritas and an eighteen-page menu make the drinking and dining possibilities practically limitless. Visa, MasterCard, American Express. Reservations for parties of five or more.

Egg Heaven

4358 East 4th Street; Long Beach; (213) 433-9277
Monday–Wednesday, 6:30 A.M.–2:30 P.M.; Thursday, 6:30 A.M.–10 P.M.; open from Friday, 6:30 A.M., until Sunday, 10 P.M.

"Imagination" is the key word here, from the art murals on the walls to the fifteen different ingredients you can choose for your personalized omelet. Cash only. No reservations. No liquor.

El Cholo

777 South Main Street; Orange; (714) 972-9900
Monday–Saturday, 11 A.M.–10 P.M.; Sunday, 10 A.M.–9 P.M.

Other locations in La Habra, downtown Los Angeles, and, as Margarita Ryan's Cantina, in Newport Beach. El Cholo is one of the finest values in Mexican dining. The menu is simple and the food served piping hot. Visa, MasterCard, American Express. Full bar.

The Filling Station

762 Pacific Avenue; Long Beach; (213) 437-3324
Monday–Friday, 7 A.M.–2:30 P.M.; Sunday, 8 A.M.–2 P.M.; Wednesday–Saturday, dinner until 9 P.M.

Eclectic menu of quiche, soups, salads, served in a simple, refreshing setting. Visa, MasterCard. No reservations. Beer and wine.

Francelli's

3404 East 4th Street; Long Beach; (213) 434-3441
Monday–Thursday, 11 A.M.–10 P.M.; Friday and Saturday, 11 A.M.–11 P.M.; Sunday, noon–11 P.M.

A mom-and-pop Italian grocery store that also happens to serve fine pizza. The deli menu offers sandwiches, pastas, and other dinners. Cash only. No reservations. Beer and wine.

Gugie's Lobster Pot
Twenty-second Street Landing; San Pedro; (213) 831-1944
Seven days, 9 A.M.–5 P.M.

Gugie's shares the pier with the winter whale-watch boats, and
you can espy some of the mammals as you eat freshly boiled
crabs or lobsters at picnic tables. Pick your own from large
tanks on the pier and Gugie's will clean and cook them for
you. Bring your own accoutrements for a rare experience. Cash
only. Beer, wine.

Hamburger Henry
4700 East Second Street; Long Beach; (213) 433-7070
3001 Wilshire Boulevard; Santa Monica; (213) 828-3000
Open twenty-four hours.

Hamburger Henry is a good, creative restaurant, where more
than forty different kinds of burgers are offered, along with a
thirty-two-item salad bar. Service is friendly and prices low.
Visa, MasterCard, American Express. Reservations recommended on weekends.

Hamburger Hut
824 Gaffey Street; San Pedro; (213) 548-9340
Daily, 7 A.M.–3 P.M.

Hamburger Hut dishes out top-notch burgers with a large variety of condiments. The interior is plain, but the hamburgers
aren't. Cash only. No reservations.

Joe Jost's Bar
2803 East Anaheim Boulevard; Long Beach; (213) 439-5446
Monday–Saturday, 10 A.M.–11 P.M.; Sunday, 11 A.M.–6 P.M.

The smoky pool hall in the back room sets the mood and the
pace at Joe Jost's. Not much of a menu, but the bar and the
back room keep the place jumping. Beer only. All major credit
cards.

Nam's Red Door Vietnamese Restaurant
2253 South Pacific Avenue; San Pedro; (213) 832-4120
Tuesday–Friday, 11 A.M.–2 P.M., 5–9:30 P.M.; Saturday,
5–9:30 P.M.

A converted house with a homey and comfortable dining room. The food is delicate and tasty, ordered mild, spicy, hot, or— watch out—very hot. Cash only. Beer and wine.

Panama Joe's Café and Bar
5100 East Second Street; Long Beach; (213) 434-7417
Monday–Saturday, 11 A.M.–11 P.M.; Sunday 10 A.M.–10 P.M.

A period flavor (complete with Tiffany lamps) and more than fifty Mexican dishes, a favorite among local residents. Visa, MasterCard, American Express. No reservations. Full bar.

Papadakis Taverna
301 West Sixth Street; San Pedro; (213) 548-1186
Monday–Friday, 11:30 A.M.–2 P.M.; dinner seven days, 5–10 P.M.

This is an authentic Greek taverna, owned and operated by John Papadakis, a former football player at USC. Excellent food, and if the mood's right, Papadakis might lead a Greek dance. Visa, MasterCard. Reservations required. Beer, wine.

The Pot Holder Café
3700 East Broadway; Long Beach; (213) 433-9305
Seven days, 7 A.M.–2 P.M.

Looks like a dive from the outside, but the inside is something else again: a huge oak bar from the Thirties, old-fashioned decorations; customers chow down on the omelets and burgers. Cash only. No reservations. No liquor.

Senfuku Restaurant
380 West Sixth Street; San Pedro; (213) 548-9695
Tuesday–Friday, 11 A.M.–2 P.M.; Tuesday–Thursday, 5–9 P.M.; Friday and Saturday, 5–10 P.M.

A Japanese restaurant offering teriyaki, tempura, and fresh seafood. Visa, MasterCard. No reservations. Beer, wine.

Sunny Spot Coffee Shop
4339 East Carson Street; Long Beach; (213) 429-6507
Monday–Friday, 5 A.M.–3 P.M.; Saturday, 5 A.M.–2 P.M.

Run-down coffeeshop, one of Long Beach's oldest; nevertheless a good place for a hearty breakfast or a filling lunch. Cash only.

Major Restaurants

Adolph's

700 Queensway Drive; Long Beach; (213) 437-5977
Monday–Friday, 6:30 A.M.–3 P.M.; 5:30–10 P.M.; Saturday and Sunday, 7 A.M.–3 P.M.; 5:30–10 P.M.

Located in the Queensway Hilton, the restaurant has a lovely marina view. The specialty is seafood; the ambience is tropical. All major credit cards. Reservations recommended.

Alpine Village Inn

833 Torrance Boulevard; Torrance; (213) 323-6520
Seven days, 11 A.M.–1 A.M.

A cheery inn that serves German-Swiss food in generous portions, with a band, animals, amusement park, and decidedly German ambience. All major credit cards. Full bar. Reservations not required.

Babouch Moroccan

810 South Gaffey Street; San Pedro; (213) 831-0246
Tuesday–Sunday, 5–10 P.M.

An authentic, six-course Moroccan meal, served with belly dancing and music.

Bobby McGee's Restaurant

6501 East Pacific Coast Highway; Long Beach;
(213) 594-8627
Monday–Thursday, 5–10 P.M.; Friday and Saturday,
5–11 P.M.; Sunday, 4–10 P.M.

The staff is dressed as storybook characters; the restaurant is chock full of antiques; and the menu offers seafood, prime rib, steak. There's an adjoining lounge for dancing; open until 2 A.M. Part of a seventeen-restaurant chain. All major credit cards. Full bar. Reservations recommended on weekends.

Café Courtney
2701 Pacific Coast Highway; Hermosa Beach;
(213) 318-2545
Monday–Thursday, 11 A.M.–9:30 P.M.; Friday, 11 A.M.–10:30
P.M.; Saturday, 10 A.M.–2 P.M., 5–10:30 P.M.; Sunday,
10 A.M.–2 P.M., 6–9 P.M.
Other locations: The Bistro, Manhattan Beach, (213) 544-0810;
Courtney Manhattan, Manhattan Beach, (213) 544-1020;
Courtney Palos Verdes, Rolling Hills, (213) 544-0771.

The place to go when you're not in the mood for authentic
haute cuisine, but want something more than a burger. Simple,
tasteful, just right. Full bar. All major credit cards.

The Main Event
24530 Hawthorne Boulevard; Torrance; (213) 373-6303
Monday–Friday, 11:30 A.M.–2:30 P.M.; Monday–Saturday,
5:30–10 P.M.

A neat little country restaurant offering Continental cuisine:
veal, seafood, lobster, pasta. American Express, Visa,
MasterCard. Reservations preferred.

Restaurant Marengo
24594 Hawthorne Boulevard; Torrance; (213) 378-1174
Monday–Friday, 11:30 A.M.–2:30 P.M.; Monday–Saturday,
6–11 P.M.; Sunday, 5–9 A.M.

An intimate, stylish French restaurant where the specialty is
Chicken Marengo, served by waiters in Napoleonic costumes.
All major credit cards. Reservations recommended.

Le Monaco Restaurant
2325 Palos Verdes Drive West; Palos Verdes Estates;
(213) 377-6775
Seven nights, 5:30–10 P.M.

A French restaurant with no surprises on the menu but a splendid view from its position on top of the hill. Full bar. All major
credit cards. Reservations suggested.

Prince of Whales Restaurant
6790 Long Beach Boulevard; Long Beach; (213) 632-1366
Seven days, 11 A.M.–2 P.M.; Tuesday–Saturday, 4–8:45 P.M.;
Sunday, 4–7 P.M.

Seafood exclusively. A full beer menu (more than forty foreign labels) and entrees for children. All major credit cards. No reservations necessary.

S. S. Princess Louise Restaurant
Berth 94; San Pedro; (213) 831-235l
Monday–Thursday, 5:30–10 P.M.; Friday and Saturday,
5–11 P.M.; Sunday, 11 A.M.–3 P.M., 4–10 P.M.

A shipboard theme restaurant with Continental cuisine. The view is disarming, and you can walk the decks before or after dining. Nightclub and cocktail lounge open till 2 A.M. All major credit cards. Reservations suggested.

La Rive Gauche
320 Tejon Street; Palos Verdes; (213) 378-0267
Tuesday–Sunday, 11:30 A.M.–3 P.M.; nightly, 5:30–10 P.M.

A rustic restaurant tucked away in the Peninsula; La Rive Gauche's French menu includes daily specials, centered around fresh fish. The Wine Spectator Award for one of the best wine lists in America (1,200 labels). Full bar. All major credit cards. Reservations recommended.

A Tout Va Bien
5730 East Second Street; Naples, Long Beach;
(213) 439-9888
Wednesday–Saturday, 6–10:30 P.M.

A small, quiet, unassuming French country inn, with formal and professional service. MasterCard, Visa, Diners. Reservations suggested.

PARK AREAS

Eldorado Park
Eldorado Park East and Nature Center; 7550 East Spring Street; Long Beach; (213) 425-8569

Eldorado Park West
2800 Studebaker Road; Long Beach; (213) 425-4712

(Check individual parks for days and times)

Eldorado Park is an eight-hundred-acre recreational facility. Park East is unstructured, with a lake for paddle boats, bike and roller-skating paths, and an archery range. Park West has an eighteen-hole golf course, tennis courts, baseball diamonds, duck pond, children's playground, and a branch of the Long Beach Public Library. The Nature Center is an eighty-acre bird sanctuary and native chaparral community. There's also a small museum with exhibits on Southern California's natural history.

Point Fermin Park/Point Fermin Marine Life Refuge
807 Paseo del Mar; San Pedro

The park is thirty-seven acres of landscaped gardens that overlook the Pacific Ocean and Los Angeles Harbor. A whale-watching station gives information to those interested. The Refuge is a tidepool area next to the Cabrillo Beach Marine Museum.

South Coast Botanic Gardens
26300 South Crenshaw Boulevard; Rancho Palos Verdes; (213) 377-0468
Daily, 9 A.M.–4 P.M.

Designed and organized by the Los Angeles Department of Arboreta and Botanic Gardens in 1960, this eighty-seven-acre garden now has specimens from all continents (except Antarctica). There's also a gift shop, displays, and gardening demonstrations.

SPECIAL ATTRACTIONS

Fisherman's Wharf
King Harbor; Redondo Beach

A nice place for small boutiques and souvenir shops and a fresh seafood meal. Additional information from the harbor restaurant at (213) 372-1171 and the Redondo Beach Chamber of Commerce at (213) 376-6912.

Marineland
6610 Palos Verdes Drive South; Rancho Palos Verdes; (213) 541-5663

Marineland overlooks the cliffs of Palos Verdes Peninsula. It's a huge aquarium and marine circus, featuring performing sea lions, whales, and dolphins. Also a Marine Care Center.

Naples Area
Second Street and Marina Drive; Long Beach; (213) 433-4811 for information

This area was developed in 1903, using its Italian namesake as a model for cottages, curving streets, and canals. It surrounds Colonnade Park, which is encircled by the Rivo Alto Canal. Lovely, romantic, perfect for a stroll.

Ports o'Call Village
Berth 77; San Pedro; (213) 831-0287

Charming, quaint, early-nineteenth-century "sea village" of small shops and restaurants. Offers a number of cruises of the harbor area.

Queen Mary/Spruce Goose
Pier J; Long Beach; (213) 435-3511

The *Queen Mary*, the largest passenger ship ever built, now calls Long Beach Harbor home, berthed proudly as a maritime museum and luxury hotel. The third-class passenger cabins have been reconstructed as a maritime heritage museum, a theater, and many other exhibits, including a celebrity exhibit. The *Spruce Goose*, the largest aircraft ever built, sits beneath a magnificent dome next door to the *Queen Mary*. Conceived and constructed by Howard Hughes, it had its maiden and final flight on November 2, 1947.

Wayfarer's Chapel
5755 Palos Verdes Drive South; Rancho Palos Verdes; (213) 377-4458

Designed in 1946 by Frank Lloyd Wright, this glass and red-wood church is a monument to Emanuel Swedenborg, Swedish theologian and mystic. Services held every Sunday at 11 A.M.

MAJOR CULTURAL POINTS OF INTEREST

Cabrillo Marine Museum
3720 Stephen White Drive; San Pedro; (213) 548-7562
Tuesday–Friday, noon–5 P.M.; Saturday and Sunday,
10 A.M.–5 P.M.

Southern California marine life on exhibit, including marine laboratories, thirty-five aquaria, pinniped and mammal rooms.

Long Beach Museum of Art
2300 East Ocean Boulevard; Long Beach; (213) 439-2119
Wednesday–Sunday, noon–5 P.M.

The museum's changing exhibits showcase Southern California contemporary art. It's located in a 1912 Craftsman-style home, with carriage house serving as bookstore and exhibition gallery.

Lomita Railroad Museum
250th Street and Woodward Avenue; Lomita;
(213) 326-6255
Open Wednesday–Sunday, 10 A.M.–5 P.M.

The museum is located in a replica of the nineteenth-century Greenwood Station of Wakefield, Massachusetts. Memorabilia from the steam era of railroading.

Los Angeles Maritime Museum
Berth 84; San Pedro; (213) 548-7618
Monday–Friday, 9 A.M.–4 P.M.; Saturday and Sunday,
12:30–4 P.M.

Housed in a remodeled ferry building in the Port of Los Angeles, this museum plots Los Angeles nautical history. The Naval Deck offers Navy memorabilia and the largest scale-model of the *Titanic* in the world.

Pasadena City Hall. This traditional baroque-style civic building was designed in 1925 and is the centerpiece of the Pasadena Civic Center. It also offers formal gardens with a fountain court-yard.

San Gabriel Valley and Pasadena

Traditional and sedate Pasadena—the image is not off the mark, but there is more to Pasadena than prize-winning floral floats every January 1. Pasadena and San Marino society, in their California Spanish-style residential mansions, long ago began the whole thing with their midwinter celebration of sunny weather, magnificent mountains, and the local soil abounding year-round with fruit and flowers.

It is no accident Pomona is not far away, nor the Valley Hunt of Pasadena organized in the 1890s, the first Tournament of Roses, complete with a jack-rabbit hunt (as a local stand-in for the fox). At first disorganized football, rugby-style, was played, and the first true Rose Bowl Game took place in 1902. The locals (Stanford) lost to Michigan 49–0. As a result, chariot racing replaced football, looking every bit like a scene from *Ben Hur*, until 1916. The locals (Washington State beat Brown 20–16) prevailed, and it has been football ever since.

The theme has always been sport and fun for all, and it is proclaimed on the beautiful Tournament of Roses posters from the 1910s and 20s. A secular celebration, it is a magnificent tradition and the grandfather of all sporting traditions in Southern California.

But there is more to Pasadena now. It can even make fun of itself, as witnessed by the annual, late-November Doo-Dah Parade, complete with the precision drill team of blue-suited, briefcase-carrying business types. No prizes, no awards, just a lot of fun and drinking at the very lively local watering holes.

The stately Tournament of Roses mansion (the Wrigley House) on South Orange Grove is five minutes from the Norton Simon Museum. Cal Tech and the Jet Propulsion Lab, the Descanso Gardens, and many other places of interest are nearby. Included is a small treasure hidden in the residential areas of San Marino—El Molino Viejo (the old mill). It was originally the grist mill for the San Gabriel Mission and now serves as the library for the California Historical Society. For a taste of original Spanish California, a few minutes at El Molino Viejo will take you back two hundred years.

Also, in San Marino, is the Huntington Library. Its gardens, representing many cultures, and its manuscript collections (Chaucer, Gutenberg, Audubon, and others) are unsurpassed. Add its first-class art and furniture collection, and the Huntington, by itself, will be a special place worth the entire trip.

Nearby Olympic events and sites are: soccer at the Rose Bowl; equestrian events at Santa Anita Park; judo at California State University, Los Angeles; and hockey at East Los Angeles College.

Inexpensive Eating Establishments

Acapulco Mexican Restaurant and Cantina
2936 East Colorado Boulevard; Pasadena; (213) 795-4248
Monday–Thursday, 11 A.M.–10 P.M.; Friday and Saturday, 11 A.M.–midnight; Sunday, 10 A.M.–11 P.M.

Famous for crab enchiladas; casual dining in a lively atmosphere that's fun for the whole family. Visa, MasterCard, American Express. Reservations weekdays only; for parties of ten or more on weekends. Full bar.

Beadle's Cafeteria
850 East Colorado Boulevard; Pasadena; (213) 796-3618
Seven days, 11 A.M.–7:45 P.M.

There's nothing at all wrong with plain old-fashioned American food, when it is as nicely prepared as it is at Beadle's. Cash only. No reservations. No liquor.

Brotherton's Farmhouse
2239 East Colorado Boulevard; Pasadena; (213) 796-5058
Tuesday–Sunday, 11:30 A.M.–8:30 P.M.

Owned and operated by the Brotherton family for fifty years, specializing in home cooking, including chicken pie that even Mother never mastered. Cash only. Reservations not required. Beer, wine.

Burger Continental
535 South Lake Street; Pasadena; (213) 792-6634
Monday–Thursday, 7 A.M.–10:30 P.M.; Friday and Saturday,
7 A.M.–11:30 P.M.; Sunday, 7 A.M.–10 P.M.

Different and exotic versions of the American hamburger. A
lovely patio. Visa, MasterCard. No reservations. Beer, wine.

Do-Nut Hole
15300 East Amar Road; La Puente; (213) 968-2912
Open twenty-four hours.

This unusual drive-through (you actually drive through the
doughnut hole) is a solution to those midnight cravings.

Konditori Restaurant
230 South Lake Street; Pasadena; (213) 792-8044
Monday–Saturday, 7:30 A.M.–5:30 P.M.

Swedish pancakes, smoked salmon and eggs, open-faced Danish sandwiches are served with care at this lovely little restaurant. Cash only. No reservations. Beer, wine.

Panchito's Mexican Kitchen
261 South Mission Drive; San Gabriel; (213) 289-9201
Tuesday–Friday, 11 A.M.–11 P.M.; Saturday, 5–11 P.M.;
Sunday, 4–11 P.M.

Built and operated by Frank Ramirez (Panchito), this delightful
restaurant boasts a secret sauce made with eighteen ingredients.
All major credit cards. Reservations for parties of ten or more.
Full bar.

Panda Inn Restaurant
3472 East Foothill Boulevard; Pasadena; (213) 793-7300
Also in Chinatown and Glendale.
Seven days, 11:30 A.M.–10:30 P.M.

Mandarin, Szechwan, Shanghainese, and Cantonese are the
dishes to try at this Chinese restaurant, which some consider
the finest in Los Angeles. Visa, MasterCard. Reservations
required. Full bar.

Sawmill
340 South Lake Avenue; Pasadena; (213) 796-8388
Monday–Thursday, 11 A.M.–10:30 P.M.; Friday and Saturday,
11 A.M.–11:30 P.M.; Sunday, 4:30–10:30 P.M.; bar until 2 A.M.

This is the place for a good, basic meal of steaks, chicken, or
seafood. A salad bar complements the main course. Live entertainment every night. Visa, MasterCard, American Express.
Reservations on a limited basis. Full bar.

Stottlemeyer's Deli
712 East Colorado Boulevard; Pasadena; (213) 792-5351
Monday–Friday, 9:30 A.M.–8 P.M.;
Saturday, 11 A.M.–8 P.M.; Sunday, 11 A.M.–7 P.M.

One of the first restaurants in Los Angeles to give sandwiches
funny names, Stottlemeyer's offers more than 150 combina-
tions. The desserts are good, too. Visa, MasterCard, American
Express. No reservations. Beer, wine.

Tokyo Lobby
927 Las Tunas Drive; San Gabriel; (213) 287-9972
Monday–Friday, 11:30 A.M.–2:30 P.M., 5–9:30 P.M.; Saturday
and Sunday, 4:30–9:30 P.M.

A Japanese restaurant that will appeal to everyone. The menu
is typical and the ambience calm. Visa, MasterCard. Reservations suggested on weekends. Beer, wine.

MAJOR RESTAURANTS

Alex's
140 Las Tunas Road; Arcadia; (213) 445-0544
Tuesday–Sunday, 4–11 P.M.

Southern Italian cuisine is offered at Alex's; good pizza and
especially tasty lasagna. Cash only. Reservations accepted, but
not necessary. Beer, wine.

Le Biarritz
4141 South Nogales Street; West Covina; (213) 964-8813
Monday–Friday, 11:30 A.M.–3 P.M., 5–10 P.M.; Saturday,
5–10 P.M.

French and Continental cuisine: fish, beef, or veal, freshly prepared and nicely served. Major credit cards. Reservations recommended. Full bar.

Chez Sateau
850 Baldwin Avenue; Arcadia; (213) 446-8806
Monday–Friday, 11:30 A.M.–2:30 P.M.; seven days, 5:30–10 P.M.; Sunday brunch, 10:30 A.M.–2:30 P.M.

Continental French cuisine. Meals are well-thought-out and nicely presented. Service is formal; it's nice to be fussed over. All major credit cards. Reservations recommended. Full bar.

The Chronicle
897 Granite Drive; Pasadena; (213) 792-1179
Monday–Saturday, 11:30 A.M.–2:30 P.M.; Monday–Thursday, 5:30–10:30 P.M.; Friday and Saturday, 5:30–11:30 P.M.; Sunday, 5–10 P.M.

Also in Santa Monica.
The Chronicle is a handsome old restaurant; good Continental cuisine in a turn-of-the-century atmosphere. Major credit cards. Reservations required. Full bar.

Maldonado's
1202 East Green Street; Pasadena; (213) 796-1126
Monday–Friday, 11 A.M.–3 P.M.; Tuesday–Thursday, dinner seating at 7 P.M.; Friday and Saturday, 6 and 9 P.M.; Sunday, 5:30 and 8:30 P.M.

Maldonado's combines delicious cuisine (seafood is a specialty) with live entertainment (harp, opera, musical comedy on different nights). Most enjoyable. Visa, MasterCard. Reservations required. Full bar.

Marianne French Restaurant
45 South Mentor Avenue; Pasadena; (213) 792-2535
Tuesday–Friday, 11:30 A.M.–2 P.M.; Tuesday–Thursday, 5:30–9 P.M.; Friday and Saturday, 5:30–10 P.M.; Sunday, 5–9:30 P.M.

Traditional French cuisine, prepared and served in a very proper setting. Try the quenelles and mousses. Major credit cards. Reservations required. Cocktails.

Miyako Restaurant
139 South Los Robles; Pasadena; (213) 795-7005
Monday–Friday, 11:30 A.M.–2 P.M.; Monday–Saturday,
5:30–10 P.M.; Sunday, 4:30–9 P.M.
Other locations in Torrance and Orange.

All the traditional Japanese dishes, nicely prepared and served by kimonoed waitresses. Visa, MasterCard. Reservations recommended. Cocktails

Monty's Steak House
592 South Fair Oaks Avenue; Pasadena; (213) 792-7776
Tuesday–Thursday, 5–11:30 P.M.; Friday and Saturday,
5 P.M.–12:30 A.M.; Sunday and Monday, 5–11 P.M.

A good steak house (the pepper steak is recommended) with a full bar and live entertainment. Major credit cards. Reservations suggested.

La Parisienne
1101 E. Huntington Drive; Monrovia; (213) 357-3359
Monday–Friday, 11:30 A.M.–2 P.M.; Monday–Thursday,
6–10 P.M.; Friday–Sunday, 5:30–10 P.M.

A very unassuming restaurant, with a good menu and generous portions of French cuisine. Seafood is especially tasty. Major credit cards. Reservations required. Full bar.

Talk of the Town Restaurant
3730 East Foothill Boulevard; Pasadena; (213) 793-6926
Monday–Saturday, 11 A.M.–2 A.M.; Sunday, 10 A.M.–2 A.M.

The favorite local hangout for Santa Anita horse players; an old, traditional steak house with full generous meals. Also fresh seafood, chicken, and veal. Visa, MasterCard, American Express. Reservations suggested. Full bar with entertainment.

Park Areas

Descanso Gardens
1418 Descanso Drive; La Canada/Flintridge; (213) 790-5571
Daily, 9 A.M.–4:30 P.M.

Something is always blooming in this 165-acre garden, especially the camellias, for which it is noted. A Japanese teahouse calmly sits in the center of the garden and there is a bookstore and gift shop.

Eaton Canyon Nature Center
1750 North Altadena Drive; Pasadena; (213) 794-1866
Park open daily, dawn to dusk. Exhibits open 9 A.M.–5 P.M.

Native California plants comprise this 184-acre compound. There is a small museum with exhibits and displays of area ecology. Self-guided tours through the canyon are welcome. Naturalist room offers nature walks, bird walks on Saturday mornings. Call center for details.

Forest Lawn Memorial Park
1712 South Glendale Avenue; Glendale;
(213) 254-3131
Open daily 8 A.M.–5 P.M.

The Southland's most famous resting grounds, Forest Lawn is a very special park, with arborways, retreats, and reproductions of three European churches: the Church of the Recessional (modeled after a tenth-century English church); the Wee o'the Heather (modeled after a fourteenth-century kirk in Glencairn, Scotland); and the Little Church of the Flowers (inspired by the English church in Thomas Gray's *Elegy Written in a Country Churchyard*).

Special Attractions

Old Town
Between Delacey Avenue, Arroyo Parkway, Holly and
Green streets; Pasadena

Gift and antique shops, galleries with exhibits by local artists.

Plaza Pasadena
300 block East Colorado; Pasadena; (213) 795-8891

A new shopping area with 122 specialty shops and three major department stores.

Rose Bowl Flea Market
Rose Bowl; 991 Rosemont Boulevard; Pasadena;
(213) 577-7208

Held on the second Sunday of each month, this is a flea-market lover's heaven. You'll find everything here, including the kitchen sink!

MAJOR CULTURAL POINTS OF INTEREST

California Institute of Technology Campus
1201 East California Boulevard; Pasadena; (213) 356-6811

This school has a fine reputation for its engineering, physics, and astronomy departments. Originally designed by Bertram Goodhue in 1930, the campus was inspired by a medieval scholastic cloister. Regularly scheduled tours Monday, Thursday, and Friday at 3 P.M., Tuesday and Wednesday at 11 A.M., starting in the public-relations department, 315 South Hill Avenue. Reservations required for parties of ten or more.

El Molino Viejo
1120 Old Mill Road; San Marino; (213) 449-5450
Tuesday–Sunday, 1–4 P.M.

Built in 1816 for the San Gabriel Mission, this building was the first water-powered mill in Southern California. It has been restored and is now the southern headquarters of the California Historical Society.

Gamble House
4 Westmoreland Place; Pasadena; (213) 793-3334
Tours are given on Tuesday and Thursday, 10 A.M.–3 P.M.; first weekend of the month, noon–3 P.M.; closed holidays.

This house, a Craftsman-style bungalow designed by Charles and Henry Greene, is an architectural delight. It was built in 1908 for the Gamble (of Procter and Gamble) family, and everything in it was specially made and/or designed for them, from the Tiffany lamps to the hand-made rugs.

The Henry E. Huntington Library, Art Galleries, and Botanical Gardens
1151 Oxford Road; San Marino; (213) 792-6141
Tuesday–Sunday, 1–4:30 P.M.; advance reservations required for Sundays, call (213) 792-6144.

Formerly the home of Henry E. Huntington, this 207-acre compound has something for everyone. The actual home is now an art gallery with such impressive paintings as Gainsborough's *Blue Boy* and Lawrence's *Pinkie*. The library houses an impressive and extensive list of English and American first editions, including a Gutenberg Bible. The gardens are beautifully landscaped and include rose and camellia gardens, and a Japanese garden, complete with koi pond and teahouse.

Los Angeles State and County Arboretum
301 North Baldwin Avenue; Arcadia; (213) 446-8251
Open daily, 9 A.M.–4:30 P.M.

This 120-acre arboretum is home to plant specimens from all over the world. They are arranged by continent of origin and surround a central spring-fed lake. Snack bar and gift shop.

San Gabriel Mission Archangel
537 West Mission Drive; San Gabriel; (213) 282-5191
Open daily, 9:30 A.M.–4 P.M.

Founded in 1771 by Fathers Pedro Cambon and Angel Somera. Originally built by Indian workers from 1791 to 1805, the current mission consists of the remains from the original structure that were restored and rebuilt in 1828 after earthquake destruction of 1812.

Norton Simon Museum
411 West Colorado Boulevard; Pasadena; (213) 449-6840
Open Thursday–Sunday, noon–6 P.M.

Old masters Rembrandt, Rubens; Goya etchings; painting and sculpture by Cézanne, Toulouse-Lautrec, Renoir, Van Gogh, Picasso, and German Expressionists. The museum shop has a comprehensive collection of art books, prints, and cards. Free parking. Group tours may be arranged in advance.

Pacific-Asia Museum
46 North Los Robles Avenue; Pasadena; (213) 449-2742
Wednesday–Sunday, noon–5 P.M.

This museum, designed by Mayberrty, Marston and Van Pelt, at the request of Grace Nicholson, offers exhibits of Far East and Pacific Basin art. Exhibits change regularly. Several gift shops on the second floor offer kitchen goods and Oriental gifts and clothing.

Orange County

"There's no city there, it's an endless sprawl without landmarks, and they stole our team." If New Yorkers say that about Los Angeles and the Dodgers, Angelenos (at least that portion from downtown to the beach) say it about Anaheim, Orange County, and the Rams. And just as quickly as Los Angeles can roll out all the reasons the image isn't accurate, Orange County can do the same. It is new, a county of vast proportions, and as seen from the freeway, it gives cause for concern. But it incorporates a diverse area from Newport Beach and Balboa on the coast; northward to Anaheim (Disneyland, Knott's Berry Farm, the Crystal Cathedral, and those Rams); to Pomona and San Bernardino County; and the spectacular mountain areas of Idyllwild, the San Bernardino National Forest, the Santa Ana Mountains, and the Cleveland National Forest.

In fact, even Ma Bell couldn't grasp it all. San Diego had to get its own area code. San Diego, another newcomer, is now "619" and Orange County kept "714." The bottom line— Orange County got the Rams and the area code. There is a *there there*, in fact, several "theres," to reverse and paraphrase that cosmopolitan critic, Gertrude Stein. And a history. In fact, both Orange County and San Diego are filled with early California history. San Diego is California's first city; and Orange County was home to early Spanish settlers, their ranches, and their life-style. A very special place, known to all thanks to the swallow, is Mission San Juan Capistrano. Located in the community of the same name, the Mission is just a few minutes off Highway 5, but secluded nonetheless.

Within a few minutes walk from the Mission is the Amtrak Station (three of the seven daily L.A.–San Diego trains stop there), and within the station area, trackside, is the charming Depot Restaurant.

And, forty-five minutes from San Juan Capistrano, in the mountains to the east, is the resort lake area of Elsinore, and within twenty-five minutes in the hills the Olympic modern-pentathlon site of Coto de Caza.

Other Olympic events and sites (and they cover a wide area, so carefully consult your map and get advice on travel time and routes) in this area are handball at California State University, Fullerton, and California State University, Pomona (in San Bernardino County); wrestling at the Anaheim Convention Center; and shooting at the Prado Recreation Park in Chino (in San Bernardino County).

INEXPENSIVE EATING ESTABLISHMENTS

Amagi
6890 Beach Boulevard; Buena Park; (714) 994-2730
Monday–Friday, 11:30 A.M.–2 P.M.; seven days, 4:30–10 P.M.;
Sunday brunch, 10 A.M.–2:30 P.M.

A fine place for a simple Japanese meal, freshly prepared, efficiently served. Sushi bar and all-you-can-eat Japanese buffet. All major credit cards. Reservations required. Full bar.

Bangkok 3
101 Palm Avenue; Balboa Peninsula; (714) 673-6521
Tuesday–Friday, 6–10 P.M.; Saturday and Sunday,
6–10:30 P.M.

Traditional Thai, with duck and fish specialties. Try the egg-rolled shrimp appetizer. American Express, Visa, MasterCard. Reservations required on weekends. Beer and wine.

Boardwalk

Surf and Sand Hotel; 1555 South Coast Highway; Laguna
Beach; (714) 497-4477 (hotel) or (714) 494-8588
(restaurant)
Monday–Thursday, 5:30–10 P.M.; Friday and Saturday,
5:30–11 P.M.; Sunday brunch, 10 A.M.–3 P.M.

Old-fashioned Laguna Beach, New England-style; quaint and
comfortable; seafood, including New England clam chowder.
All major cards. Reservations recommended for weekends.
Full bar. Entertainment in lounge.

Bouzy Rouge Café

3110 Newport Boulevard; Newport Beach; (714) 673-3440
Monday–Thursday, 5:30–10 P.M.; Friday and Saturday, 5:30–
11 P.M.; Sunday, 5–9 P.M.; Saturday breakfast and lunch, 8
A.M.–3 P.M.; Sunday brunch, 10 A.M.–2:30 P.M.

A friendly neighborhood café featuring a taste of many European cuisines. The wine bar, offering vintage wine by the
glass, is unusual. MasterCard, Visa, American Express. Reservations required.

El Cholo

777 South Main Street; Orange; (714) 972-9900
Monday–Saturday, 11 A.M.–10 P.M.; Sunday, 10 A.M.–9 P.M.

Other locations in La Habra, Orange, and Margarita Ryan's
Cantina, Newport Beach. A loud, fast, and fun Mexican restaurant where the service is efficient, the food tasty, and the
prices refreshingly low. Visa, MasterCard, American Express.
Full bar.

Hansa House

1840 South Harbor Boulevard; Anaheim; (714) 750-2411
Seven days, 11 A.M.–3 P.M., 4:30–9 P.M.

A filling, tasty, all-you-can-eat smorgasbord. Daily specialties.
MasterCard, Visa, American Express. Banquet facilities. Full
bar.

Ichabod Crane's
651 West Whittier Boulevard; La Habra; (213) 694-1988;
(714) 992-2336
Monday–Friday, 11 A.M.–3 P.M.; Sunday–Thursday, 5–9 P.M.;
Friday and Saturday, 5–10 P.M.; Sunday 10 A.M.–3 P.M.

An English-style dinnerhouse. Warm, comfortable. All major
cards. Reservations suggested. Full bar. Dancing.

Mr. Peng's No. 2
9730 Garden Grove Boulevard; Garden Grove;
(714) 530-1311
Seven days, 11 A.M.–10 P.M.

The basics such as mu shu pork, pan-fried dumplings, and
some not-so-basics—seasonal fresh fish. American Express,
MasterCard, Visa. Full bar.

Mrs. Knott's Chicken Dinner Restaurant
8039 Beach Boulevard; Buena Park;
(714) 827-1776 (Ext. 316)
Seven days, 7–11:30 A.M.; Sunday–Friday, noon–9 P.M.;
Saturday, 7 A.M.–10 P.M. (summer hours)

Owned by Knott's Berry Farm, but located outside the gates
of the park. The tender chicken and fresh-baked pies are mem-
orable. Be prepared to wait in line. All major cards. Reservations for parties of twelve or more. No liquor.

Nanbankan
24291 Avenida de la Carlota; Laguna Hills; (714) 855-8135
Monday–Friday, 11:30 A.M.–2 P.M.; seven days, 5–10 P.M.
11330 Santa Monica Boulevard; West Los Angeles;
(213) 478-1591
Seven days: 5:30–10:30 P.M.

Japanese; features teppan (cooking at the table); also a regular
dining room and sushi bar. Visa, MasterCard, American Express. Beer and wine.

Saddleback Inn Dining Room

1660 East First Street; Santa Ana; (714) 835-3311
Monday–Friday, 11 A.M.–3 P.M.; Monday–Saturday,
5–10:45 P.M.

A hacienda where the kitchen combines food from the Old
West with contemporary dishes; basic American fare mixed
with Mexican. All major cards. Full bar. Live music.

Seafood Broiler Restaurant and Market

1199 North Euclid Avenue; Anaheim; (714) 778-5000
Sunday–Thursday, 11 A.M.–10 P.M.; Friday and Saturday,
11 A.M.–10:30 P.M.

Various other locations throughout Los Angeles and Orange
County areas. Fresh fish is offered daily in this combined
restaurant-indoor fish market. Visa, MasterCard, American
Express. No reservations. Full service bar.

MAJOR RESTAURANTS

Ambrosia

695 Town Center Drive; Costa Mesa; (714) 751-6100
Monday–Saturday, 6 P.M.–10 P.M.; lunch,
11:30 A.M.–2:30 P.M. Closed Sundays.

Elegant, extravagant, and expensive, Ambrosia takes good care
of customers. Included in Le Premier, a three-part restaurant.
French. All major credit cards. Full bar. Coat and tie. Reservations required.

Bessie Walls Fine Food and Spirits

1074 North Tustin Avenue; Anaheim; (714) 630-2812
Monday–Friday, 11 A.M.–3 P.M.; Sunday–Thursday,
5–10 P.M.; Friday and Saturday, 5–11 P.M.; Sunday brunch,
10 A.M.–3 P.M.

Early California cuisine served in a 1920s Spanish home. A
combination of American and Mexican food, with seafood,
chicken, "steakchilada," plus more. All major credit cards.
Reservations suggested. Full bar.

La Brasserie
202 South Main Street; Orange; (714) 978-6161
Monday–Friday, 11:30 A.M.–2 P.M.; Monday–Saturday,
5–10 P.M.

American-French, cooked and served delicately and with skill.
A charming restaurant. American Express, MasterCard, Visa.
Reservations suggested. Full bar.

The Cellar Restaurant
305 North Harbor Boulevard; Fullerton; (714) 525-5682
Tuesday–Saturday, 6:30–11 P.M.

In the cellar of the charming old California Hotel, this restaurant is a delight. Nouvelle cuisine, served with a flourish. All
majors. Full bar.

Chez Cary
571 South Main Street; Orange; (714) 542-3595
Daily, 6:30–10 P.M.

First-rate French cuisine, served by an efficient crew in a lovely
and luxurious setting. All majors. Reservations recommended.
Prefer coat and tie. Full bar.

The Crab Cooker
2200 Newport Boulevard; Newport Beach; (714) 673-0100
Sunday–Thursday, 11 A.M.–9 P.M.; Friday and Saturday,
11 A.M.–10 P.M.

A plain setting, with plain accoutrements; only fresh fish served,
as good as it is casual. Also to-go. Cash or check. Wine and
beer. First come, first served.

The Five Crowns
3801 East Coast Highway; Corona del Mar; (714) 760-0331
Monday–Thursday, 5–11 P.M.; Friday and Saturday,
5–12 P.M.; Sunday, 10:30 A.M.–3 P.M.; 4–12 P.M.

This English restaurant, in a refurbished inn, is Lawry's of
Orange County and, as you may expect, excellent. MasterCard,
Visa, American Express. Reservations required. Full bar.

Marrakesh
1100 West Pacific Coast Highway; Newport Beach;
(714) 645-8384
Monday–Thursday, 6–10 P.M.; Friday–Sunday,
5:30–10:30 P.M.
Also in Studio City.

An authentic Moroccan restaurant; seven-course meals served sans silverware, of course. All major credit cards. Reservations required. Full bar.

Park Areas

Newport Dunes Aquatic Park
East Coast Highway and Jamboree Road; Newport Beach;
(714) 644-0510

A lovely place to bring the family, this aquatic park is a fifteen-acre lagoon where you can rent sailboats and paddleboats. There's also a picnic area, campgrounds, dressing rooms, and a launching ramp.

Sherman Library and Gardens
2647 East Pacific Coast Highway; Corona del Mar;
(714) 673-2261

This is a beautiful botanical garden and library that specializes in the history of the Pacific Southwest. A tea garden offers pastries and coffee. There's also a small gift shop.

Special Attractions

California Alligator Farm
7671 La Palma Avenue; Buena Park; (714) 522-2615

A fascinating reptile zoo, where you'll find not only alligators, but also crocodiles, lizards, and snakes. (Don't worry, they're all in glass cages or in pens.) There are also regularly scheduled shows and a small gift shop.

Disneyland
1313 South Harbor Blvd.; Harbor Boulevard exit/Santa Ana Freeway; Anaheim; (714) 533-4456

The most famous theme park in the world, Disneyland truly has something for everyone. The different areas in Walt Disney's Magic Kingdom are Main Street USA, Adventureland, New Orleans Square, Frontierland, Bear Country, Fantasyland, and Tomorrowland. Restaurants and concessions are in all the special areas. Souvenir booths and shops abound. Special shows (like the Electric Light Parade) are scheduled. And there are roving minstrels and Disneyland characters. A very special place and fun for all.

Knott's Berry Farm
8039 Beach Boulevard; Buena Park; (714) 952-9400

Another of the Southland's famous theme parks, Knott's Berry Farm is a replica of the Old West, with several different areas: Ghost Town, Fiesta Village, Roaring '20s Airfield, the Knott's Good Time Theater, and (just for kids) Camp Snoopy. Rides, museums, exhibits, concessions, souvenir shops, and Mrs. Knott's fried chicken make this an all-day fun affair.

Lion Country Safari
8800 Irvine Center Rd; Irvine Center Drive exit/San Diego Freeway; Laguna Hills; (714) 837-1200
Daily, 9:45 A.M.–3:30 P.M.

A five-hundred-acre preserve where the animals are left to roam while you drive through the compound. There's also a petting village, animal nursery, and a Zambezi River cruise.

Movieland Wax Museum
7711 Beach Boulevard; Buena Park; (714) 522-1154
Sunday–Thursday, 10 A.M.–8 P.M.; Friday and Saturday, 10 A.M.–10 P.M.

Over two hundred life-size, exquisitely detailed movie and TV stars, in wax, on exhibit. The California Plaza Restaurant, on the museum grounds, is a nice place to stop for a bite to eat.

South Coast Plaza
3333 Bristol Street; Costa Mesa; (714) 546-6683

A beautifully designed shopping mall located just off the San Diego Freeway. It has large department stores and small boutiques; you won't walk away from here empty-handed.

Whale Watching
Dana Wharf Sport Fishing; 34675 Golden Lantern;
Dana Point; (714) 496-5794

A seasonal (winter) activity, this is an interesting, fun, and educational tour. The whales come in right off Dana Point.

MAJOR CULTURAL POINTS OF INTEREST

Balboa Pavilion
400 Main Street; Balboa; (714) 673-5245

This pavilion, built in 1905, is the center of marine recreation for Newport Beach. Designated a California Point of Historical Interest, it has a restaurant, gift shop, oceanview bar, and arcades; it is the Newport terminal for Catalina Island tours. Take the ferry across to Balboa Island for a Balboa Bar ice cream.

The Crystal Cathedral
12141 Lewis Street; Garden Grove; (714) 971-4000

Dr. Robert Schuller's Crystal Cathedral is breathtaking. Designed by Philip Johnson and John Burgee, the cathedral is 415 feet long, 207 feet wide, and 128 feet high, made of white steel trusses and tempered silver glass and seats 1,861.

Mother Colony House
414 North West Street; Anaheim; (714) 774-3840
Wednesday, 3–5 P.M.; Sunday, 1:30–4 P.M.

This white clapboard house, circa 1857, was the first house built in Anaheim. It contains an exhibit of Anaheim's pioneer history.

Mission San Juan Capistrano
Camino Capistrano and Ortega Highway; San Juan
Capistrano; (714) 493-1111
Daily, 7:30 A.M.–5 P.M.

This mission was founded in 1776 by Father Junípero Serra. The finished stone church was destroyed in 1812 by an earthquake. It has undergone a complete restoration and the stone church is now replicated. Famed for its returning swallows.

Muckenthaler Cultural Center
1201 West Malvern Avenue; Fullerton; (714) 738-6595

This 1923 Spanish Baroque house, donated to Fullerton by the Muckenthaler family, now houses art exhibits, classes, receptions, and theater-on-the-green.

Newport Harbor Art Museum
859 San Clemente Drive; Newport Beach; (714) 759-1122

This museum houses a permanent collection of twentieth-century art specializing in Southern California artists, and changing exhibits of contemporary art. The Sculpture Garden Café is a nice place to get a light meal, and there is also a gift shop.

Malibu

Malibu—from the unique J. Paul Getty Museum on the Pacific Coast Highway (Highway 1) just north of Sunset Boulevard to Trancas Canyon and the Ventura County line—is an area of contrasts.

The Getty Museum is both beautiful and traditional. The large, dark cobblestones of the access road enforce a five-mile-per-hour speed limit. The villa is a breathtaking recreation of the ancient Roman villa of the Papyri in Herculaneum, covered by the volcanic ash of the great eruption of Mt. Vesuvius in A.D. 79. This modern vision has withstood the pounding Pacific seas, the torrential winter rains, the local Malibu fast life, and the Los Angeles smog. In fact, the ocean breezes keep the Getty, and the rest of Malibu, a year-round retreat and haven from the urban rush of Los Angeles proper.

Topanga Canyon, with its rustic image, its laid-back restaurants, and its clubs is just a few miles north, also off Highway 1. And the Malibu County area, home to entertainers, celebrities, and their entourages, is about fifteen to twenty

minutes farther north on Highway 1. It's this enclave that gives
Malibu its fast-life image. A beautiful joining of low rugged
hills and mountains and the Pacific Ocean, this area is dotted
with secluded coves and beaches.

Beginning with Topanga Canyon, several canyon roads lead
off Highway 1 into the rugged Santa Monica Mountains, and
many scenic routes are to be found. Otherwise, one continues
north on Highway 1 along the rugged coast to Ventura.

Olympic events and sites in this area are water polo at
Pepperdine University, just a few minutes north of Malibu
Colony. The modern, Mediterranean-style campus buildings
rise dramatically on a hill inland from the highway.

INEXPENSIVE EATING ESTABLISHMENTS

Alice's Restaurant
23000 Pacific Coast Highway; Malibu; (213) 456-6646
Monday–Friday, 11:30 A.M.–10 P.M.; Saturday and Sunday,
10 A.M.–11 P.M.

Organic food the American way: hamburgers, sandwiches, eggs,
omelets—with a conscience. Visa, MasterCard. Full bar. Reservations accepted.

The Chart House
18412 West Pacific Coast Highway; Malibu; (213) 454-9321
Monday–Thursday, 5–10:30 P.M.; Friday, 4–12 P.M.; Sunday,
3–10:30 P.M.

Beautiful, romantic, right on the ocean. Usually a long wait.
The steaks, chicken, and fish are evenly cooked and nicely
priced. All major credit cards. First come, first served. Full
bar.

Chris' Kitchen
18763 Pacific Coast Highway; Malibu; (213) 456-8383
Seven days, 7 A.M.–6 P.M.

Eggs, burgers, fish and chips, sandwiches, along with surfers
and beach bunnies. Cash only. No alcohol.

Colony Coffee Shop
23706 Pacific Coast Highway; Malibu; (213) 456-8546
Monday–Saturday, 7 A.M.–7 P.M.; Sunday, 8 A.M.–7 P.M.

Superstar residents of Malibu Colony come to have a burger here; a popular coffee shop, with comfortable atmosphere and good food. Cash only. Beer and wine.

Sand Castle Restaurant
28128 West Pacific Coast Highway; Malibu (Paradise Cove); (213) 457-2503
Seven days, 6 A.M.–3 P.M., 5–10 P.M.

A romantic spot, right on the ocean; fine seafood. All major cards. Reservations. Full bar.

MAJOR RESTAURANTS

Carlos and Pepe's and Nantucket Light
22706 Pacific Coast Highway; Malibu; (213) 456-3105
Sunday–Thursday, 11:30 A.M.–11 P.M.; Friday and Saturday, 11 A.M.–midnight

Good seafood, a full salad bar, and yet another panoramic ocean view. All major credit cards. No reservations. Full bar.

Inn of the Seventh Ray
128 Old Topanga Canyon Road; Topanga; (213) 455-1311
Seven days, 6–10 P.M.: Monday–Friday, 11:30 A.M.–3 P.M.; Saturday, 11 A.M.–3 P.M.; Sunday brunch, 9:30 A.M.–3 P.M.

Dine in a converted church on grounds where trees thrive and brooks meander. Food strictly organic, often mellow. Visa, MasterCard. Beer and wine. Reservations for dinner.

La Scala Malibu
3835 Cross Creek Road; Malibu; (213) 456-1979
Tuesday–Thursday, 11:30 A.M.–10:30 P.M.; Friday and Saturday, 11:30 A.M.–11 P.M.

The beachside counterpart of La Scala in Beverly Hills, with the fine Italian cuisine of its sister. American Express, MasterCard, Visa. Reservations accepted. Full bar.

Moonshadows
20356 Pacific Coast Highway; Malibu; (213) 456-3010
Monday–Thursday, 5–11 P.M.; Friday and Saturday, 5 P.M.–
midnight; Sunday, 4–11 P.M.

Another fine on-the-beach steak house; steaks, salads, and a
romantic view. All major credit cards. No reservations. Full
bar.

PARK AREAS

Leo Carillo State Beach/Point Mugu State Park
Pacific Coast Highway and Mulholland Highway; Malibu;
(213) 706-1310

Point Mugu State Park, situated across from Leo Carillo State
Beach, offers seventy miles of trails, perfect for hikes and
picnics. Camping hookups are available. There's good surfing
at the north end of Carillo Beach.

Malibu Pier Sport Fishing Landing/Surf Rider State Beach
23000 Pacific Coast Highway; Malibu; (213) 456-8030

The landing (built in 1903 by Frederick Rindge; rebuilt 1946)
on Malibu Pier offers regular day-and-half-day surface fishing
cruises. Call for further information. There is also a bait and
tackle shop; fishing licenses are sold. Next door is Surf Rider
State Beach, where surfing is good in August and September;
a convenient location to watch is right from the pier.

Point Dume
Kaanan Dume Road; Malibu

This is mostly a residential area with a secluded beach. It was
named for Father Dumetz, a Jesuit at the Ventura Mission.
Located just southwest of Zuma Beach Park.

Santa Monica Mountains
Mulholland at Pacific Coast highways

A fabulous view of both Los Angeles City and the San Fernando Valley through this semiwild chain of canyons.

Topanga State Park
20825 Entrada Road; Topanga; (213) 455-2465

Over nine thousand acres of trails through knolls, waterfalls, and wooded glens. A true picture of Los Angeles' bygone habitat.

Zuma Beach
Entrance at Zuma Bay Road and Pacific Coast Highway; Malibu

Zuma Beach is one of Malibu's largest: it's over three miles long. There's great surfing here.

SPECIAL ATTRACTIONS

Malibu Creek State Park
28754 Mulholland Highway; Agoura; (213) 706-1310

Excellent hiking on fifteen miles of trails, Malibu Creek, Century Lake, oaks, chaparral, and volcanic rock formations on four thousand acres.

Paradise Cove
Zumirez Drive (28200 Pacific Coast Highway); Malibu Riviera

A private beach—romantic, very away-from-it-all.

Pepperdine University
24255 West Pacific Coast Highway; Malibu; (213) 456-4000

A beautiful, nondenominational four-year college on a hill overlooking the Pacific Ocean. A lovely lookout of the area.

Topanga Canyon
Topanga Canyon Boulevard between Pacific Coast Highway and Mulholland Drive

The term "rustic canyon living" could have been coined with Topanga in mind. One of the best sightseeing drives in Los Angeles, about ten miles of windy, lulling road.

MAJOR CULTURAL POINTS OF INTEREST

California Institute of the Arts (CAL ARTS)
24700 McBean Parkway; Valencia; (805) 255-1050

Walt Disney's endowment created the school in 1970. A four-year institution with schools in film, dance, theater, art, and music.

J. Paul Getty Museum
17985 Pacific Coast Highway; Malibu; (213) 459-8402 (for reservations)

This is a replica of a Roman seaside villa, with colonnaded walkways, mosaics, frescoes, and Roman-style landscaping. This Mediterranean complex sits atop a hill overlooking the Pacific Ocean. The galleries house European paintings from the Renaissance through Baroque periods, and French decorative arts. There's a tearoom for light meals, and a bookstore. Admission is free, but you must make advanced parking reservations, or take a taxi, or an RTD bus. You are not allowed to park in the neighborhood and walk in the door.

Malibu Art and Design
3900 South Cross Creek Road; Malibu; (213) 456-1776
Monday–Saturday, 10 A.M.–6 P.M.; Sunday, noon–5 P.M.

A combination general store and art gallery. The store stocks household and personal items, and the gallery exhibits local artists' works.

Tidepool Gallery
22762 West Pacific Coast Highway; Malibu; (213) 456-2551
Tuesday–Sunday, 11 A.M.–5:30 P.M.

This is a terrific seashell store that also sells artwork.

Ojai and Lake Casitas

The Ojai (pronounced Oh-high) Valley is eighty-four miles north of downtown Los Angeles by way of Highway 101 and Highway 33 north. The valley is nestled about ten miles from the coast and Ventura at the base of the Los Padres National Forest, which rings it on the north and east with rugged mountain peaks ranging to over six thousand feet.

Lake Casitas twists among the rolling hills of the valley's sparsely populated west end.

There are four roads in and out: the southern route, Highway 33 from Ventura and the coast, is the easiest and most traveled; the eastern route is Highway 150 from the Santa Clara Valley and Santa Paula (Highway 126, which connects with Highway 5); the northern route is Highway 33 north into the Los Padres National Forest; and the western route is Highway 150 past Lake Casitas and over the Casitas Pass to Highway 101 just south of Santa Barbara. Each of the latter three has its special appeal: the eastern route descends through the high meadows of the upper Ojai and passes under the rocky ledges of Topa Topa; the northern route leads to rugged campsites and creeks and follows a steeply ascending, hairpin-twisting course; and the western route provides at its first summit a spectacular eastward view over Lake Casitas and toward the face of Topa Topa. From this view, one senses why the last few surviving California condors have chosen the nearly inaccessible ledges of Topa Topa's jagged, sheer face as their nesting home.

Ojai retains a small-town atmosphere, and indeed it isn't an overwhelming quantity of any man-made thing that gives the valley its special quality. There are a few jewels, like the Ranch House Restaurant, that sparkle in this seductive natural setting. One feels close to the mountains and the clear skies and sequestered within the chaparral-covered folds of the steep nearby mountainsides.

The Chumash Indian's word for moon is A-hwai, and in the mission days there was a ranch Aujai. You can draw your own conclusions when you feel for yourself the balmy night air of the Ojai.

INEXPENSIVE EATING ESTABLISHMENTS

Antonio's

106 South Montgomery; Ojai; (805) 646-6353
Daily, 11:30 A.M.–9:00 P.M. (Mondays to 8:30 P.M.)

A charming patio restaurant with typically Mexican cuisine, California style. A nice selection of Mexican beers, moderately good margaritas. Across the street from the Ojai Art Center and the Ojai Valley Museum. MasterCard and Visa. Full bar.

Chez Bernard's

139 East Ojai Avenue; Ojai; (805) 646-8830
Daily, 11–3 P.M.; 5–10 P.M.; Sunday brunch, 9 A.M.–3 P.M.

Pizzas done Mediterranean style in one of three wood-burning brick ovens to be found in California. Also baguettes, salads, and sandwiches served on an outdoor patio. A short, but pleasant wine list, and beer. MasterCard, Visa.

The Gaslight

11432 N. Ventura Avenue; Ojai; (805) 646-5990
Tuesday–Sunday, 5–10 P.M. Early Bird dinners Tuesday–Thursday and Sunday, from 5–7 P.M.

A serviceable, pleasant restaurant with beef and veal dishes, augmented by a few German specialties. Popular on weekends with lots of foot-stomping dancing. All major credit cards. Banquet facilities. Entertainment and dancing Friday and Saturday, 9 P.M.–1:30 A.M. Full bar.

The Nest

108 South Montgomery; Ojai; (805) 646-8111
Tuesday–Sunday, 7 A.M.–2:30 P.M., 5–9 P.M.; Sunday brunch, 8 A.M.–2 P.M.

Lynn Wachter has created an intimate restaurant that began as a lunch room in a cozy, antique living-room setting. Delicious salads (the Arbolada and the Tico) and dishes derived from family cooking are featured. MasterCard and Visa. Full bar.

Major Restaurants

L'Auberge
314 El Paseo; Ojai; (805) 646-2288
Saturday and Sunday, 11 A.M.–2:30 P.M.; Wednesday–
Monday, 5:30–9 P.M.

Paul Franssen of L'Auberge was formerly at the Santa Barbara
Biltmore for sixteen years. In 1981, he opened his excellent
French restaurant in a renovated 1910 Ojai residential building.
The wine list is short, but excellent; and there are fish, fowl,
and beef specialties. The quality is consistently very good. For
lunches and warm-weather dining, the terrace under the scrub
oak tree offers a lovely view of the Ojai Valley. MasterCard
and Visa. Wine and beer. Reservations.

The Ojai Valley Inn
Ojai Avenue (no street address; approximately 2 miles west
of the town arcade); Ojai; (805) 646-5511
Daily, 8–10 A.M. (Sunday till 11 A.M.), noon–3 P.M.,
7–9 P.M.

All breakfasts and lunches are buffets; Sunday-night dinner is
the grand buffet. This is also an expensive, but first-class
American-plan hotel. The highlight is the view over the rolling
fairways of the golf course and the surrounding mountains. No
credit cards. Full bar. Reservations.

Pierpont Inn
Sanjon Road; Ventura; (805) 643-6144
Seven days, Breakfast, 7:00 A.M.–10:30 A.M.; Lunch, 11:30
A.M.–2:00 P.M.; Dinner, 6:00 P.M.–8:45 P.M.; Sunday brunch
8 A.M.–3 P.M.

This one isn't in Ojai, but on a bluff overlooking the Ventura
Beach approximately seventeen miles toward Los Angeles from
Ojai (off Highway 101). A charming hotel and restaurant. The
feature on the menu is abalone steak, a favorite of locals since
the days of the Chumash Indians. MasterCard, Visa, American
Express. Entertainment and dancing Thursday–Saturday. Full
bar.

The Ranch House
South Lomita Avenue; Ojai; (805) 646-2360
Wednesday–Saturday, 6 and 8:30 P.M.; Sunday, 1, 3:30, 6, and 8:30 P.M.

With or without the Olympics, the Ranch House is worth the trip. The wine list, particularly for California wines, is superb and very fairly priced. The service, including the friendly wine stewards, is unparalleled for courtesy and restraint. Alan Hooker, the founder and guiding light, may occasionally be seen. However, he's more likely to be hidden away working on a new recipe. The menu is short, but creative, with totally fresh ingredients and always of consistently high quality. Herbs are grown in their own garden which wraps around the bamboo paths, fish pond and outdoor dining terraces. If you call about one week in advance, they'll have a white-fish mousse ready for your appetizer. If you don't, it won't matter, you'll still lose your cares and worries. MasterCard, Visa, American Express. Wine and beer. Reservations.

PARK AREAS

Channel Islands National Park and Visitor's Center
1901 Spinnaker Drive; Ventura Harbor; (805) 644-8157

The nation's newest national park comprises the four Santa Barbara Channel Islands. Tidepools, flora and fauna exhibits. Tours available through Island Packer Cruises in Ventura, (805) 642-1393.

Los Padres National Forest
Ojai Ranger Station; 1190 East Ojai Avenue; Ojai; (805) 646-8293

A rugged mountain area to the north and east of Ojai of 1,900,000 acres. At the east end the rocky outcrop of Topa Topa can be seen from all points in the valley. A 6,170-foot peak, the nesting home of the California condor, it catches the late-afternoon light and flushes with delicate pinks and blues. Deer, quail, and other small game abound, and there is fishing and hunting in season. Three areas of special note:

Wheeler Gorge
7 miles north of Ojai on Highway 33, along Matilija Creek
A steep, twisting creek and road, dotted with small swimming holes and picnic areas.

Lion's Campground
Off Highway 33, 25 miles to the north of Ojai past Wheeler Gorge
On Sespe Creek by way of the Rose Valley road

Pine Mountain
30 miles north of Ojai, off Highway 33
Nine miles on Pine Mountain Road to a campground at an altitude of 7,000 feet.

SPECIAL ATTRACTIONS

Old Spanish Days
122 North Milpas; Santa Barbara; (805) 963-8101

Every year in early August, it's La Fiesta in Santa Barbara. There are many reasons for going to Santa Barbara anytime of year, including the Mission Santa Barbara [(805) 682-4713]; the Spanish and Moorish–style Santa Barbara courthouse building on Anacapa Street; the Museum of Natural History [(805) 682-4711] and its seventy-foot blue whale; the botanic gardens and its sixty acres of native flora [(805) 682-4726], and the adobes and Spanish buildings of the old Presidio area. [For further information, call the Santa Barbara Conference and Visitor's Bureau at (805) 965-3021.]

Valley of Shangri-La
East end of the Ojai Valley; Highway 150

This road leads out of the east end, to the lovely ranch meadows of the upper Ojai, toward Santa Paula. At the lookout point at the top of this sharply twisting road is the Valley of Shangri-La as seen by Ronald Colman in the film, *Lost Horizon*.

MAJOR POINTS OF CULTURAL INTEREST

Krotona
Krotona Hill; (805) 646-2653

Krishnamurti made this his home for many years. The Krishnamurti Oak, so named for his frequent talks under its branches, is located on the eastward slope of Krotona Hill, a few hundred feet above the Ranch House. The Krotona Library is the largest theosophical library on the West Coast.

Mission San BuenaVentura
211 East Main Street; Ventura; (805) 644-3993

A quiet retreat founded by Father Junípero Serra in 1782, this mission has been carefully restored. It has lovely gardens.

The Ojai Music Festival
Ojai City Park; Call Ojai Valley Chamber of Commerce; (805) 646-3000

The annual Ojai Music Festival takes place in late May and features not only chamber and classical music but other forms, from jazz to classical guitar. It is performed, under the spreading sycamores, in a small intimate amphitheater. Over the years Stravinsky, Robert Craft, Lucas Foss, and others have served as Festival directors.

PART 3

A Year-round Guide
to Southern California

In the preceding Parts 1 and 2 of this Guide the reader has been introduced to Southern California hotels, transportation, and services, and to the 1984 Olympic events, with a guide to "What to Do Before and After an Event."

In the following Part 3, the reader will be given a year-round guide to dining, watering holes, theater and music, clubs and dancing, excursions, shopping, health and beauty, museums and places of cultural interest, sports, and annual events.

Some of the entries in the dining and other sections of Part

The entrance to Rex II Ristorante on the ground floor of the Oviatt Building, an art deco masterpiece on South Olive Street, downtown Los Angeles. *Ratkovich & Bowers*

3 may overlap with entries in the "What to Do Before and After an Event" in Part 2. These overlapping entries will provide additional information and make this guide easier to use, especially in light of the widespread locales and diverse geography of the Olympic events and of the many Southern California communities.

Dining in Los Angeles
by Dick Roraback, Restaurant Writer

Los Angeles—home of the alfalfaburger, the margarita, and the onion ring—as the dining capital of the world?

The Parisian raises an eyebrow in utter disbelief. The Cantonese is incredulous. The San Franciscan snorts, the New Yorker sneers. The Angeleno smiles and pats his happy stomach.

It may not be true. Not yet. But forces are at work, from within and without, converging on Southern California with irresistible energy and originality. It is the stuff—or at least the foodstuff—of revolution.

From within, the bounty of the West is being reshaped and refined into something increasingly, if a little grandly, recognized as "California cuisine." Definitions come and go, as the process sends out shoots here, pulls in horns there. Authors Neal Weiner and David Schwartz, though, come closest to the pulse of the movement, calling it a blend of nouvelle cuisine, traditional American fare, and West Coast imagination, all with an emphasis on fresh, light, and wholesome.

The ingredients, of course, were here already ("California," writers critic Colman Andrews, "is the richest state in the Union in gastronomic raw materials"). More recently came the desire. "The young led the way," says Los Angeles Times critic Lois Dwan, "rebelling against poor food in expensive places."

A cornucopia of home-grown goodies; a confluence of brilliant young chefs; a growing awareness of dining as something far more than stuffing one's face—who could ask for anything more?

Californians could. And did. In the sun, sand, surf, and cinema center of the world, they demanded more than good food at moderate prices. What they wanted along with their meal was fun. They got it.

Viscount Newport, along with countless overseas visitors, is astounded and enchanted with the uniquely L.A. dining experience, and articulates it better than most. "People want to be entertained," said Newport, a restaurateur himself (Porter's in London), "and the Californians do it better than anyone. I'm not talking only about decor. The place can be plain as mud, but there's an air of excitement, an atmosphere that hits you in the face as you walk through the door."

There are, of course, the great restaurants where one pays homage to—and top dollar for—exquisite dishes and their preparation: L'Orangerie, the Tower, l'Ermitage, Rex Il Ristorante. There are also the great restaurants where the food is equally superb (and expensive) but the atmosphere is somewhat less formal: Spago, Michael's ("California French"), Scandia, Ma Maison [the unlisted number: (213) 655-1991].

In the main, however, there are innumerable (and affordable) places where the dishes are less classic, still excellent, but the atmosphere, ambience, and/or decor will knock your socks off. Lawry's California Center comes immediately to mind—often called Los Angeles' most "typical" restaurant, though it's one of a kind: a Spanish-colonial garden oasis with strolling mariachis. Then there are, at random among (literally) 25,000 others: Trader Vic's, with its "Polynesian" punch-and-potent rum concoctions; the ultra-chic China Club, where pork-and-celery is called "Autumn of Himalaya" and rice is "Jade Stones"; the raucous Lucy's El Adobe, with its movie stars and politicians; Gladstone's 4-Fish, whose owner, Bob Morris, says, "I want people to ooh and ah"; Marengo, where the waiters dress as Bonaparte's legions; Bobby McGee's, with a salad bar in a bathtub; the Overland Stage, with its bear, buffalo, and rattlesnake entrees.

One stops, and just in time: "Sometimes the people could be eating dried grass," observes Newport, "but they enjoy it." It is often (but not always) true that the hokier the restaurant, the worse the food, and Los Angeles practically invented hoke. Rest assured, though, that when dried grass is made palatable, it will be done in Los Angeles. And probably by an immigrant.

The "foreigners" (as we all are, give or take a generation or two) constitute the second great influence on the Los Angeles dining tradition, an influence even more powerful than "the force within."

Our city has long since superseded New York as America's—indeed, the world's—greatest fondu, unsurpassed as a melting pot. After the Anglos moved in on the Hispanics (who had moved in on the Shoshone Indians, who may have moved in on some Nordic types), the Hispanics are back in force. This time, moreover, they are accompanied by the Asians, the Africans, the Middle Easterners, the Europeans—all yearning to eat well and often. Collectively, they are the majority: Japanese, Chinese, Filipinos, Vietnamese, Samoans; Italians, Greeks, Scots, Armenians, Germans; Liberians, Moroccans, and Egyptians; Lebanese, Israelis, and Iranians; Mexicans, of course, and Guatemalans and Cubans.

And collectively, they have infused Los Angeles with a vitality, an excitement unmatched in America since turn-of-the-century Manhattan.

Naturally, each nationality initially prefers its own authentic restaurants, to the great enrichment of the local dining scene. A Korean restaurant springs up here, a Hungarian place there, a Swedish konditori across the street. Sushi coexists with hot dog; burritos become as ubiquitous as burgers.

In time, there is assimilation, but more important, there is cross-fertilization. Results are sometimes startling, always fascinating.

Chaos, on Vermont Avenue, serves Cuban-Chinese food. A Yugoslavian cook makes Dan Tana's one of our better Italian restaurants. An Afghan couple runs the Olde Manhattan Spaghetti Faire. The best chef in town, Austrian Wolfgang Puck of Spago, serves pizzas he learned to make in France. A place opens in Redondo Beach called Pancho and Wong's. Ajeti's serves "Albanian Natural Foods."

Dynasty, a Beverly Hills coffee house by day and an Indonesian restaurant by night, is run by a Chinese. Carlos & Charlie's is run by a Jewish grandmother who serves tequila, shrimp, and Bronx cheesecake. La Petite Chaya and C'Est Japon boast Franco-Japanese cuisine. The Calcutta Cricket Club shares a common bar with McGinty's Irish Pub.

Someone opens a place called Yangzee Doodle. El Libertad springs up, an El Salvadoran restaurant run by a Japanese who also serves teriyakiburgers. Coriander in Studio City bills itself as a "French/Italian/Thai/American/Seafood" restaurant.

Doubling the blessing, Los Angeles' ethnic restaurants, of which there are thousands and thousands, help keep the prices down with less loss in quality.

So do the chain restaurants, many of which are first-rate (Velvet Turtle; Acapulco y Los Arcos, with an eighteen-page menu; Seafood Broiler; Hungry Tiger; Jolly Roger; El Pollo Loco; International House of Pancakes; etc.).

So do the hamburger places, a many-splendored variety starting with the renowned Cassell's and Hampton's, continuing through the Nucleus Nuance with its "Ra, the Untouchable Burger" (and bulging out at Chasen's, where a hamburger costs $16.50 cooked, but $20 raw).

So do the delicatessens (Nate 'n' Al's, Art's, and Canter's star), and so do the vegetarian restaurants (Meyera is a classic, but who can resist the Inn of the Seventh Ray, or the Golden Temple of Conscious Cookery?).

Mitigating against economy, on the other hand, are the distances between restaurants of one's choice. Los Angeles County is bigger than the states of Delaware and Rhode Island combined, and while Angelenos think nothing of driving forty miles for a good meal, visitors generally are without cars and the public-transport system is woeful.

This need not be a major concern, however. Excellent restaurants are virtually everywhere, and several main arteries fairly burst with them: La Cienega Boulevard and Melrose Avenue (expensive); Vermont and Fairfax avenues (ethnic); Ventura Boulevard in the San Fernando Valley (something for everyone).

Further, one needn't bother dressing up. Except for some of the major restaurants (and even including many of them), attire is informal almost to the point of underwear. So, too, is the service, perhaps not as efficient as elsewhere but as friendly as your next-door neighbor.

So don't hesitate. Jump right in. Chances are you'll be both surprised and pleased.

Chances are, too, that by the next Olympics, you'll be boasting that, in 1984, you ate in the Dining Capital of the World.

Restaurants

American

Carl Andersen's Chatam
10930 Weyburn Avenue; Westwood; (213) 208-4321
Monday–Saturday, 11 A.M.–9 P.M..

Good for a home-cooked meal. Lunch features sandwiches, dinner an accent, such as Danish shrimp, steak tartare. Home-made pastries. Inexpensive. Reservations required for dinner. Visa and MasterCard.

The Chart House
Marina del Rey, Malibu, Redondo Beach, Long Beach, Westwood
Monday–Thursday, 5:30–11 P.M.; Friday and Saturday, 5–11:30 P.M.; Sunday, 5–10 P.M.

Favorite place for young couples in love and seafood in a romantic ambience. Great cocktails and wonderful Mud Pie. Moderate. First come, first served. All major credit cards.

The Chronicle
897 Granite Drive; Pasadena; (213) 792-1179
2640 South Main Street; Santa Monica; (213) 392-4956
Monday–Thursday, 6–10:30 P.M.; Friday and Saturday, 6–11:30 P.M.; Sunday, 5–10 P.M. Lunch, Monday–Friday, 11:30 A.M.–2:30 P.M.

Steaks or seafood in a dining experience from long ago, when service was excellent and ambience genteel. The food is fresh and well-prepared. Expensive. All major credit cards. Reservations preferred.

Greenblatt's
8017 Sunset Boulevard; Hollywood; (213) 656-0606
Open seven days, 9 A.M.–2 A.M.

"The wine merchant that fronts as a deli" is the motto of
Greenblatt's, and you will find both in abundance: a nicely
stocked deli, many different salads and pastries, and a complete
liquor store. Upstairs, a dining room. Orders to go. Moderate.
MasterCard and Visa.

Hampton's Kitchen
1342 North Highland Avenue; Hollywood; (213) 469-1090
4301 Riverside Drive; Burbank; (213) 845-3009
Seven days. Call for hours.

For hamburgers in a garden-like setting. Don't forget dessert.
Moderate. All major credit cards. For parties of six or more,
reservations suggested.

Indian Hill Market
555 West Foothill Boulevard; Claremont; (714) 621-3200
Monday–Saturday, 6:30–11 A.M., 11:30 A.M.–2:30 P.M.,
5:00–10 P.M.; Sunday, Lunch, 10 A.M.–2 P.M.;
Buffet, 5–9 P.M.

Save yourself for Sunday champagne brunch; you can eat enough
to cover the rest of the week. Weekday entertainment starting
9 P.M. Moderate. American Express, MasterCard, Visa. Full
bar.

Johnnie's Patio Restaurant
4017 South Sepulveda Boulevard; Culver City;
(213) 397-6654
Seven days, 10 A.M.–3:30 A.M.

Johnnie's specialty: hot pastrami on a French roll. Class sandwiches in casual atmosphere, plus burgers, fish, chicken, and
fries. Tabletop jukeboxes provide "entertainment." Inexpensive. Beer.

Lawry's The Prime Rib
55 North La Cienega Boulevard; Beverly Hills;
(213) 652-2827
Monday–Thursday, 5–11 P.M.; Friday and Saturday,
5 P.M.–midnight; Sunday, 3–11 P.M.

Out-of-towners like Lawry's simple dinner of prime rib (different-size cuts), spinning salad, mashed potatoes, and Yorkshire pudding, served grandly and promptly. Moderate. Reservations required. All major credit cards. Full bar. Recommend coat and tie.

Morton's
8800 Melrose Avenue; Los Angeles; (213) 276-5205
Monday–Saturday, 6–11:30 P.M.

Popular among show-biz folk, noisy and fun. Simple meals— fish and veal—served in a casual atmosphere. Expensive. All major credit cards. Reservations required. Semi-dressy.

Musso and Frank Grill
6667 Hollywood Boulevard; Hollywood; (213) 467-7788
Monday–Saturday, 11 A.M.–11 P.M.

Ideal for a fresh, home-cooked dinner, for a drink at the huge bar, or for a quick meal at the counter. A landmark of the old Hollywood. Moderate. All major credit cards. Reservations appreciated for larger parties.

The Palm
9001 Santa Monica Boulevard; West Hollywood;
(213) 550-8811
Monday–Friday, noon–10 P.M.; Saturday, 5–10:30 P.M.;
Sunday, 5–9:45 P.M..

Steaks, fresh seafood (especially lobster), fries, and desserts, lots of noise, sawdust on the floors. A real treat if you like New York. Moderate-expensive. Reservations required. All major credit cards. Full bar.

Reuben E. Lee
151 East Coast Highway; Newport Beach; (714) 675-5811
Monday–Thursday, 11:30 A.M.–10 P.M.; Friday,
11:30 A.M.–11 P.M.; Saturday, noon–11 P.M.; Sunday,
10 A.M.–10 P.M.

Multilevel dining: a Seafood Deck for fresh catches (prime rib
and chicken also are on the menu); the Sternwheeler for a
dinner show; the Wheelhouse for private parties. Moderate.
All major credit cards. Full bar.

Tail o' the Cock
477 South La Cienega Boulevard; Beverly Hills;
(213) 273-1200
12950 Ventura Boulevard; Sherman Oaks; 877-0889
Seven days, Monday–Thursday, 11 A.M.–10 P.M.; Friday and
Saturday, 11 A.M.–11 P.M.; Sunday, 10 A.M.–10 P.M.

A pleasant place to go for a simple American meal, served
without fanfare but with formality. Brunch is especially good.
Piano bar. Moderate. All major credit cards. Reservations recommended.

Tick Tock
1716 North Cahuenga Boulevard; Hollywood;
(213) 463-7576
Wednesday–Saturday, 11:30 A.M.–2 P.M., 4–8 P.M.;
Sunday, noon–8 P.M.

Standard American food: low prices and good quality. Inexpensive. All major credit cards. Wine and beer.

Tony Roma's
9404 Brighton Way; Beverly Hills; (213) 278-1207
Other locations in Encino, Santa Monica, Newport Beach; and
Palm Springs.
Monday–Friday, 11 A.M.–2 A.M.; Saturday, noon–2 A.M.;
Sunday, 3 P.M.–2 A.M.

There's always a crowd, but if you wait it out, you won't be disappointed. Portions of ribs and chicken are huge; be sure to split an order of onion rings. Inexpensive. MasterCard and American Express. Entertainment nightly.

Village Inn
127 Marine Street; Balboa Island; (714) 675-8300
Monday–Thursday, 6:30 A.M.–10:30 P.M.; Friday,
6:30 A.M.–11:30 P.M.; Saturday, 9:30 A.M.–11:30 P.M.;
Sunday, 10:30 A.M.–11:30 P.M.

A casual restaurant that fits right into the atmosphere on Balboa Island, the Village Inn is a comfortable English-style pub. The menu, reasonably priced, includes chicken, beef, fish, and burgers. Inexpensive-moderate. All major credit cards. Full bar.

Chinese

Ah Fong's
424 North Beverly Drive; Beverly Hills; (213) 276-1034
Other locations in Hollywood and Westwood.
Sunday–Thursday, noon–11 P.M.; Friday and Saturday,
noon–midnight.

Actor Benson Fong decided to become a restaurateur and opened Ah Fong's, serving basic Cantonese Chinese food. It's a good place to go if you don't want to drive all the way to Chinatown. Inexpensive. Visa and MasterCard. Full bar.

La Chinoise
23600 Rockfield Boulevard; Lake Forest; (714) 830-9984
Monday–Friday, 11 A.M.–3 P.M.; seven days, 5—11 P.M.

Continental (French) cuisine, prepared Chinese-style. The menu is different, the service is efficient, and the dining experience refreshingly new. Moderate-expensive. All major credit cards. Reservations required.

Fung Lum

222 Universal Terrace Parkway; Universal City;
(213) 760-4603
Monday–Thursday, 11:30 A.M.–2:30 P.M., 5–10 P.M.; Friday
and Saturday, 11:30 A.M.–2:30 P.M., 6–10 P.M.; Sunday,
11 A.M.–10 P.M.

The finest Chinese restaurant in the city—for ambience. The
food is a little expensive—and a little above-average—but
look out the full plate-glass windows at the San Fernando
Valley below. Try the specialty, barbecued ribs unlike any in
Los Angeles. Moderate-expensive (for Chinese). All major
credit cards.

Green Jade

750 North Hill Street; Chinatown; (213) 680-1528
Sunday–Thursday, 11:30 A.M.–3 P.M., 4:30–9 P.M.; Friday
and Saturday, 5–9:30 P.M..

Green Jade serves everything from very spicy hot-and-sour
soup to chicken chow mein. Nice, basic. Moderate. Visa and
MasterCard. Beer and wine.

Madame Wu's Garden

2201 Wilshire Boulevard; Santa Monica; (213) 828-5656
Sunday–Thursday, 11:30 A.M.–10 P.M.; Friday,
11:30 A.M.–11 P.M.; Saturday, 5–11 P.M.

One of the city's better-known Chinese restaurants; good food,
nice menu, excellent service. Proprietress Sylvia Wu enhances
the decor. Moderate. All major credit cards. Reservations required. Full bar.

Mandarin

430 North Camden Drive; Beverly Hills; (213) 272-0267
Monday–Friday, 11 A.M.–11 P.M.; Saturday and Sunday,
5–11 P.M.

Szechwan, Hunan, Peking, and Shanghai food in a calm and
beautiful setting. Moderate-expensive. All major credit cards.
Reservations required. Full bar.

Miriwa
750 North Hill Street; Chinatown; (213) 687-3088
Seven days, 10 A.M.–2:30 P.M., 5–9:30 P.M.

Miriwa is best tried early Sunday morning for dim sum. Otherwise prepare to wait for a table. Always packed, and always good. The dim sum are spicier and more flavorful than elsewhere in the neighborhood. Dinners in large portions. Moderate (though some entrees are high-rent); inexpensive lunch. All major credit cards. Reservations required for dinner. Full bar. Hours may be extended for Olympics, so call ahead.

Mouling Garden West
11620 Wilshire Boulevard; West Los Angeles;
(213) 477-5041
Sunday–Thursday, 11:30 A.M.–10:00 P.M.; Friday and Saturday, 11:30 A.M.–11 P.M.

Szechwan and other dishes always fresh and beautifully served. The atmosphere is stately and elegant. Moderate. All major credit cards. Full bar.

Mr. Chow L.A.
344 North Camden Drive; Beverly Hills; (213) 278-9911
Monday–Friday, noon–2:30 P.M.; seven days,
6 P.M.–midnight.

A chichi place to eat Chinese in the heart of Beverly Hills. Good food at elevated prices. Expensive. All major credit cards. Full bar.

Shanghai Winter Garden
5651 Wilshire Boulevard; Mid-Wilshire; (213) 934-0505
Monday–Sunday, 11:30 A.M.–3 P.M.; Monday-Sunday,
4–10:30 P.M.

Combines wonderful Shanghai-style food with an equally nice atmosphere. Try the Kung-pao chicken. Moderate. All major credit cards. Reservations required. Full bar.

Trader Vic's
9876 Wilshire Boulevard; Beverly Hills; (213) 274-7777
Sunday–Thursday, 4:30 P.M.–12:30 A.M.; Friday and
Saturday, 4:30 P.M.–1 A.M.

If you like dining in a tropical paradise, the Polynesian-style
food always is fresh, the service quick and polite, the meal
satisfying. Expensive. All major credit cards. Full bar. Reservations required.

Continental

Le Bistro
246 North Canon Drive; Beverly Hills; (213) 273-5633

Le Bistro Garden
176 North Canon Drive; Beverly Hills; (213) 550-3900
Monday–Friday, noon–3 P.M.; Monday–Saturday,
noon–midnight; (Bistro Garden: seven days,
11:30 A.M.–midnight).

Le Bistro is ultrachic, superglamorous, and very expensive; to
see and be seen in. Le Bistro Garden offers much the same,
with less formality. Don't leave without trying the chocolate
soufflé. Expensive. All major credit cards. Full bar. Reservations required. Gentlemen must wear jackets.

Carlos & Charlie's
8240 Sunset Boulevard; Hollywood; (213) 656-8830
Monday–Friday, 11:30 P.M.–1 A.M.; Saturday and Sunday,
5–midnight.

Carlos & Charlie's is loud, lively, and fun. Meals are a combination of American and a bit of Mexican. The restaurant and
bar is always crowded, and there's a private disco upstairs for
dancing into the night. Moderate. All major credit cards. Full
bar.

Chasen's
9039 Beverly Boulevard; Los Angeles; (213) 271-2168
Tuesday–Sunday, 6 P.M.–1 A.M.

When Elizabeth Taylor was making a movie in Russia, she had Chasen's chili flown in. An old Hollywood establishment, noted for simple but expensive meals—and for tradition. Expensive. No credit cards. Checks accepted with proper identification. Reservations advisable. Jackets for gentlemen. Full bar.

Chez Cary
571 South Main Street; Orange; (714) 542-3595
6:30–10 P.M. seven days (lounge opens at 4 P.M.).

First-rate haute cuisine, backed by efficient and professional service. The wine "book" offers more than 800 labels. Expensive. All major credit cards. Reservations recommended. Full bar. Jackets and ties for gentlemen preferred.

The Cove
3191 West 7th Street; Mid-Wilshire; (213) 388-0361
Monday–Friday, 11:30 A.M.–11 P.M.; Saturday,
4:30 P.M.–midnight; Sunday, 4:30–10 P.M.

Mostly German, definitely romantic. The Cove's specialty of Schnitzel Black Forest is a treat. So are the strolling violinists. Moderate. All credit cards. Reservations recommended. Full bar.

The Original Hollywood Brown Derby
1628 North Vine Street; Hollywood; (213) 469-5151
Monday, 11 A.M.–3 P.M.; Tuesday–Sunday, 11 A.M.–10 P.M.

Sit in a booth, twinkling lights swirling around you; picture yourself as a Hollywood star of the forties. Meats, fish, and Cobb salad all are freshly prepared and efficiently served. Cheese bread is extraordinary. Moderate-expensive. All major credit cards. Full bar.

Homer and Edy's Bistro
2839 South Robertson Boulevard; Los Angeles;
(213) 559-5102
Tuesday–Saturday, 6–11 P.M.; Sunday, 5–10 P.M.

Creole food, featuring gumbos, courtbouillon, chicken, beef.
Plus Dixieland jazz and New Orleans oyster loaf.

Jimmy's
201 Moreno Drive; Beverly Hills; (213) 879-2394
Monday–Friday, 11:30 A.M.–3 P.M.; Monday–Saturday,
6 P.M.–midnight.

Very expensive; also very good. French Continental cuisine in
a serene, elegant dining room where you always feel special.
All major credit cards. Reservations required. Full bar with
entertainment. Jackets for gentlemen.

Phoenicia
343 North Central Avenue; Glendale; (213) 956-7800
Monday–Friday, 11:30 A.M.–3 P.M.; Tuesday–Sunday,
5–10 P.M.

Intimate and formal. The food is nicely prepared and the wine
list is adequate; a favorite among local residents. Moderate.
All major credit cards.

Rangoon Racquet Club
9474 Santa Monica Boulevard; Beverly Hills;
(213) 274-8926
Monday–Friday, 11:30 A.M.–3 P.M.; Monday–Saturday,
6 P.M.–midnight.

Rangoon Racquet Club is, oddly enough, busy and formal at
the same time. A pristine interior accentuates the food, which
is good. Beef, chicken, fish are all offered. Expensive. All
major credit cards. Full bar.

Scandia Restaurant
9040 Sunset Boulevard; West Hollywood; (213) 278-3555
Tuesday–Saturday, 11:30 A.M.–3 P.M., 6 P.M.–12:30 A.M.;
Sunday, 11 A.M.–3 P.M., 5 P.M.–1 A.M.

Scandia is romantic. Even better, the food is delicious. An
absolutely delightful place for a late supper. Full bar. All major
credit cards. Reservations required.

Stratton's
10886 Le Conte Avenue; Westwood; (213) 208-8880
Tuesday–Sunday, 11:30 A.M.–3 P.M.; Tuesday–Thursday,
5:30–10 P.M.; Friday, 5:30–11 P.M.; Saturday, 5–11 P.M.;
Sunday 5–10 P.M..

The Continental cuisine at Stratton's is good; the tile and stone
patio makes the experience even better. Located next door to
the Westwood Playhouse, pleasant place to stop before a show.
Expensive. All major credit cards. Full bar.

Trumps
8764 Melrose Avenue; West Hollywood; (213) 855-1480
Monday–Saturday, 11:55 A.M.–3 P.M.; Tea, 3:30–6 P.M.;
Monday–Thursday, 6:30 P.M.–midnight; Friday and Saturday,
6:30 P.M.–12:30 A.M.

A converted artist's studio—light, airy, and very casual. Trumps
also offers something for every culinary taste, prepared by
Michael Roberts, one of Los Angeles' finest chefs. Expensive.
All major credit cards. Full bar. A harpist performs during tea.

The Windsor
3198 West 7th Street; Mid-Wilshire; (213) 382-1261
Monday–Friday, 11:30 A.M.–midnight; Saturday,
4:30 P.M.–midnight.

Traditional luxury in service and menu, which is French-Con-
tinental. Don't pass up the pastries. Expensive. All major credit
cards. Full bar. Jackets for gentlemen.

French

Au Chambertin
708 Pico Boulevard; Santa Monica; (213) 392-8738
Tuesday–Sunday, 6–11 P.M.

A special French restaurant, owned and operated by Lap Huynh
and his Vietnamese family. The food is always nicely prepared
and the menu includes truffle soup and feuilletage. A pre-
theater dinner, prix-fixe and à la carte. Inexpensive-moderate.
MasterCard, Visa. Full bar. Reservations required.

Bagatelle
8690 Wilshire Boulevard; Beverly Hills; (213) 659-0782
Monday–Friday, 11:30 A.M.–2:30 P.M.; Monday–Saturday,
6 P.M.–10 P.M.

What once was a small sandwich bar has blossomed into cer-
tified French cuisine. Small, intimate, elegant. Expensive. Visa,
MasterCard. Wine and beer.

Bernard's
515 South Olive Street; Downtown Los Angeles;
(213) 612-1580
Monday–Friday, 11:30 A.M.–2 P.M.; Monday–Thursday,
6–10 P.M.; Saturday, 6–11 P.M.

Located in the renovated Biltmore Hotel, Bernard's is a stately,
lovely restaurant; seafood prepared in classic and nouvelle
methods. Harp music keeps the mood romantic. Expensive.
All major credit cards. Reservations required. Jackets for
gentlemen.

The Cellar
305 North Harbor Boulevard; Fullerton; (714) 525-5682
Tuesday–Saturday, 6:30–11 P.M.

The Cellar actually is the cellar of the Villa del Sol. Top-notch
nouvelle cuisine and atmosphere. A favorite in Orange County.
Moderate. All major credit cards. Full bar.

Chez Helene
1029 West Washington Boulevard; Venice; (213) 392-6833
Tuesday–Saturday, noon–3 P.M.; Tuesday–Sunday,
6:30–10 P.M.

A very intimate French restaurant, this is one of the best in
Venice. Lamb, chicken, and a very special chocolate cheesecake. Moderate. All major credit cards. Beer and wine.

L'Affair
11024 Sepulveda Boulevard; Mission Hills; (213) 365-5939
Monday–Friday, 11:30 A.M.–2:30 P.M.; seven nights,
5:30–10:30 P.M.

A very nice French restaurant, specializing in fresh fish. Moderate. All major credit cards. Full bar. Reservations required.

L'Ermitage
730 North La Cienega Boulevard; Los Angeles;
(213) 653-5840
Monday–Saturday, 6:30–10:30 P.M.; (during Olympics,
6–10:30 P.M.; Sunday also).

Los Angeles' standards for formal French dining were begun at L'Ermitage, founded by the late Jean Bertranou. It remains atop the city's haute-cuisine establishments. Expensive. All major credit cards. Reservations required. Full bar.

L'Orangerie
903 North La Cienega Boulevard; Los Angeles;
(213) 652-9770
Seven nights, 6:30–10:30 P.M.

L'Orangerie is one of those special places that offers classic food prepared nouvelle style, romantic ambience. Menu varies from vegetables with tomato sauce to steak, chicken, veal, and duck. Expensive. All major credit cards. Reservations required. Full bar.

La Serre
12969 Ventura Boulevard; Studio City; (213) 990-0500
Monday–Friday, noon–2; Monday–Saturday, 6–10:30 P.M.

A bright spot in Valley cuisine; La Serre offers extraordinary haute cuisine amid lush greenery. Expensive. MasterCard, Visa, American Express. Full bar. Reservations a must.

La Toque
8171 Sunset Boulevard; West Hollywood; (213) 656-7515
Monday–Saturday, 6:30–10:30 P.M.

Chef-owner Ken Frank offers a prix-fixe menu and serves delightful meals in a French countryside setting. Prix-fixe: moderate; à la carte: expensive. All major credit cards. Full bar. Reservations required.

Le Dome
8720 Sunset Boulevard; West Hollywood; (213) 659-6916
Monday–Friday, noon–2 A.M.; Saturday, 6 P.M.–2 A.M.

This favorite of the music industry offers elegant informality.
The menu is varied and interesting.

Le Monaco
2325 Palos Verdes Drive West; Palos Verdes Estates;
(213) 377-6775
Seven nights, 5:30–10 P.M.

A beautiful setting, magnificent sunsets over the Pacific; the
standard menu offers no surprises. Moderate. All major credit
cards. Full bar.

Le St. Germain
5955 Melrose Avenue; Hollywood; (213) 467-1108 (09)
Monday–Friday, noon–2; Monday–Saturday, 6–11 P.M.

Casual elegance in the manner of a country inn. Modern French
cuisine. Expensive. All major credit cards. Full bar.

Les Anges
14809 Pacific Coast Highway; Santa Monica;
(213) 454-1331
Tuesday–Sunday, 6:30–9:30 P.M.

An intimate beach restaurant with formal dining and excellent
cuisine moderne. Very expensive, but most agree worth it.

Ma Facon
1000 Wilshire Boulevard; Santa Monica; (213) 394-2718
Tuesday–Sunday, 6:00–10:00 P.M.; Friday and Saturday,
6–11 P.M.

Nouvelle cuisine served in a luxurious Baroque setting of silk
and velvet. Specialties include lamb and duck. Expensive. All
major credit cards. Full bar.

Ma Maison
8368 Melrose Avenue; Los Angeles; (213) 655-1991
Monday–Saturday, Noon–2:30; 6:30–10 P.M.

Ma Maison, noted for a celebrity clientele, unlisted phone number and, originally, Wolfgang Puck (who has since opened La Chinoise and Spago), also boasts French country cooking by new Chef Claude Segal. If you can manage a reservation, you won't forget the experience. Expensive. All major credit cards. Full bar. Reservations required. Casual chic.

Moustache Cafe
8155 Melrose Avenue; West Hollywood; (213) 651-2111
Monday–Saturday, 11:30 A.M.–1 A.M.; Sunday,
11:30 A.M.–midnight.
Other locations in Beverly Hills and Westwood.

The right place for casual French dining, with prices that won't keep you from enjoying your meal. Served in a bistro-type atmosphere (the Melrose Moustache has a lovely outdoor patio), the menu is eclectic, offering omelets, crepes, salads, and full entrees. Moderate. Visa and MasterCard. Reservations recommended. Full bar.

Robaire's
348 South La Brea Avenue; Mid-Wilshire; (213) 931-1246
Tuesday–Thursday, 5–10:30 P.M.; Friday and Saturday,
5–11 P.M.; Sunday, 5–10 P.M.

One of Los Angeles' oldest bistro-style French restaurants; reliable, nicely priced meals. Moderate. All major credit cards. Full bar. Reservations recommended.

Studio Grill
7321 Santa Monica Boulevard; Hollywood; (213) 874-9202
Monday–Friday, noon–2:15; Monday–Thursday,
6–10:15 P.M.; Friday and Saturday, 6–11:15 P.M.

Beyond a nondescript facade, the restaurant is transformed into its own world. The food, mostly French, some Continental, is always fresh with light sauces. Homemade desserts are sublime. Complete wine list. Moderate-expensive. All major credit cards. Reservations required. Full bar expected by Olympics time.

Health Foods

Chez Naturel
11838 Ventura Boulevard; Studio City; (213) 763-1044
Monday–Thursday, 11:00 A.M.–10:30 P.M.; Friday and
Saturday, 11:00 A.M.–11:30 P.M.; Sunday,
10 A.M.–10:30 P.M.

For once, a natural-food restaurant with some taste. No chemicals here. Inexpensive. All major credit cards. Beer and wine. Reservations required for parties of five or more.

Forty Carrots
3333 Bristol Street; Costa Mesa; (714) 556-9700
Monday–Friday, 11 A.M.– 9 P.M.; Saturday, 11 A.M.–6 P.M.;
Sunday, 10:30 A.M.–5 P.M.

A very informal natural-food restaurant, with fresh-baked muffins, quiche, and a salad bar. Inexpensive. MasterCard and Visa. Beer and wine. No reservations.

Good Earth
1002 Westwood Boulevard; Westwood; (213) 208-8215
Sunday–Thursday, 9–11 P.M.; Friday and Saturday,
9 P.M.–midnight.

This is one of a chain of health-food restaurants, all offering freshly made, and organically grown, food and pastries. MasterCard and Visa. Beer and wine. Reservations required for large parties only.

Inn of the Seventh Ray
128 Old Topanga Canyon Road; Topanga; (213) 455-1311
Seven days, 6–10 P.M.; Monday–Friday, 11:30 A.M.–3 P.M.;
Saturday, 11 A.M.–3 P.M.; Sunday brunch, 10 A.M.–3:30 P.M.

Up in Topanga, in what was once a church, Inn of the Seventh Ray serves organic vegetables, fresh fish, eggs and chickens without hormones. Sit beside a running stream and beneath tall, shady trees. Mystical but enjoyable. Moderate. Visa, MasterCard. Beer and wine. Reservations required for dinner.

Lindberg's Nutrition
3945 Crenshaw Boulevard; Los Angeles; (213) 290-1273
Many other locations throughout Los Angeles area.
Monday–Saturday, 11 A.M.–3 P.M.

Lindberg's is a vitamin-health food store with a small coffee-shop-type restaurant (some booths and a counter). The salads and sandwiches and homemade soups are tasty and fresh. Inexpensive. MasterCard and Visa. No alcohol.

Meyera
3009 Main Street; Santa Monica; (213) 399-1010
Seven days, 6–10 P.M.

Meyera is an elegantly plain restaurant serving truly gourmet vegetarian meals with a touch of French. Homemade breads and pastries are especially pleasing. Expensive. All major credit cards. Reservations recommended. Beer and wine.

Old World
8782 Sunset Boulevard; West Hollywood; (213) 652-2520
Other locations in Westwood and Beverly Hills.
Sunday–Thursday, 8 A.M.–1 A.M.; Friday and Saturday,
8 A.M.–2 A.M.

Hardwood floors, smoking and nonsmoking sections, fresh-baked pastries, and an eclectic natural-foods menu: hamburgers, salads, and omelets. Everything meshes. Moderate. Visa, MasterCard, American Express. No reservations. Full bar.

Indian/Middle Eastern

Bengal Tiger Indian Restaurant
1710 North Las Palmas; Hollywood; (213) 469-1991
Sunday–Thursday, noon–10:30 P.M.

A family-run Indian restaurant; excellent breads, chicken, and curries. Especially nice for lunch. Inexpensive. Visa, MasterCard, American Express. Reservations recommended on weekends. Beer, wine.

Canard de Bombay

476 South San Vicente Boulevard; Los Angeles;
(213) 852-0095
Monday–Friday, 11:30 A.M.–2:30 P.M.; Monday–Thursday,
5:30–10 P.M.; Friday and Saturday, 5:30 P.M.–midnight.

English-Indian curries, plus tandoori, biryani, and pullai dishes.
Moderate. All major credit cards. Reservations recommended
on weekends.

Dar Maghreb

7651 Sunset Boulevard; Hollywood; (213) 876-7651
Monday–Friday, 6–11 P.M.; Saturday, 5:30–11 P.M.; Sunday,
5:30–10:30 P.M.

One of the city's most beautiful Moroccan restaurants. Exotic
meals eaten without utensils; lavish rooms, surrounded by waterfalls. Expensive. Visa, MasterCard. Reservations suggested. Cocktails.

Fez Moroccan

5910 Warner Avenue; Huntington Beach; (714) 840-3024
Daily, 5–10 P.M.

Moroccan cuisine with five-, six-, seven-, eight-, and nine-
course dinners. Inexpensive. Visa, MasterCard. Reservations
suggested on weekends. Beer, wine.

Koutoubia

2116 Westwood Boulevard; West Los Angeles;
(213) 475-0729
Tuesday–Sunday, 6–10 P.M.

Subdued decor, fine, complex Moroccan dishes, such as b'stilla,
lamb brochette, and couscous. Moderate. All major credit cards.
Reservations recommended. Beer, wine.

Marrakesh

1100 West Pacific Coast Highway; Newport Beach;
(714) 645-8384
13003 Ventura Boulevard; Studio City; (213) 788-6354
Monday–Friday, 6–10 P.M.; Friday–Sunday, 5:30–10:30 P.M.

Marrakesh is magnificently appointed, and the prix-fixe Moroccan menu is nicely priced. The meal, including soup, salad, choice of fish, chicken, rabbit, or squab, is efficiently served by djellabah-clad waiters wearing fezzes. Moderate. Major credit cards. Full bar. Reservations required.

Raja Restaurant
8875 West Pico Boulevard; West Los Angeles;
(213) 550-9176
Seven days, 6–11 P.M.

Wonderful, tasty curries are the specialty, plus lamb, beef, seafood, and great breads. Inexpensive-moderate. Visa, MasterCard, American Express. Reservations recommended. Beer, wine.

Taj Mahal
163 North La Cienega Boulevard; Beverly Hills;
(213) 659-3810
Monday–Saturday, 11:30 A.M.–2:30 P.M.; Sunday–Thursday, 6:30–10:30 P.M.; Friday and Saturday, 6 P.M.–midnight; Happy Hours, 10:30 P.M.–2:00 A.M.

Curry dishes, tandoori lamb and chicken, and other popular Indian offerings, along with Continental cuisine. Moderate. All major credit cards. Reservations recommended. Full bar.

Italian

Adriano's Ristorante
2930 Beverly Glen Circle; Los Angeles; (213) 475-9807
Tuesday–Saturday, 11:30 A.M.–2:30 P.M.; Sunday,
11 A.M.–3 P.M.; Tuesday–Thursday, Sunday, 6–10:30 P.M.;
Friday and Saturday, 6–11 P.M.

On a hill at the top of Bel-Air, Adriano's is a classy, traditional Italian restaurant. The menu offers seafood, veal, quail, and pastas. Desserts are good and rich. Expensive. MasterCard, Visa, American Express. Reservations required. Full bar.

Alfredo's
666 Anton Boulevard; Costa Mesa; (714) 540-1550
Monday–Friday, 11:30 A.M.–2 P.M.; Monday–Saturday,
6–10 P.M.; Friday and Saturday, 6–11 P.M.; Sunday brunch,
10 A.M.–2 P.M.

Chef Christian Rassinoux offers seafood, poultry, and veal, as
well as pasta. The wine list is especially full. Expensive. All
major credit cards. Reservations recommended. Cocktails.

Anna Maria Ristorante
1356 South La Brea Avenue; Mid-Wilshire; (213) 935-2089
Tuesday–Friday, 11 A.M.–10 P.M.; Saturday and Sunday,
4–10:30 P.M.
Other location: 418 Wilshire Boulevard, Santa Monica,
(213) 395-9285

More family-style Italian than posh; a nice, clean restaurant
with heated patio. Meals are generous and fresh, strictly Neapolitan. Seafood, other daily specials, good pastas and pizzas.
Moderate. All major credit cards. Wine and beer. Reservations
recommended.

Antonello Ristorante
3800 Plaza Drive; Santa Ana; (714) 751-7153
Monday–Friday, 11:30 A.M.–2 P.M.; Monday–Thursday,
6–10 P.M.; Friday and Saturday, 6–11 P.M.

One of the finest Northern Italian restaurants south of Los
Angeles. There is something for everybody: fish, veal, beef,
chicken, and pastas, all served in a homey setting. Moderate.
All major credit cards. Reservations recommended. Full bar.

La Barbera's
11813 Wilshire Boulevard; West Los Angeles;
(213) 478-0123
Seven days, 11 A.M.–1:30 P.M.

If you can stand the wait, you'll likely love La Barbera's.
Always crowded (mostly with students from UCLA), La Barbera's gives you lots of food for a very small price. Especially
tasty pizzas. Inexpensive. Cash only. No reservations. Cocktails.

Casa Monica
1110 Montana Avenue; Santa Monica; (213) 451-0765
Thursday–Friday, 11:30 A.M.–2 P.M.; Monday–Friday,
5:30–9:30 P.M.; Friday and Saturday, 5:30–10:30 P.M.

A cozy and comfortable Italian restaurant offering both Italian
and Continental cuisine. Veal, fresh fish, and fresh desserts.
Moderate. All major credit cards. Reservations for four or more
only.

Chianti Ristorante
7383 Melrose Avenue; West Hollywood; (213) 653-8333
Seven days, 5:30–11:30 P.M.

Romantic decor with booths and etched glass. Service tends
toward the pompous, but the food is well-prepared and without
surprise. Expensive. Visa, MasterCard, American Express.
Reservations required. Full bar.

Giuseppe!
8256 Beverly Boulevard; Los Angeles; (213) 653-8025
Monday–Friday, 11:30 A.M.–3 P.M.; Monday–Thursday,
6–11 P.M.; Friday and Saturday, 6–midnight

Giuseppe Bellisario, owner and maître d'hôtel, will greet you
in charming fashion. The menu is a chalkboard with different
specialties every day; an absolute delight. Expensive. All major
credit cards. Reservations required. Full bar.

Mangia
10543 West Pico Boulevard; West Los Angeles;
(213) 470-1952
Monday–Thursday, 11:30 A.M.–9:30 P.M.; Friday and
Saturday, 11:30 A.M.–10:30 P.M.

Mangia was born as a take-out counter for antipastos, but grew
by demand. Now it's a full-fledged restaurant with covered
patio. The food, from cold antipastos to homemade pastas, is
light and freshly prepared. Pleasant greenhouse-type setting.
Moderate. Visa, MasterCard, American Express. Reservations
required. Beer, wine.

Mario's

1001 Broxton Avenue; Westwood; (213) 208-7077
Monday–Thursday, 11:30 A.M.–11:30 P.M.;
Friday, 11:30 A.M.–12:30 A.M.; Saturday, 4 P.M.–12:30 A.M.;
Sunday, 4–11:30 P.M.

Mario's is a favorite of students; tasty food at low prices. Serves Neapolitan Italian, including pastas, pizza, and salads. Always crowded. Moderate. All major credit cards. Reservations recommended. Beer and wine.

Martoni's

1523 North Cahuenga Boulevard; Hollywood;
(213) 466-3441
Monday–Friday, 11:30 A.M.–3 P.M.; Monday–Saturday,
5 P.M.–1 A.M.

A comfortable, traditional restaurant full of authentic Southern Italian tastes and aromas. Generous portions of hearty food. Moderate. Reservations recommended. All major credit cards. Full bar.

Orlando & Orsini Ristorante

9575 West Pico Boulevard; Los Angeles; (213) 277-6050
Monday–Friday, noon–3 P.M.; Monday–Saturday, 6–11 P.M.
Other location: Cafe Roma, Beverly Hills, 274-7834.

Fine Italian cuisine served in a warm and comfortable atmosphere. Popular with the entertainment-industry set. Expensive. Visa, MasterCard, American Express. Reservations recommended.

Peppone Restaurant

11628 Barrington Court; Brentwood; (213) 476-7379
Tuesday–Friday, 11:30 A.M.–2:30 P.M.; Tuesday–Saturday,
5:30–11:30 P.M.; Sunday, 4:30–11:30 P.M.

Always crowded and reservations are hard to come by, but the meal is never a disappointment. Chef Gianni Paoletti offers chicken, pastas, and fresh fish. An impressive wine selection. Prices medium to high. Major credit cards. Reservations required for dinner. Full bar.

Rex Il Ristorante
617 South Olive Street; Downtown Los Angeles;
(213) 627-2300
Monday–Friday, noon–2 P.M.; Monday–Saturday, 7–10 P.M.

Some enjoy Rex for rich art-deco atmosphere; others for fine cucina nuova. A sumptuous setting inside the renovated Oviatt building; dark wood, Lalique glass fixtures and etched metalwork. Expensive. All major credit cards. Reservations required. Full bar.

La Scala
9455 Santa Monica Boulevard; Beverly Hills;
(213) 275-0579
Other locations in Beverly Hills and Malibu.

La Scala is dependable, warm, and elegant. You won't find anything unusual or different on the menu, but classics such as Chicken Marengo and steak and peppers are excellent. The wine list, featuring owner Jean Leon's own wines, also is topnotch. Expensive. All major credit cards. Full bar. Reservations required.

Valentino
3115 Pico Boulevard; Santa Monica; (213) 829-4313
Friday, noon–3 P.M.; Monday–Saturday, 5:30–11:30 P.M.

An oasis on Pico Boulevard, Valentino is the finest Italian restaurant in the city. The menu offers standards, such as veal, gnocchi with pesto, calamaretti, fresh fish; new and special dishes are listed every few months. Owner Piero Selvaggio's wine list is extraordinary, numbering between 800 and 1000 labels. Expensive. All major credit cards. Reservations required. Full bar.

Verdi
1519 Wilshire Boulevard; Santa Monica; (213) 393-0706
Tuesday–Sunday, from 5:30 P.M. (flexible close)

This "ristorante di musica" is an experience. The dining room sits on two levels, directed toward center stage, where Verdi's 22-person company sings opera and musical comedy. All very professional; so is the kitchen, offering homemade pastas, fresh seafood and meat dishes. Expensive. Visa, MasterCard, American Express. Reservations required. Full bar.

Japanese

Amagi
6890 Beach Boulevard; Buena Park; (714) 994-2730
6114 West Sunset Boulevard; Hollywood; (213) 464-7497
Monday–Friday, 11:30 A.M.–2 P.M.; seven days, 4:30–10 P.M.;
Sunday brunch, 10 A.M.–2:30 P.M.

Amagi is special; the dining room is large but romantic, the sushi bar intimate, and the waitresses, in full kimono, sweet and efficient. But the best thing about Amagi is the food. Moderate. All major credit cards. Reservations required. Full bar.

Benihana of Tokyo
14160 Panay Way; Marina del Rey; (213) 821-0888
Many other locations throughout Los Angeles.
Monday–Friday, 11:30 A.M.–2:30 P.M.; 5:30–10:30 P.M.;
Saturday, 5:30–11:30 P.M.; Sunday, 5–11 P.M.

Benihana is show-biz Japanese; many like it. The evening's entertainment is by your chef, who cuts, slices, and cooks with spinning knives and flying shrimp. It's fun. Moderate. All major credit cards. Reservations recommended.

Hanabishi
343 East First Street; Downtown Los Angeles;
(213) 680-1989
Friday–Wednesday, 11:30 A.M.–3 P.M.; 5–10:30 P.M.

A small, unassuming place with great sushi. Don't forget the sake. Inexpensive. MasterCard, Visa. Beer and wine.

Hiro Sushi
1621½ Wilshire Boulevard; Santa Monica; (213) 395-3570
Monday–Friday, noon–2:30 P.M.; Sunday, Monday,
Wednesday, Thursday, 5:30–10:30 P.M.; Friday and
Saturday, 5:30–11 P.M.

Hiro Sushi offers a friendly sushi bar, or dinners in a small dining area. Inexpensive. MasterCard, Visa. Reservations required for five or more. Beer and wine.

Horikawa
111 South San Pedro Street; Little Tokyo; (213) 680-9355
3800 South Plaza Drive; Santa Ana; (714) 557-2531
Monday–Friday, 11:30 A.M.–2 P.M., 5:30–10:30 P.M.;
Saturday, 5–11 P.M.; Sunday, 5–10 P.M.

Five different rooms for everything from sushi to teppan-style cooking. There also is a chef's dinner (kaiseki) to be ordered in advance. Expensive. All major credit cards. Full bar.

Imperial Gardens
8225 Sunset Boulevard; Hollywood; (213) 656-1750
Seven days, 6–10 P.M.

This is a show-biz favorite with respectable (and authentic) Japanese food. Sushi at the bar; tatami rooms for special dinners. There also is a cocktail lounge for entertainment and dancing. Moderate-expensive. All major credit cards. Reservations recommended. Full bar.

The Inagiku Oriental Plaza
Bonaventure Hotel (Fifth and Flower streets); Los Angeles; (213) 614-0820
Tuesday–Friday, 11:30 A.M.–2:30 P.M.; daily, 5:30–10:00 P.M. Closed Monday.

A very elegant restaurant, on the eighth walkway in the Bonaventure Hotel. Most notable is the tempura, fresh and light. Moderate. All major credit cards. Full bar. Reservations recommended.

Miyako Restaurant
139 South Los Robles; Pasadena; (213) 681-3086
Monday–Friday, 11:30 A.M.–2 P.M.; Monday–Saturday,
5:30–10 P.M.; Sunday, 4–9:30 P.M.

Other locations: Del Amo Center, Torrance, and Town and Country, and Orange.

This is a very safe, simple Japanese restaurant. Moderate. Visa, MasterCard. Reservations recommended. Full bar.

Nanbankan
24291 Avenida de la Carlota; Laguna Hills; (714) 855-8135
Monday–Friday, 11:30 A.M.–2 P.M.; seven days, 5–11:30 P.M..

Features teppan and sushi bar. Moderate. Visa, MasterCard, American Express. Beer and wine. Reservations recommended.

O-Sho Sushi
10914 West Pico Boulevard; West Los Angeles;
(213) 475-3226

O-Sho offers good teriyaki specials and a full sushi bar. Simple and unassuming. Moderate. Visa, MasterCard. Reservations not required. Full bar.

Teru Sushi
11940 Ventura Boulevard; Studio City; (213) 763-6201
Monday–Friday, noon–2:30 P.M.; Monday–Thursday, 5:30–11 P.M.; Friday and Saturday, 5:30–11:30 P.M.; Sunday, 5–10 P.M.

Always busy, and rightfully so; the sushi here is wonderful and the teriyaki specials aren't bad either. Moderate. All major credit cards. Reservations for six or more only.

A Thousand Cranes Japanese Restaurant
120 South Los Angeles Street; Little Tokyo; (213) 629-1200
Seven days, 11:30 A.M.–2 P.M., 6–10 P.M.; Monday–Friday Breakfast, 7–10 A.M.

Standard Japanese cuisine served in a serene setting of reflection ponds, shrubs, and flowers. A fairly good sushi bar, tableside cooking, and excellent tempura. Expensive. All major credit cards. Reservations required.

Yamashiro
1999 North Sycamore Avenue; Hollywood; (213) 466-5125
Seven days, 11:30 A.M.–3 P.M.; Monday–Thursday, 5:30–
10:30 P.M.; Friday, 5:30–11:30 P.M.; Saturday, 5–11:30 P.M.;
Sunday, 5–10:30 P.M.

People go for the view (a breathtaking one, from atop a Hollywood hill), but the food is average or worse. Moderate-expensive. All major credit cards. Full bar. Reservations recommended on weekends.

Yamato Restaurant
2025 Avenue of the Stars (Century Plaza Hotel); Century City; (213) 277-1840
Monday–Friday, 11:30 A.M.–2:30 P.M., 5–11:30 P.M.;
Saturday, 5–11:30 P.M.; Sunday, 4:30–11 P.M.

A very good Japanese restaurant; nicely prepared meals; a pretty setting and hustling service. There is a sushi bar and also teppan-style cooking. Special tatami rooms for a private romantic meal. Expensive. All major credit cards. Reservations required. Full bar.

Korean/Thai

Dong Il Jang
3455 West Eighth Street; Mid-Wilshire; (213) 383-5757
Seven days, 11 A.M.–10:30 P.M.

Good, simple, basic Korean food, including kim-chee soup, meats, fish, and vegetables. Inexpensive. American Express, Visa, MasterCard. Reservations required. Beer and wine.

Kang Suhr
3332 West Olympic Boulevard; Mid-Wilshire;
(213) 735-4884
Seven days, 11:30 A.M.–10:30 P.M.

Kang Suhr has a long, full menu with plenty of variety. Standards such as mandu kuk and bul kogi are offered. It's the right place if you can't figure out just exactly what you want.

Inexpensive. American Express, MasterCard, Visa. Full bar. Reservations required for dinner.

Korean Gardens
950 South Vermont Avenue; Mid-Wilshire; (213) 388-3042
Seven days, 11:30 A.M.–11 P.M.

Famous for barbecued meats; you cook them yourself on a small hibachi. Korean Gardens also offers soups, tripe, chicken and, naturally, kim-chee. Inexpensive. All major credit cards. Beer and wine. Reservations required.

New Peking
913 South Vermont Avenue; Mid-Wilshire; (213) 389-6764
Monday–Saturday, 10:30 A.M.–11 P.M.

Plain and basic, offering barbecued ribs cooked in paper, fish and vegetables, and some Chinese traditionals, such as chop suey and chow mein. Inexpensive. MasterCard, Visa. Reservations not required. Beer and wine.

Original Thai BBQ
4055 West Third Street; Los Angeles; (213) 383-8571
Monday–Thursday, 11 A.M.–10 P.M.; Friday and Saturday, 11 A.M.–11 P.M.; Sunday, noon–10 P.M.

As its name implies; also seafood dishes. Inexpensive. Visa, MasterCard. Reservations recommended on weekends. Beer and wine.

Siamese Garden
301 Washington Street; Marina del Rey; (213) 821-0098
Monday–Tuesday, Thursday–Friday, 11:30 A.M.–3 P.M. Saturday, 11:30 A.M.–11 P.M.; Monday–Tuesday, Thursday, 5–10 P.M.; Sunday, 3:30–10 P.M.; Friday and Saturday, 5–11 P.M.

This Thai restaurant offers such specialties as seafood, spring rolls, beef satay, Thai noodles, and barbecued chicken. Moderate. All major credit cards. Beer and wine. Reservations recommended.

Siamese Princess
8048 West Third Street; Los Angeles; (213) 653-2643
Seven nights, 5:30–11 P.M.; Monday–Friday,
11:30 A.M.–2:30 P.M.

The dining room will match the excellence of its kitchen. It's
the favorite of many, with offerings of fish, meats, and vegetables. Moderate. All major credit cards. Reservations recommended. Beer and wine.

Thai Gourmet
9650 Reseda Boulevard; Northridge; (213) 701-5712
Monday–Saturday, 11 A.M.–10 P.M.

Thai Gourmet features the Esarn cooking of northeastern Thai-
land, whence chef Monkgorn Kaiwsai hails.

Tepparod
4649 Melbourne Avenue; Los Angeles; (213) 669-9117
Seven days, 11 A.M.–3 P.M.; Sunday–Thursday, 5–10 P.M.;
Friday and Saturday, 5–11 P.M.

Tepparod is one of the city's oldest Thai restaurants and one
of the best. The basics, plus new and different dishes, are
offered. Inexpensive. Visa, MasterCard. Reservations not required. Beer and wine.

Mexican

Acapulco & Los Arcos
733 East Broadway; Long Beach; (213) 435-2487
Many other locations throughout Los Angeles area.
Seven days, 11 A.M.–10 P.M., until 11 P.M. Friday
and Saturday.

A chain that offers good basic Mexican dishes in pleasant
atmosphere with reasonable prices. Inexpensive. Visa,
MasterCard, American Express. Full bar. Reservations for parties of five or more.

Antonio's
7472 Melrose Avenue; West Hollywood; (213) 655-0480
Tuesday–Friday, noon–2:30 P.M.; Tuesday–Saturday,
5–11 P.M.

The menu here is different and unusual, everything freshly
prepared and tasty. Wandering mariachis enhance the experience. Inexpensive. Visa, MasterCard, American Express. Full
bar. Reservations recommended.

El Cholo
1121 South Western Avenue; Los Angeles; (213) 734-2773
Monday–Thursday, 11 A.M.–10 P.M.; Friday, 11 A.M.–11 P.M.;
Sunday, 11 A.M.–9 P.M.
Other locations in La Habra, Orange, and Newport Beach.

El Cholo has been around more than 50 years, and for good
reason: a substantial menu; food served quickly and piping hot;
always tasty. A lovely outdoor patio is a special place to be
during the warmer months. All major credit cards. Reservations
suggested.

El Torito Restaurant and Cantina
13715 Fiji Way; Marina del Rey; (213) 823-8941
Various other locations.
Sunday–Thursday, 11 A.M.–11 P.M.; Friday and Saturday,
11 A.M.–midnight.

El Torito specializes in ambience. The restaurant in the Marina
sits on the boardwalk, overlooking the water, and the setting
is very nearly irresistible. The usual Mexican fare is not bad
either. Moderate. All major credit cards. Full bar. Reservations
for parties of ten or more.

The Gardens of Taxco
1113 North Harper Avenue; West Hollywood;
(213) 654-1746
Tuesday–Thursday, and Sunday, 4:30–11 P.M.; Friday and
Saturday, 4:30–midnight.

Dining at Gardens of Taxco is different from other Mexican
restaurants: there is no menu; authentic meals are based on

menus from Mexico City fare; and wandering mariachis add to the mood. It's all topped off with a custard dessert. Inexpensive. Visa, MasterCard, American Express. Beer and wine. Reservations for four or more.

La Fonda
2501 Wilshire Boulevard; Mid-Wilshire; (213) 380-5055
Monday–Friday, 11 A.M.–2 P.M.; seven days, 5:30 P.M.–2 A.M.

La Fonda is all atmosphere and fun. Tempo is set by an excellent mariachi band. Settle in for a few margaritas. Moderate. All major credit cards. Reservations recommended. Full bar.

Lucy's El Adobe
5536 Melrose Avenue; Hollywood; (213) 462-9421
Monday–Saturday, 11 A.M.–11:30 P.M.

Wall photos of former Governor Jerry Brown, Linda Ronstadt, and other luminaries munching on tacos or chatting with Lucy. A favorite of Paramount Studios people, right across the street. Lucy's doesn't offer anything new or different, but it does offer Hollywood. Inexpensive. Visa, MasterCard. Full bar. Reservations for parties of six or more.

Macho's
939 Broxton Avenue; Westwood; (213) 208-8050
Monday–Thursday, 11 A.M.–midnight; Friday, 11 A.M.–1 A.M., Saturday and Sunday 4–11 P.M.

Macho's is noisy, crowded, fun. Good place for drinks and chips, or for a full meal. The restaurant has many levels, but it's always crowded. Typical. Inexpensive. All major credit cards. No reservations. Full bar.

Panchito's Mexican Kitchen
261 South Mission Drive; San Gabriel; (213) 289-9210
Tuesday–Friday, 11 A.M.–11 P.M.; Saturday, 5–11 P.M.; Sunday, 4–11 P.M.

Frank Ramirez, Panchito himself, is a special part of his restaurant. The building, located on the site of San Gabriel's first city hall, was built by him, and he's as good in the kitchen as he is in construction. He's concocted a special 18-ingredient salsa that he uses to soak his meats and seafood in an extraordinary Mexican restaurant. Inexpensive. All major credit cards. Reservations for parties of ten or more. Full bar.

Pancho's

3615 Highland Avenue; Manhattan Beach; (213) 545-6670
Monday–Thursday, 11 A.M.–11 P.M.; Friday and Saturday,
11 A.M.–midnight; Sunday brunch, 10 A.M.–3 P.M.

This is an oceanside version of a Mexican restaurant; beautiful rooms, a full bar, and fresh seafood dishes. Inexpensive. Visa, MasterCard. Reservations not required.

Seafood

The Crab Cooker

2200 Newport Boulevard; Newport Beach; (714) 673-0100
Sunday–Thursday, 11 A.M.–9 P.M.; Friday and Saturday,
11 A.M.–10 P.M.

The Crab Cooker is low on atmosphere but high on freshness. The restaurant itself is plain—paper plates, plastic utensils— but who cares when the fish tastes as if it were caught when you ordered. Inexpensive. Cash only. First come, first served. Wine and beer.

Diamond Seafood Restaurant

724 North Hill Street #131 Food Center; Chinatown;
(213) 617-0666
Seven days, 11:30 A.M.–11 P.M.

Diamond Seafood has other good dishes on the menu, but seafood clearly is its forte. Whether you like it hot and spicy or plain, you won't be disappointed. Ambience loud, service tends to be grouchy, food will save it all. Moderate. All major credit cards. Reservations for large parties only. Beer and wine.

Famous Enterprise Fish Company
174 Kinney Street; Santa Monica; (213) 392-8366
Monday–Thursday, 11:30 A.M.–10 P.M.; Friday and Saturday,
11:30 A.M.–11 P.M.; Sunday, 10:30 A.M.–10 P.M.

The "famous" is for a mesquite grill which produces tasty and
light charcoal-broiled fish. A nautical theme adds to the fun.
Moderate. Visa, MasterCard, American Express. Reservations
for parties of six or more only.

Gladstone's 4 Fish
17300 Pacific Coast Highway; Pacific Palisades;
(213) 454-3474
Sunday–Thursday, 7 A.M.–11 P.M.; Friday and Saturday,
7 A.M.–midnight.

The beach view is the thing here; it will capture your heart as
you dine on fresh fish broiled over a mesquite grill. There is
also a good bar. Full menu from opening. Moderate-expensive.
Visa, American Express, MasterCard. Dinner reservations only.

Hymie's Fish Market
9228 West Pico Boulevard; Los Angeles; (213) 550-0377
Monday–Thursday, 6–10 P.M.; Friday and Saturday,
6–10:30 P.M.; Monday–Friday, 11:30 A.M.–2:30 P.M.

There is not a good table at Hymie's, but never mind. The
food counts: superb and fresh. It's prepared without sauce to
preserve the flavor. Moderate. All major credit cards. Reservations recommended. Full bar.

Jack's at the Beach Restaurant
2700 Wilshire Boulevard; Santa Monica; (213) 829-2846
Monday–Friday, 11:30 A.M.–2:30 P.M.; daily 5:30–10:30 P.M.

Jack's at the Beach really isn't at the beach. The Pacific Ocean
Park pier is gone and Jack's had to move, but the restaurant
still serves good, hearty meals of fresh seafood in a traditional,
formal setting. Moderate. All major credit cards. Reservations
required. Full bar.

Land's End Restaurant

323 Ocean Front Walk; Venice; (213) 392-3997
Seven days, 5:30–10 P.M.; Sunday brunch, 10 A.M.–2:30 P.M.
Cocktails and hors d'oeuvres, Saturday, noon–4:30 P.M.

Seafood on a French menu; simple setting, including patio.
Inexpensive. Visa, MasterCard, American Express. Reservations on weekends. Full bar.

Maxwell's by the Sea

317 South Pacific Coast Highway; Huntington Beach Pier;
(714) 546-2555
Sunday–Thursday, 8 A.M.–10 P.M.; Friday and Saturday,
8 A.M.–11 P.M.

A very full, varied seafood menu; should be able to please
even the most difficult palate. Dinner includes the usual—
soup or salad; potatoes, rice, or pasta; vegetables—and the
unusual: popovers. Moderate. All major credit cards. Reservations suggested. Full bar, entertainment nightly.

Mon Kee Live Fish and Seafood Restaurant

679½ North Spring Street; Chinatown; (213) 628-6717
Sunday–Thursday, 11:30 A.M.–9:45 P.M.; Friday and Saturday,
11:30 A.M.–10:15 P.M.

The name should tip you off. Nothing here but plain tables
and lots of fabulous fish, so fresh it tastes as though it's just
been caught. Inexpensive-moderate. Visa, MasterCard. Reservations for six or more. Beer and wine.

Reuben E. Lee

151 East Coast Highway; Newport Beach; (714) 675-5811
Monday–Thursday, 11:30 A.M.–10 P.M.; Friday,
11:30 A.M.–11 P.M.; Saturday, noon–11 P.M.; Sunday,
10 A.M.–10 P.M.

Reuben E. Lee is fun and cheerful. The Seafood Deck offers
seafood and meats; the Sternwheeler has a dinner show; the
Wheelhouse is reserved for private parties, all built into a
former Mississippi riverboat. Moderate. All major credit cards.
Full bar.

The Seafood Broiler
5545 Reseda Boulevard; Tarzana; (213) 996-0100
Sunday–Thursday, 11 A.M.–10 P.M.; Friday and Saturday,
11 A.M.–10:30 P.M.
Eleven Southern California locations.

A restaurant-fresh fish market where the freshest of seafoods—
white sea bass, red snapper, oysters, clams—is barbecued.
Also offers a great seafood salad. Inexpensive. Visa,
MasterCard, American Express. No reservations. Beer, wine.

Woody's Wharf
2318 Newport Boulevard; Newport Beach; (714) 675-0474
Monday–Thursday, 11 A.M.–10 P.M.; Friday and Saturday,
11 A.M.–11 P.M.; Sunday, 10 A.M.–10 P.M.; bar until 2 A.M.

A waterfront saloon where people, plenty of them, congregate
for food and drink. French-style fresh seafood and shellfish
along with veal and steak. Inexpensive. Visa, MasterCard,
American Express. Reservations for large parties only. Full
bar.

Watering Holes and Clubs

A few cautionary notes. Before starting out, verify the address, the opening and closing hours, and the dress code by telephone. Also ask about the *precise* location: for example, Wilshire Boulevard runs from downtown to the ocean in Santa Monica, and the same for Sunset Boulevard. San Vicente Boulevard is actually two totally unconnected streets, one in the Hollywood area and the other in Brentwood and Santa Monica. Sepulveda proceeds in sections from the San Fernando Valley to areas south of the airport.

You will need a stiff one if you head for a bar on Wilshire and find yourself at the right street address, but the *wrong* town. Some of these avenues and boulevards extend twenty miles or more.

Also, do not forget the drunk-driving code. CHIPS (the California Highway Patrol) is unrelenting. And the freeways are doubly hazardous if you are not in control.

So, choose carefully, plan ahead, and you will be able to discover some watering holes of distinction and charm. Celebrity-gazing spots such as Trumps or Kathy Gallagher's; Yee Mee Loo in Chinatown, so cramped and dark that even Miles Archer and Sam Spade would enter cautiously; a series of lovely pubs in Santa Monica; and local favorites like Monahan's in Pasadena and Ercoles in Manhattan Beach.

Many fine margarita places as well, from the Los Arcos chain to Lucy's El Adobe celebrity hangout on Melrose in Hollywood. Then, there are the traditional bars: the El Padrino at the Beverly Wilshire Hotel and the hangout for Hollywood's old guard, Musso and Frank's Grill.

Don't forget that California wines are widely available,

sometimes a fine selection by the glass. And good beer selections, probably the widest anywhere at Barney's Beanery in Hollywood.

Following is just a sampling of a few favorite watering holes and clubs.

Tom Bergin's
840 South Fairfax; Mid-Wilshire; (213) 936-7151
Tom Bergin's West
11600 San Vicente Boulevard; West Los Angeles;
(213) 820-3641

Bergin's is a great Irish drinking bar, with lots of people, noise, and signatures on the wall. Bergin's West has the added attraction (for those who care) of being a home for singles.

Charmers Market
175 Marine Street; Santa Monica; (213) 399-9160

A delightful place to spend an hour sipping wine on the covered outdoor patio—pick your own from the selection inside the market. But watch out, everything is expensive.

China Club
8338 West Third Street; Los Angeles; (213) 658-6406

A trendy place; the "in" people of Los Angeles sauntering up to the outer-space-Japanese-decor bar. Entertainment weekly. Check local listings for details.

Chrystie's Bar & Grill
8442 Wilshire Boulevard; Beverly Hills; (213) 655-8113

Once dilapidated and charming, now pristine and charming. It's a great place for an after-show drink.

The Ginger Man
369 North Bedford Drive; Beverly Hills; (213) 273-7585

A hot spot for Beverly Hills singles and couples. Especially crowded after work on Friday, but that's the fun.

Hard Rock Café
The Beverly Center; 8600 Beverly Boulevard; West
Hollywood; (213) 276-7605

The sister restaurant of London's Hard Rock Café, and owned
by Peter Morton (of Morton's). Everyone in town knew this
place would be popular once the doors opened, and everyone
was right. The bar is huge. The restaurant is fun, 1950s-style,
and the music pulsates loudly. Occasional live entertainment;
check local listings.

Joe Allen
8706 West Third Street; Los Angeles; (213) 274-7144

Once *the* place to be seen; still, years later, pretty full on a
Friday or Saturday night. A successful transport of New York
feeling to Southern California.

Kathy Gallagher
8722 West Third Street; West Hollywood; (213) 271-9930

A stately New York-style bar and grill with fresh flowers everywhere. A nice place to go for a less frenetic drink; but late-
night can be busy. Kitchen open until 1:30 A.M.

La Cage aux Folles
643 North La Cienega; West Hollywood; (213) 657-1091
Closed Sunday.

More a restaurant/nightclub than a watering hole. Like the
movie of the same name, offers all you expect of a drag-queen
show. It's fun. The revue changes every eight weeks.

Oscar's Pub and Restaurant
8210 Sunset Boulevard; Hollywood; (213) 654-3457

A cheery, homey English pub-restaurant, fine for British ale.
Jazz Wednesday through Saturday. Closed Sunday.

The Polo Lounge
9641 West Sunset Boulevard (Beverly Hills Hotel); Beverly
Hills; (213) 276-2251

Once the only place the stars came out at night, the Polo Lounge now has competition, but stays exciting.

TGI Friday's
13470 Maxela Avenue; Marina del Rey; (213) 822-9052
Also in Woodland Hills.

A classic singles bar that made Marina del Rey famous.

Yesterday's
1056 Westwood Boulevard; Westwood; (213) 208-8000

Caters to the younger crowd in a big way: huge dining room and full-length bar; a cocktail lounge upstairs. Noisy and crowded and upbeat.

West Beach Café
60 North Venice Boulevard; Venice; (213) 399-9246

A chic beach establishment offering nouvelle California cuisine and a gallery's worth of works by prominent local artists.

Theater and Music

Contrary to rumor, Los Angeles is alive with music and theater experiences. There are an overwhelming number of concert sites and programs, including those at the Music Center, the Hollywood Bowl, Universal Amphitheater, the Forum, the Greek Theater, and more. Nothing quite matches a balmy summer evening, nestled under a comforter (the temperature can drop 30 degrees from the daytime high) listening to a Hollywood Bowl concert.

At the Bowl, many bring a picnic meal and wine. But for those who want to reserve "tailgate parties" for football, there are many restaurants and clubs for before and after the concert to be found elsewhere in this guide.

Larger Theaters

Huntington Hartford Theater
1615 North Vine Street; Hollywood; (213) 462-6666

A Broadway-sized (1,038-seat) house that often attracts touring companies of popular New York productions. Offers mostly drama and comedy, and an occasional small-scale musical.

L.A. Stage Company
1642 North Las Palmas Avenue; Hollywood; (213) 461-2755
(377 seats)
L.A. Stage Company West
205 North Canon Drive; Beverly Hills; (213) 461-2755
(348 seats)

The Jacques Lipchitz sculpture in the foreground is framed by the Dorothy Chandler Pavilion, one of three buildings that comprise the Music Center, in downtown Los Angeles, the site for the Academy Arts every April.

Comfortable, medium-sized theaters; both offer politically flavored comedy and drama that takes a stand.

Los Angeles Music Center
135 North Grand Avenue; Downtown; (213) 972-7211

The Center Theater Group operates both the 2,100-seat Ahmanson Theater and the 750-seat Mark Taper Forum in the Music Center. The Ahmanson has a subscription season and tends to present nonmusical, often traditional fare. Nearly every production features a cast of household names. The smaller Taper generates and develops new plays, provides grants to playwrights, and operates an experimental space, the Mark Taper, Too, at the John Anson Ford Cultural Center [(213)

972-7372], in Hollywood. The Music Center is also the site of the Dorothy Chandler Pavilion, home of the Los Angeles Philharmonic and the L.A. Civic Light Opera.

Los Angeles Public Theater
366 North La Cienega Boulevard; Los Angeles; (213) 659-6415

The L.A. Public Theater runs a season of serious works, both revivals and premieres, at the Coronet Theater. The schedule is adventurous, not always geared to big-name stars, although familiar faces frequently appear, often from the world of television.

Pantages Theater
6233 Hollywood Boulevard; Hollywood; (213) 460-4411, 465-4100

A 2,900-seat converted movie house that generally books tried-and-true, crowd-pleasing musicals.

Shubert Theater
2020 Avenue of the Stars; Century City; (213) 553-9000

This 1,829-seat space is usually occupied by large-scale Broadway musicals or plays. Popular shows can run for a year or more.

South Coast Repertory Theater
655 Town Center Drive; Costa Mesa; (714) 957-4033

Both the 507-seat Mainstage auditorium and the 160-seat Second Stage Theater offers a blend of classics and contemporary plays. SCR's interest in works by new playwrights, usually staged in the smaller, flexible space, has made it an increasingly important artistic force.

Westwood Playhouse
10886 Le Conte Avenue; Westwood; (213) 553-9000

An intimate (498-seat) booking space for one-man revues, small musicals, and dramas.

Smaller Theaters (Equity Waiver—under 100 Seats)

Cast Theater and **Cast-at-the-Circle**
804 North El Centro Avenue; Los Angeles; (213) 462-0265

A popular, highly visible pair of Equity Waiver theaters (under 100 seats) that house an enormous range of theatrical activity. The eclectic array of productions includes everything from performance art to revivals.

Los Angeles Actors' Theater
1089 North Oxford Avenue; Los Angeles; (213) 464-5500

Offers a subscription season of Off-Off-Broadway-style fare, often politically oriented, in two spaces—one main stage equipped to seat up to 174, the other (half-stage) a snug 40.

Matrix Theater
7657 Melrose Avenue; Los Angeles; (213) 852-1445

Home of Actors for Themselves, the Matrix (99 seats) offers mostly serious dramas, along with occasional spoofs, using important stage talents.

Odyssey Theater
12111 Ohio Avenue; West Los Angeles; (213) 826-1626

A well-known venue for original shows that can't be seen anywhere else in the city. The emphasis is on experimental, sometimes avant-garde theater, done in three flexible spaces.

Theater Theater
1715 Cahuenga; Hollywood; (213) 871-0210

Once housed in a tiny Melrose Avenue space, Theater Theater presents critically respected and audience-pleasing shows in its present larger facility. Plays tend to be serious, sometimes shocking. Truly daring theater.

Music

Hollywood Bowl
2301 North Highland Avenue; Hollywood; (213) 876-8742

The summer home of the Los Angeles Philharmonic, the Hollywood Bowl (seating 17,619) offers classical music under the stars. Picnic before the concert. A preseason Fourth of July fireworks celebration is an annual event. The season runs July through September and features gala closing events.

Irvine Meadows Amphitheater
8800 Irvine Center Drive; Laguna Hills; (714) 977-1300

A relatively new amphitheater, Irvine Meadows offers pop music in a beautifully designed setting. Reserved seats are available, as is lawn seating.

Pacific Amphitheater
100 Fair Drive; Costa Mesa; (714) 720-0979

The Southland's newest amphitheater, Pacific offers music of all types. It has reserved and nonreserved seats, and lawn seating.

The Palace
1735 North Vine Street; Hollywood; (213) 462-3000

This medium-size theater covers the rock spectrum, with the emphasis on new wave.

Perkins Palace
129 North Raymond; Pasadena; (213) 796-7001

Rock music is the offering at this music hall.

Royce Hall
UCLA Campus; Westwood; (213) 825-9261

Undergoing a complete renovation at this time, Royce Hall is scheduled to reopen for the Olympics. Major touring attractions, recitals, and concerts.

Universal Amphitheater
Universal Studios; Universal City; (213) 980-9421

Newly renovated and now covered, the Amphitheater offers major pop music and comedy acts throughout the year. Perhaps the best pop-music revue in town.

Smaller Clubs

Since the hours for these clubs may frequently change, the editors have not attempted to provide details regarding performance times. Instead, the reader should call for information regarding specific featured acts and performance times.

Baked Potato
3787 Cahuenga Boulevard West; North Hollywood;
(213) 980-1615

Jazz. The menu features countless variations on the baked potato. Haven for some of the best studio musicians, where many of them go for jam sessions.

Club Lingerie
6507 Sunset Boulevard; Hollywood; (213) 466-8557

Hollywood's trendiest showcase books everything from punk to blues, reggae to rockabilly.

The Country Club
18415 Sherman Way; Reseda; (213) 881-5601

Heavymetal, rock, and pop.

Crazy Horse Steakhouse and Saloon
Newport Freeway, Dyer Road Exit; 1580 Brookhollow Dr.;
Santa Ana; (714) 549-1512

Country music, steaks, and beer.

The Comedy Store
8433 Sunset Boulevard; Hollywood; (213) 656-6225

A showcase and testing ground for up-and-coming comedians.

Concerts by the Sea
100 Fisherman's Wharf; Redondo Beach; (213) 379-4998

Jazz, mixed with soothing ocean waves. The biggest names in jazz make their way to this club, which is laid out like a little theater five rows deep.

Golden Bear
306 Pacific Coast Highway; Huntington Beach; (714) 536-9600

Folk, pop, jazz, rock; across from the pier.

Hop Singh's
4110 Lincoln Boulevard; Marina del Rey; (213) 822-4008

Leans toward jazz, with some pop and blues.

Improvisation
8162 Melrose Avenue; West Hollywood; (213) 651-2583

A weekend showcase (Thursday–Saturday) for comedians. It also features music and the work of new songwriters.

L.A. Cabaret
17271 Ventura Boulevard; Encino; (213) 501-3737

Touted as "The Valley's Newest Hot Spot," L.A. Cabaret offers live music during the week and dance parties on Sunday and Tuesday nights, when there is no cover charge.

Lighthouse
30 Pier Avenue; Hermosa Beach; (213) 372-6911

Mix of rock and jazz.

McCabe's Guitar Shop
Pico at 31st Street; Santa Monica; (213) 828-4403

A small stage and card-table seats are arranged behind the guitar shop, where folk music (and a little jazz) is performed.

The Palomino Club
6907 Lankerseim Boulevard; North Hollywood;
(213) 764-4010

The granddaddy of all country and western honky tonks. The
Palomino serves up steaks, beer, the biggest names in country
music. Now-famous acts came from Bakersfield and other
nearby towns in the old days to play for a few dollars a night.
Then "Hollywood" discovered it all on its doorstep, but the
Palomino hasn't changed.

Roxy Theater
9009 Sunset Boulevard; Hollywood; (213) 276-2222

A small, intimate music club that has recently been transformed
into a small, intimate theater. Music is promised to return.

Dancing

Beverly Cavern
4289 Beverly Boulevard; Hollywood; (213) 662-6035

New Wave dance club Wednesday–Sunday. Live bands Friday
and Saturday; Ladies night on Wednesday.

Chippendale's
3739 Overland Avenue; West Los Angeles; (213) 202-8850

The first club in the city to introduce the now-famous male
strippers to an all-women audience. When the show's over,
the men are allowed in and the coed dancing begins. When
the athletic male strippers perform, a wide range of ladies offer
tips and frenetic encouragement.

The Fake Club
1743 Cahuenga Boulevard; Hollywood; (213) 462-9858

A private club, located in the Continental Club. It's somewhat
sleazy, but there's lots of New Wave music, imported English
music, and funk. Check for times.

Fantasia Disco
Bonaventure Hotel; 404 South Figueroa Street; Los Angeles; (213) 689-4777

A middle-of-the-road disco. Happy hour from 4 P.M. and after-hours dancing. There's a *Playboy*-centerfold search contest every Tuesday. Fashionable attire mandatory.

Le Hot Club
15910 Ventura Boulevard; Encino; (213) 986-7035

Funk and New Wave music, break dancing.

Roosevelt Hotel
7000 Hollywood Blvd.; Hollywood; (213) 469-2442

The Garden Room of the Roosevelt, a formerly grand hotel now somewhat seedy, showcases local talent, from comedy to rock. Call for specifics for Tuesday through Saturday shows.

Sasch
11345 Ventura Boulevard; Studio City; (213) 769-5555

This is a good-sized club with a nice floor, live rock 'n' roll, and canned Top 40 to dance to.

The Scat Club
at Chippendale's; 3739 Overland Avenue;
West Los Angeles; (213) 202-8850

New Wave dance night, including romantic, Motown, ska, and synth-pop music. There are also videos. Tuesday nights only.

Sports Teams

While the Olympics will dominate the sports scene, not only in Southern California but throughout the world, during 1984, the local year-round sports scene offers the greatest array of teams and individual talent to be found anywhere. All the major professional teams are included in the following, and the two major universities, USC and UCLA. These two schools have each won more NCAA championships and produced more Olympians than any other university or college.

And there are many other outstanding local college and university teams, including Cal State Fullerton (baseball and basketball), Long Beach State (basketball and track and field), and Pepperdine (volleyball, water polo, and basketball).

There are major annual events, including the Rose Bowl, the Winston Western 500, and the Long Beach Grand Prix, and they are listed in the Annual Events section.

And, for the horseracing, there is Hollywood Park in Inglewood [(213) 419-1500], Santa Anita in Arcadia, [(213) 574-7223], and Del Mar in San Diego County, [(619) 481-1207].

Pros

Angels Baseball
Anaheim Stadium; 800 W. Katella Avenue; Anaheim; (714) 634-2000

Gene Autry's California Angels are still bridesmaids, but popular in Orange County.

Boxing
Olympic Auditorium; Los Angeles; (213) 749-5171

The Rose Bowl in scenic Arroyo Seco just north of downtown Pasadena. *The Tournament of Roses Committee*

The Olympic dates from 1925. Jimmy Lennon, the classic ring announcer, does the announcing. Boxing every Thursday year-round.

Dodgers Baseball
Dodger Stadium; 1000 Elysian Park Avenue; Los Angeles; (213) 224-1400

The Dodgers are the biggest draw in town—or in sports and major-league baseball for that matter. Dodger Blue is more pervasive than smog. Dodger Stadium is a lovely spot for an evening with palm trees and a golden sunset to be seen over the outfield seats.

L.A. Express Football
Memorial Coliseum; Exposition Park; Los Angeles;
(213) 546-5622

The USFL's local entry in a landscape that produces great
football talent, the Express are just another pretty face mask,
but there is promise.

L.A. Raiders Football
Memorial Coliseum; Exposition Park; Los Angeles;
(213) 322-5901

The Raiders, victorious in war, the Super Bowl, and in the
courtroom, are in the Coliseum for keeps. At least it seems
that way. Local heroes from Pac 10 schools and USC and
UCLA dot the lineup. For characters and character, and good
old free-spirited football, no one is better.

L.A. Rams Football
Anaheim Stadium; 800 West Katella Avenue; Anaheim;
(714) 937-6767

The Rams are back in contention and in Anaheim, having said
good-bye to the venerable Coliseum.

Kings Hockey
Forum; Manchester Boulevard; Inglewood; (213) 674-6000

Perennial struggles and hopeful fans for the local National
Hockey League Team.

Laker Basketball
Forum; Manchester Boulevard; Inglewood; (213) 674-6000

Laker fans are as fanatic as the Dodger fans. Celebrities inhabit
the best seats while young millionaires race up and down the
court. A team of great quality and great individuals, including
a few old Bruins, Jabbar and Wilkes.

Strings Tennis
Forum; Manchester Boulevard; Inglewood; (213) 674-6000

This team-tennis sport has never made it and still struggles.

Lazers Soccer
Forum; Manchester Boulevard; Inglewood; (213) 674-6000

The Lazers are in the MISL, the Major Indoor Soccer League, and their season runs from October to March. The Aztecs, formerly of the NASL, have folded and no replacement team has reentered the league.

Universities

UCLA Bruins
Westwood
Tickets: (213) 825-2101
Bruin Bench: (213) 825-3944

The Bruins now play football at the Rose Bowl in Pasadena (through the 1981 season at the Coliseum). The scenic area around this grand old stadium is ideal for tailgate parties.

All other sports are at the UCLA campus in Westwood. Basketball in Pauley Pavilion with its ten NCAA championship banners, and track and field at Drake Stadium, named in honor of Ducky Drake (student athlete, coach, and now trainer at UCLA), who once coached two UCLA students to the Decathlon gold and silver medals at the same Olympiad—Rafer Johnson and C. K. Yang.

USC Trojans
Heritage Hall; University Park
Tickets: (213) 743-2620
Cardinal and Gold Club: (213) 743-2771

The Trojans and their famous mascot, Traveller II (an Arabian stallion), still ply their football fortunes at the Coliseum, adjacent to their campus and to Exposition Park, with its rose gardens and museums. USC is the nation's number-one all-time football bowl team in victories and winning percentages.

Heritage Hall contains more trophies and championship memorabilia than any other hallowed athletic hall. From 1930 to 1968 the Trojans won twenty-four national track-and-field championships over this thirty-nine-year span, and many Olympians represented the USA from those teams, originally coached by the legendary Dean Cromwell.

Annual Events

Barnsdall Park Art Festival

Art demonstrations, puppet shows, and other outdoor festivities. Held every July in Barnsdall Park, Hollywood.

Calabasas Pumpkin Festival

The tiny town of Calabasas celebrates autumn every year with a pumpkin festival. Located in the southwestern corner of the San Fernando Valley, this onetime stagecoach stop still has a rural, homey atmosphere.

Chinese New Year

Fireworks, dragon parades, and festivities held every February in Chinatown. Call Chinatown Chamber of Commerce, (213) 628-1828.

Cinco De Mayo

Festivities surrounding the fifth of May commemorating the defeat of the French by Mexico in 1862. Various locations around Los Angeles. For more information call (213) 265-9661.

Laguna Beach Arts Festival

Artwork, crafts, and food on sale at this outdoor fair held in Laguna Beach during July. Call Laguna Beach Arts Festival, (714) 494-1145.

Laguna Beach Winter Festival

Annual surfing contest as well as art, theater, and horse show. Usually held in late February in Laguna Beach. Call the Laguna Beach Chamber of Commerce at (714) 494-1018.

Long Beach Grand Prix

Indy Car drivers roar through the streets of Long Beach every year in late March. For information call (213) 437-0341.

Los Angeles County Fair

This is the largest county fair in the United States. It has an annual eighteen-day run from mid-to-late September at the Fairgrounds in Pomona. Call Los Angeles County Fair Association, (714) 623-3111.

Los Angeles International Film Exposition (FILMEX)

A two-week, noncompetitive festival held July 15–20 at various area movie theaters. It features tributes, retrospectives and film from around the world. Call FILMEX, (213) 469-9400.

Oktoberfest

A festival celebrating autumn in Torrance's Alpine Village. Bands, beer gardens, and good food. For more information, call (213) 327-4384. Friday, Saturday, and Sunday, September 10–October 30.

Renaissance Pleasure Faire

A lively pageant recreating a sixteenth century country fair. This year's event at Paramount Ranch, Agoura, will be held from May 5th to June 10th. For information call (213) 851-9750.

Tournament of Roses Parade and Rose Bowl

Held usually on New Year's Day at the Rose Bowl in Pasadena, this granddaddy of football bowl games is preceded earlier in the day by a parade of bands, floats, and personalities along Colorado Boulevard. The game is a confrontation between the Big Ten and Pacific Ten conference winners.

Westwood Sidewalk Arts and Crafts Show

Held during spring and fall on the streets of Westwood; browse, shop, and listen to music.

Winston Western 500

This major stock-car race is held annually in November at Riverside International Raceway, at 22255 Eucalyptus Avenue in Edgemont. (714) 653-1161.

Southern California Getaways:

One-Day and Overnight Excursions

by Jerry Hulse, Travel Editor

I hope you have a day or two to spare, before, after, or even during the Olympics. Obviously, you may want to visit the celebrated attractions: Disneyland, Marineland, Universal Studios, the *Queen Mary,* Knott's Berry Farm, Huntington Library, ad infinitum. You may want to visit communities. If I were asked for my opinion, I would suggest a trip north to Santa Barbara and the little Danish town of Solvang as well as Hearst's Castle, near San Luis Obispo. If time permitted, I would motor inland to Palm Springs and south to San Diego, a city with the finest in leisure-style living, along with a huge helping of culture and hedonism (the Old Globe Theater, symphonies, nightclubs, waterfront restaurants, man-made islands). Because of its excellent weather (possibly the *best* in the world), San Diego is an outdoor land of bays and beaches, hiking trails, and unusual hotel/resorts.

While other cities seem bent on destroying old buildings, San Diego jealously guards its Victorian gems. A case in point: Heritage Park, an eight-acre arena near Presidio Hill where handsome old gingerbread structures are secure from the wrecker's ball. One of San Diego's old/new sections is the downtown complex, Gaslamp Quarter. Several years ago, dozens of turn-of-the-century buildings were prettied up for posterity in a sixteen-block area, with brick sidewalks and gas lamps that glow each evening. The Gaslamp Quarter is a joy for the visitor: boutiques, galleries, antique shops, and restau-

The Hotel del Coronado on Coronado Island in San Diego. This Victorian-style resort hotel was opened in 1887 and is now a modern-day vacation getaway a few hours from Los Angeles.

rants (Southern California's oldest Chinese restaurant, Wong's Nanking Café, does business here). The Quarter is also the home of the San Diego Ballet Company and Gaslamp Theater. Appealing, too, is nearby Seaport Village and the adjacent Embarcadero Park, unveiled on the site of the old Coronado ferry landing.

Huge aircraft carriers and small destroyers stand at anchor in San Diego's bay; submarines move stealthily out to sea and excursion boats leave regularly on sightseeing journeys that skirt the commercial docks, tuna clippers, yacht harbors, and San Diego's navy and marine installations. The city's greatest attraction, though, is its zoo, where animals appear in near-natural surroundings: pigmy chimps from Africa, koalas from New Zealand, golden marmosets, Indian rhinos, and the okapi from the Congo, altogether more than five thousand specimens representing the largest collection of wild animals in the entire world. A few miles north is a sister compound, the eighteen-hundred-acre San Diego Wild Animal Park, where visitors ride monorails to catch glimpses of addax and antelope, gazelles and gnus, zebras, buffalo, gorillas, and ring-tailed lemurs.

San Diego's attractions include nearly seventy golf courses, Old Town, thoroughbred racing at Del Mar, and opera, plus California's oldest missions. Visitors explore Mission Bay with its resort hotels, marinas, beaches, and boat docks. Spread across 4,600 acres, Mission Bay is billed as the world's biggest water playground (wind surfing, sailing, fishing, swimming). It is the home of Sea World as well as one of my favorite resort hotels, Vacation Village (Japanese-style bridges close the gap across man-made lagoons; tiki torches glow at night). Another is the wonderful Del Coronado Hotel, with its Victorian turrets and towers (it was here that the then Duke of Windsor is reputed to have met the woman for whom he would later surrender the British throne).

Across the border from the Del Coronado lies Tijuana with its bullring, jai-alai auditorium, restaurants, and hotels. Visited annually by more Americans than any foreign city in the world, Tijuana spills over with bazaars on either side of Avenida Revolución, offering imports both European and Oriental: Swiss watches, French perfumes, Japanese silks, Italian knits.

Back in San Diego County, surfers crowd on some of California's finest beaches. A case in point is La Jolla Cove and Windansea, ranked among professionals as second only to the surfing in Hawaii. The lovely village of La Jolla is an anachronism, a flashback to the good times, the refined times of earlier years when such little enclaves of America still functioned with grace and dignity. Nowhere is this demonstrated more dramatically than at Hotel La Valencia, once shelter for the cinematic likes of Greta Garbo, Clark Gable, Lillian Gish, Charles Laughton, Jack Warner, and Gregory Peck. The hotel's Spanish-tile floors gleam spotlessly beneath wrought-iron chandeliers; young lovers, silver-haired matrons, and retired navy admirals dine in the patio restaurant in a setting out of an F. Scott Fitzgerald novel. Indeed, the era of *The Great Gatsby* comes quickly to mind. A national women's magazine once described La Valencia as "one of the ten best hotels in California to stay with one's husband—or someone else's."

La Jolla provides the sort of atmosphere that inspires one to sculpt and to write, and so it is populated by many artists and literary folk. Visitors laze in the sun, look in on the art galleries or the Scripps Institute of Oceanography, and dine in excellent restaurants. Cliffsides burst with bougainvillea; peaceful coves and flowered yards unfold; strollers fill their souls with gorgeous sunsets while gulls wheel gracefully in the slowly darkening heaven.

Meanwhile, up the coast at Laguna Beach, paintings come to life with dramatic reality during the annual Festival of Arts and Pageant of the Masters. Each summer evening the works of renowned artists—from da Vinci to Gainsborough to Norman Rockwell—are recreated at Irvine Bowl. The show's tableaux are depicted by the local druggist, the grocer, doctors, housewives. Even schoolchildren appear nightly as saints and sinners, dancers and Madonnas. Laguna's residents are the stars of the show, the designers, the makeup artists, the program sellers. In conjunction with the pageant, paintings are displayed by local artists at an outdoor gallery. By nightfall, the 2,500-seat amphitheater becomes a frame for living paintings—some spotlighted by a Pacific moon. Like La Jolla, Laguna is a picture-postcard town that brings to mind some Mediterranean village. Sorrento, perhaps. Or Saint-Jean-Cap-Ferrat.

Traveling inland, legions of visitors take in Palm Springs (can you name another resort with a poodle parlor that operates alongside a beauty salon?). Palm Springs is America's best-known sandpile. Still, it took a golfing President, Dwight Eisenhower, to focus world attention here. Palm Springs boasts more than 6,000 swimming pools, dozens of golf courses, hundreds of tennis courts, and thousands of hotel rooms. Without argument, two of the peachiest resorts are La Mancha (villas with private swimming pools and push-button fireplaces) and Ingleside Inn, the gathering place for film stars, politicians, and European royalty. Show-biz personalities stake their claims on the various golf links in a ritual that finds them hurrying back each autumn. After seeing The Springs over several seasons, I accepted the lures and moved there myself. My reasons? The clean air, the relaxed way of life. Now jackrabbits cross my path whenever I walk the dog and often at night I hear coyotes howling in the hills. Whenever someone asks me what Palm Springs is *really* like, I tell them about Palm Canyon, with its elegant shops . . . how the San Jacinto range rises so dramatically . . . how the evening sun sets sand dunes a-flame . . . how the stars shine so brightly . . . how. . . . But come see for yourself.

But don't forget the coast, north to Santa Barbara. Recently I was struck by the thought, Why would anyone wish to travel all the way to the Côte d'Azur or the Italian Riviera when Santa Barbara's coastline is every bit as lovely, if not lovelier? I am attracted by Santa Barbara's Spanish influence (its magnificent mission), the Mediterranean blueness of the Pacific, the relaxed attitude that prevails here, and the well-being one feels from just being alive in this world of ocean and mountain greenery. In the past twenty-five years the population has increased dramatically, but the same historic buildings exist: the graceful Queen of Missions, the Spanish-Moorish courthouse, the old adobes, art galleries, and the Presidio, over which the flags of three nations have flown (Spain, Mexico, and the United States).

In Santa Barbara polo is still featured on Sunday, although Sunday is special for other reasons: a day given over to arts-and-crafts shows and long, leisurely brunches at the city's fine hotels and resorts. A favorite is El Encanto, perched in mountains overlooking Santa Barbara and the Pacific with its Channel Islands. El Encanto resembles a country place one discovers behind Nice or Cannes, especially at times when the wisteria is in bloom and the nights are warm and starlit. Its restaurant is the perfect choice for Sunday brunch, particularly the terrace, with its wrought-iron railing, green turf, yellow umbrellas, classical melodies, and potted posies. The sense of romance prevails inside El Encanto as well: fans spin in the ceiling and a piano is heard in a distant corner (guests have the choice of 100 white stucco cottages scattered across nine acres blooming with bougainvillea, hibiscus, and geraniums). A similar sense of well-being prevails at Montecito Inn and the renowned Santa Barbara Biltmore, with its distinctive Spanish flavor. A harpist performs each afternoon in the lounge at the Biltmore and a Latin trio grinds out romantic nonsense for the cocktail crowd.

While mission bells ring, vacationers stroll along El Paseo (*the avenue* in Spanish); they explore Stearns Wharf and a sixty-five-acre botanical garden, the Andrew Clark Bird Refuge, the Museum of Natural History, a children's zoo, art galleries, Dos Pueblos Orchid Farm, and nearly fifty antique shops with such fetching names as The Old Oak Tree and On Consignment.

Those with time to spare take in Los Padres National Forest, the sun-blessed Santa Ynez Valley, the flower fields of Lompoc, and the charming little village of Solvang—a touch of Scandinavia rising from the rich California soil. A page from Hans Christian Andersen, Solvang comes complete with gas lamps and windmills as well as homes and shops that are vividly reminiscent of faraway Denmark (some with storks nesting in the chimneys). Beyond Solvang awaits Hearst's Castle, the haunting Big Sur coast, Carmel, and Monterey . . . and so many, many other storied destinations that it would take weeks, indeed years, to see it all.

One-Day Excursions

Disneyland
Harbor Boulevard exit; Santa Ana Freeway; Anaheim; (714) 999-4565

The world-famous theme park, all seventy-six acres, in a kingdom of magic and fantasy. Main Street USA, Adventureland, Frontierland, New Orleans Square, Bear Country, Fantasyland, and Tomorrowland.

Forest Lawn Memorial Park
1712 South Glendale Boulevard; Glendale; (213) 254-3131

Well-known resting place of former Hollywood luminaries. Also contains reproductions of European churches, garden retreats, and famous sculptures. Admission free.

Henry E. Huntington Library, Art Gallery and Botanical Gardens
1151 Oxford Drive; San Marino; (213) 792-6141

This extensive collection of rare books and manuscripts donated by railroad tycoon Henry E. Huntington. This was his

Camp Snoopy is one of many attractions at Knott's Berry Farm in Buena Park, Orange County.

residence. Famous artworks include Gainsborough's *Blue Boy* and Lawrence's *Pinkie*.

Hollywood Hills and Sign

On the hills above Hollywood reside many entertainment industry notables. High over their roofs is one of the most famous landmarks in Los Angeles—the Hollywood sign. It can be seen from many parts of the city, but for a better view, take Beachwood Drive to Ledgewood Drive to Durand Drive. For information: call the Hollywood Chamber of Commerce, 6324 Sunset Boulevard, (213) 469-8311.

Knott's Berry Farm

8039 Beach Boulevard; Buena Park; (714) 952-9400

The oldest theme amusement park in the world. Now 150 acres and divided into Old West Ghost Town, Fiesta Village, Roaring 10's Airfield, and Camp Snoopy.

Los Angeles Zoo
5333 Zoo Drive; Los Angeles; (213) 666-4090

Wild animals grouped according to continent of origin over seventy-five acres. There is also a children's zoo and an animal nursery.

Mann's Chinese Theater
6925 Hollywood Boulevard; (213) 273-3360

Another landmark of note is Mann's Chinese Theater. Its courtyard contains the footprints, handprints, and signatures of over 160 film stars.

Marineland
6610 Palos Verdes; Rancho Palos Verdes; (213) 541-5663

An offering of sea animals, live shows, and a Marine Care Center.

Queen Mary
Pier J; Long Beach; (213) 435-3511

The R.M.S. *Queen Mary*, the largest passenger ship ever built, now resides in permanent dry dock and serves as a maritime museum and luxury hotel.

Six Flags Magic Mountain
Magic Mountain Parkway; (off Interstate 5); Valencia;
(805) 255-4111

Fast, scary, white-knuckling rides are featured in this two-hundred-acre amusement park. One admission fee covers all rides and attractions. Fun for the whole family.

Spruce Goose
Pier J; Long Beach; (213) 435-3511

The largest aircraft ever built is on display next to the *Queen Mary*. Built in 1942 by Howard Hughes, this prototypical air cargo transport seaplane took its one and only flight November 2, 1947.

Universal Studios Tour
Hollywood Freeway and Lankerseim Boulevard offramp; Universal City; (213) 877-1311

A "behind-the-scenes" tour, three and one-half hours long, of a major Hollywood studio backlot. Food concessions and gift shops abound, as well as staged demonstrations and stops such as Prop Plaza.

SCENIC OUTDOORS

Angeles National Forest
150 South Los Robles; Pasadena; (213) 577-0050, (213) 684-0350

Hundreds of miles of creeks, eight natural and artificial lakes, one thousand miles of roads, hiking, and riding trails, all make up this well-visited national forest located directly north of Los Angeles.

Cleveland National Forest

Extends from five miles above the Mexican border northwest into Orange and Riverside counties. It has peaks as high as six thousand feet, deserts, chaparral thickets, and abandoned mines. (619) 293-5050.

Descanso Gardens
1418 Descanso Drive; La Canada/Flintridge; (213) 790-5571

Famous for its collection of camellias, set among a flowing stream, waterfalls and Japanese teahouse. Admission fee. Open daily 9 A.M.–4:30 P.M.

Exposition Park
Figueroa Street at Exposition Boulevard; Los Angeles; (213) 744-7400

Site of the 1932 Olympics, this beautiful park is the location of two major museums: The California State Museum of Science and Industry and the Los Angeles County Museum of History. The Memorial Coliseum and Los Angeles Sports Arena are also here, as well as picnic areas and rose garden.

Griffith Park
Visitor's Center: 4730 Crystal Springs Drive; Los Angeles; (213) 665-5188

The largest city park in the United States. It contains the Los Angeles Zoo, four golf courses, Griffith observatory, fifty-two miles of bridle and hiking trails and picnic grounds.

Laguna Beach/Newport Beach

Laguna Beach is a succession of small coves: Moss Street, Crescent Bay, Brooks Street, and Laguna beaches; Shaw's and Treasure coves. All are picturesque, sizable, and directly accessible from Pacific Coast Highway. Parking is scarce.

North of Laguna Beach, take any sign reading "Balboa Peninsula" and you will find expansive, beautiful beaches at the end of numbered streets. Each of these beaches is great for swimming and surfing, and one, the famous Wedge, is renowned for its huge body-surfing waves. Newport Beach is an affluent, upwardly mobile community that cherishes its beaches as well as its art galleries, restaurants, and shops. (714) 644-8211.

Los Angeles State and County Arboretum
301 North Baldwin Avenue; Arcadia; 446-8251

Plant specimens from all over the world are housed here on this 120-acre arboretum. Tall palms, lush plantings, demonstration gardens. Domestic horticulture at its best. Admission fee.

Los Padres National Forest
(805) 968-1578

Over 1,900,000 acres of rugged, wild forestland. It is the second largest forestland in California. Between Santa Barbara

and Goleta, Highway 154 will take you into the forest. Closer
to the Los Angeles Basin, the Fraser Park exit of Interstate 5,
north of Gorman, also provides access.

Malibu Beaches

Beautiful stretches of coastline north of Santa Monica off Highway 1. There are public beaches, a secluded residential colony,
tidepools, and a fishing pier.

Point Vicente
Palos Verdes Drive; one-half mile south of Hawthorne
Boulevard; Palos Verdes

Point Vicente presents a beautiful view of the Pacific. There
is a lighthouse and an exclusive residential coastal community.
Marineland is nearby. There are popular sky-diving areas, and
rolling green fields stretch from highway to impressive ocean
cliffs.

San Bernardino National Forest
Interstate 10 or 15 to most areas; (714) 383-5588

There is year-round enjoyment to be had here. Numerous creeks,
lakes, and trails dot the forest. Arrowhead/Big Bear are among
the popular vacation playgrounds. Reservations are available
at most campgrounds and at Ticketron outlets.

San Clemente
(714) 492-1131

Just south of San Juan Capistrano is another beautiful beach
city. San Clemente offers boating, surfing, sailing, diving, and
fishing, as well as trap and skeet shooting. President Nixon's
Western White House made it famous. The Nixon Library is
now located there.

San Juan Capistrano
(714) 493-1111

South of Los Angeles, accessible from Highway 1 or Interstate
5 is San Juan Capistrano. Known for its historic mission, the
town also features a breathtaking coastline. The swallows ar-

rive on March 19 and leave in the fall. Historic sites include late-nineteenth-century Santa Fe Railroad station and other adobe buildings.

Will Rogers State Historic Park
14253 Sunset Boulevard; (213) 454-8212

Originally the home of cowboy-humorist Will Rogers, this 187-acre park is now open to the public. The extensive grounds are excellent for hiking and picnicking. On Saturdays and Sundays during the summer, one may even watch a polo match.

Overnight or Longer Excursions

Baja California/Tijuana

A popular excursion for visitors to San Diego, Mexico's Tijuana is a free port known for its shopping. A dense, noisy metropolis, its restaurants and shops add color and excitement to a trip to San Diego.

South from Tijuana is the Baja Peninsula. It has hundreds of miles of desolate, pristine beaches. Popular for years with surfers, beach lovers, and fishermen, Baja is a rapidly developing state. Along the Pacific Coast, particularly in Ensenada, one encounters many modern, clean hotels and restaurants.

Big Bear/Lake Arrowhead

Nestled in the San Bernardino Mountains are Southern California's prime recreational areas, Big Bear and Lake Arrowhead. Together they provide seasonal boating, swimming, hiking, and water and snow skiing. Accommodations, from cabins to hotels, are available. In addition, Lake Arrowhead has a modern lakeside shopping mall. Big Bear's Visitor Bureau, (714) 886-5878. Lake Arrowhead Chamber of Commerce, (714) 337-3715.

Catalina and the Channel Islands

A pretty, cove-fringed island set twenty-six miles off the coast of California, Catalina is perfect for a weekend getaway or longer. Restaurants, excursions, shops, fishing, and skin diving are available. The back region of the island still has herds of bison, boars, and goats. For more information call: (213) 510-1520 at the Visitor's Information Center.

Farther north and still at sea are the Channel Islands. They are a string of tiny islands comprising about 18,000 acres. Reachable only by boat, they offer an escape to dramatic coves, vistas of open ocean and its wildlife. All-day boat trips from Ventura, (805) 642-1393.

Death Valley

The lowest spot in the continental United States, Death Valley is also one of the hottest. Temperatures commonly reach 120 degrees on summer days. It is an area of various landscape ranges, from alkali flats to the peaks of the Panamints. Visit Death Valley from mid-October to mid-May when temperatures are in the seventies. There is a Visitors Center in Furnace Creek, where exhibits, slide shows, and guided walks provide orientation to the surrounding sights. The Furnace Creek Inn and Ranch offers tennis, golf, riding, and swimming; (619) 786-2345 for reservations. For Death Valley Visitor's information, (619) 786-2331.

Las Vegas

This is a tale of two cities. First, The Strip, with Caesars Palace, MGM Grand, Sands, Tropicana, and Sahara hotel-casinos. It never shuts down. Second, Las Vegas, the town, with its boating, swimming, water skiing on nearby Lake Mead, its golf, horseback riding, and tennis. Tours of Hoover Dam, Death Valley, and the Grand Canyon originate here. The choices abound, the hotels and restaurants excellent. (702) 457-1467.

Ojai/Santa Barbara

Up Highway 1, north of Los Angeles, is the small rural community of Ojai. It attracts artists as well as lovers of the outdoors. It is filled with boutiques, shops, and galleries. The Oaks at Ojai caters to those intent on getting in shape and features an extensive fitness program.

Farther north on Highway 101 is beautiful Santa Barbara, a city noted for Spanish architecture, a California mission, scenic wharves, and beaches. The Arlington Theater, situated on red-tiled Main Street, is architecturally noteworthy. (805) 965-3021 for information.

Inland, and yet more northern, is Solvang, known as "Little Denmark, USA." Food and pastries here are prepared from old Danish recipes. Shops carry Danish goods and have an Old World ambience. During summer months an outdoor theater fest provides nighttime entertainment. (805) 688-3317 for information.

Palm Springs/Idyllwild

Palm Springs has long been a winter campground of the elite, with its shimmering pools, its golf courses, and its nightlife. There is an aerial tram that takes you to the top of Mt. San Jacinto, from which the entire desert panorama comes into view. Palm Springs Visitor's Bureau, (619) 327-8411.

Nearby is the tiny village of Idyllwild. It offers picturesque Alpine vistas, a pleasant change from the vast stretches of desert around it. Idyllwild Chamber of Commerce, (619) 659-3259.

San Diego

Situated about 150 miles down the coast from Los Angeles, this major California city features a benevolent climate, great beaches, a beautiful harbor, excellent restaurants. Right in the heart of the city is Balboa Park, which contains art museums, sports facilities, theaters, and a world-famous zoo without cages, the San Diego Zoo. Within its 125 acres are the rarest animals in the world. Balboa Park also houses the San Diego Museum of Art and Timken Gallery. There is horseracing at Del Mar and a large number of golf and tennis facilities.

Opulent homes necklace wide stretches of beach and the blue Pacific. Seaworld, and oceanarium, covers over eighty acres in Mission Bay Park. There are several shows daily featuring dolphins, seals, and killer whales. Rides and exhibits all center on sea life. (619) 232-310l. San Diego Chamber of Commerce (619) 232-0124.

San Simeon

San Simeon sits atop a knoll overlooking the Pacific Ocean. It is the site of sprawling Hearst Castle, built by newspaper tycoon William Randolph Hearst. There are pools, gardens, and statuary everywhere. There are four tours of castle and grounds available. Reservations must be made via Ticketron. A good place to stay while visiting San Simeon is in Cambria. Located six miles south of Hearst's Castle, this peaceful town is a haven for artists and campers. San Simeon State Beach offers excellent campsites and picnic areas. (805) 927-4621 for Hearst Castle information; and (805) 927-3500 for visitor information.

Sierra Nevada

The Sierra Nevada mountain range contains a forest of giant sequoia trees and miles of lofty peaks. Some trees in Sequoia Park are over 3,500 years old and rise over 270 feet.

Bordering to the north is Kings Canyon Park, boasting giant sequoias. Beautiful vistas and crystal caves abound. Both parks contain over 1,300 miles of mountains, canyons, lakes, and waterfalls. During the spring thaw, river rafting is popular on the Kern River.

Shopping

by Marylou Luther, Fashion Editor

For $35 an hour, the woman who selects Carol Burnett's clothes will take you shopping at the trendiest boutiques on Rodeo Drive, where she knows every salesperson and every bargain.

For $100 and two and a half hours of your time, you can "have your colors done" by women who swear they can make you feel better by putting you in the right color.

And in between, you can visit one of the city's famous shopping malls and be entertained by strolling troubadours or street dancers free of charge. This is, after all, the home of the late Victor Gruen, the architect who pioneered the idea of the shopping mall.

Ah, the shopping mall, where The Broadway's clothes meet Mrs. See's candy, and it's love at first bite.

One of the best things about shopping in Los Angeles is the comfort factor. The big crowds that bombard the Bloomingdale's regular in New York or the Filene's bargain hunter in Boston are so dispersed in this sprawling megalopolis that it's possible to go from shop to shop, boutique to boutique, department store to department store, without once being jostled, bumped, pushed, shoved, or otherwise humiliated. And inside the emporium of your choice, you can usually go from notions to negligees without once getting your toes stepped on.

One of the best things about shopping in Los Angeles is the casual spirit. Shopping is taken very seriously, for instance, in New York, where you are expected to dress for the occasion. (You put on your best clothes so you can take them off.) Shopping is taken very casually in Los Angeles, where some of the city's most celebrated women shop in their tennis clothes.

Even the salespeople in many of the stores dress down rather than dress up. The major stores make it easy for you to distinguish between salespeople and other customers, however, by providing employees with store nametags. And at least one of the city's major department stores, Bullock's, will have translators in residence by Olympics time for visitors who might be able to ask "how much" but are having trouble converting European sizes into American sizes, for example, or asking directions from one department to another. (The Bullock's in the Beverly Center already is staffed with linguists who speak eleven different languages.)

If you're from a country where people arrive at "the best price" by bargaining, you might be disappointed to learn that prices are firm, and not negotiable, at all major stores. Smaller shops, especially in the downtown area, consider bargaining a way of life. You might be glad to know that comparison shopping is not necessary here; most major stores charge similar prices for brand-name merchandise.

If you're interested in patronizing manufacturers who are official Olympics licensees, look for a label that says "Manufacturer under license to the LAOOC." The label may or may not have the five Olympics rings on it. If in doubt, Olympics organizers suggest calling the manufacturer. If that sounds a bit farfetched, try asking the salesperson. He or she just might know.

Certain cities are famous for certain products. London, for example, has its Burberry raincoats and Savile Row suits. France has its Maud Frizon shoes and Chanel perfumes. Italy has its Fendi furs and Gucci moccasins. L.A. has its Nudie's of North Hollywood and Frederick's of Hollywood.

The former is the namesake shop of the man known as the king of cowboy couture. (His custom-made gold-lamé suit for Elvis Presley cost $10,000 and he drives a white Cadillac embellished with steer horns and 1,200 silver dollars, rifles, six-shooters, derringers, and silver statuettes of horses and horseshoes. His customers include President Reagan, Roy Rogers, and the late John Wayne.) Frederick's of Hollywood is the passionate purple store originated by Frederick Mellinger, who's the undisputed king of X-rated lingerie. His customers include Nebraska housewives and Sunset Strippers. Both stores are considered national monuments of a sort by such famous French designers as Thierry Mugler and Claude Montana, who see them as treasure houses of American high tack. The success of Nudie's and Frederick's also is responsible for whole networks of western shops and trashy lingerie boutiques in many areas of the city.

Some of the best buys in Los Angeles are the sweatshirts and T-shirts from student stores at UCLA and USC. At AS-UCLA Students Store, 308 Westwood Plaza, for example, the famous UCLA (pronounced OOKLA by the French, who covet them) sweatshirts range from $13.50 to $18.50.

For young Olympians interested in redressing the 1950s, the place to go is Melrose Avenue in West Hollywood, where both new and used clothes from that era are available. The Venice Beach Boardwalk, where casual California wear is easily available at good prices, and the Rose Bowl Swap Meet, Pasadena's favorite flea market, are also treasure troves for the young.

If you happen to be small by American standards, you might find just what you're looking for in Chinatown or Little Tokyo, both located in downtown Los Angeles and both well-known for stocking short sizes for men and petites for women. Melrose Avenue, Venice Beach, the Rose Bowl, Chinatown, and Little Tokyo all are recommended for soaking up the local culture as well as serious shopping.

European visitors often seek out American lingerie as gifts for the folks back home. It's not that pantyhose are difficult to find elsewhere or that the French have lost their market for sexy bras and lacy garter belts, it's that America is one of the few places in the industrialized world that offers cotton underthings, things such as pantyhose with cotton crotches, panties and bras made of both knitted and woven cotton, cotton stockings, cotton leotards, cotton garter belts, cotton camisoles, and cotton slips.

Perhaps the most famous all-cotton apparel item of all time—one born right here in the state of California—is still going strong. It's Levi Strauss' original 501 jean, the one the miners wore when they went for the gold back in 1849.

Shopping Guide

ARCO Plaza
Fifth and Flower Streets; Downtown Los Angeles;
(213) 625-2132

This shopping and dining area is located beneath the twin
towers of the Atlantic Richfield and Bank of America towers.
You'll find mostly smaller shops and boutiques, art galleries,
bookstores, and lots of places to grab a quick bite. This is also
the location of the Los Angeles Visitors Information Center
and the RTD Center.

Beverly Center
La Cienega and Beverly boulevards; Los Angeles;
(213) 854-0070

One of Los Angeles' newest malls, this one has two full levels
of stores (from large, like Bullock's and Broadway, to small,
like Sanrio and Sasch). You'll find everything you need here:
clothes, accessories, home furnishings, beauty products, and
vitamins. The top level is reserved for concessions, restaurants,
and a fourteen-theater movie complex (Beverly Cineplex) that
offers art films.

Broadway Plaza
700 W. Seventh Street; Downtown Los Angeles;
(213) 624-2891

The Broadway Plaza combines with the Hyatt Regency and an
office tower to create a mélange of activity. The shopping
available is varied, with large department stores (like Broadway
and Joseph Magnin) and smaller boutiques and bookstores.

Century City Fashion Square
10250 Santa Monica Boulevard; Century City;
(213) 552-8155

An open-air mall, and a fine one. This fashion square offers
many nice shops, including Bullock's and Broadway, Joseph
Magnin and Judy's, and smaller shops like Papagallo, Clothes-
line, and Nickelodeon. There's something for everyone at Century Square, and lots of choices for a quick meal as well.

The Cooper Building
860 South Los Angeles Street; Los Angeles; (213) 622-1139

In the heart of the downtown garment district, this discount
paradise offers the intrepid shopper eleven floors and over
eighty shops to choose from. Factory outlets and stores selling
discounted designer clothing are inside.

Del Amo Fashion Center
3525 Carson; Torrance; (213) 542-8525

Del Amo offers 355 different stores in its expansive center.
The big ones include Broadway, Sears, Penney's, Robinson's,
Bullock's, and I. Magnin. There are also lots and lots of smaller
shops and thirty restaurants from which to pick.

Farmer's Market
Third and Fairfax; Los Angeles; (213) 933-9211

A roofed open-air mart, this place is a delight to the senses.
Fresh fruits and vegetables, meats, cheese, flowers, candies,
pastries and breads abound. There are lots of different concessions where one can grab a quick meal, and across the parking
lot to the other side, you'll find shops and boutiques.

Fox Hills Mall
200 Fox Hills Mall; Sepulveda and Slauson boulevards;
Fox Hills; (213) 390-7833

The two big department stores at Fox Hills are May Company
and J. C. Penney. The rest of the mall is made up of 129
different merchants selling everything from shoes to diamonds.

Glendale Galleria
135 Glendale Galleria; Central and Colorado; (off Ventura and Glendale freeways); (213) 246-2401

There are 160 shops and boutiques at the Glendale Galleria, including Broadway, Buffum's, Ohrbach's, Penney's, and the brand-new Nordstrom's.

Grand Central Market
317 S. Broadway; Downtown Los Angeles; (213) 624-2378

An indoor shopping bazaar where all kinds of food are available, at very reasonable prices. Fresh meats, fruits, and vegetables are most popular, but ready-to-eat food isn't so bad either.

Loehmann's
(Adjacent to Farmer's Market); 6220 West Third Street; Los Angeles; (213) 933-5675

This famous nationwide discount chain specializes in removing the labels and dropping the price. All kinds of clothes available from formal to swimwear plus "the Back Room" designer section with slightly higher prices. Hard work and crowded group dressing rooms, but tremendous savings. Other locations include three in Los Angeles, plus Fullerton and Reseda.

Main Street
Santa Monica

A lovely place for a leisurely Sunday walk, but the leisure will be mixed with youthful and fun-loving spirit. Roller skaters—not so many as Venice, though—joggers, and cyclists will pass by. There are trendy and smart stores (Colors of the Wind and the Gallery), restaurants (Wolfgang Puck's Chinois-on-Main and the Chronicle), the decorator shops (Bobi Leonard). Pioneer Boulangerie and Napoleons at the north end and Charmers Market, the Rose Café, and Via Dolce Confectioners at the south end (at the Venice border) offer between them a variety of delicatessen, gourmet, bakery, and ice-cream treats. Whether its truffles, croissants, cheese, pasta, or imported beer

and California wines, you will be rewarded with many plea-
sures, great and small.

Melrose Avenue (in West Los Angeles)

The Melrose Avenue area is youthful, L.A. chic and perfect
for strolling. In contrast to the gold-coast, international qual-
ities of Rodeo Drive and the Rodeo Collection, Melrose features smaller, designer-owned shops and has strong Los Angeles
westside flavor.

And there are numerous excellent restaurants and water
holes, ideal for celebrity gazing, mixed in with the clothing,
antique, and art shops.

Among the shops are:

Azar Wood

8101 Melrose Avenue; West Los Angeles; (213) 653-5609

This small store features clothing by Los Angeles couturier
designer Wayne Woods. The collection includes casual wear
and a selection of silks for women.

You'll also find a few thrift shops along the avenue including:

Les Enfants

8332 Melrose Avenue; West Los Angeles; (213) 651-0527

Unusual clothing and jewelry for children only, at least those
with chic and trendy tastes.

Faire la Cuisine (adjoining **Fred Segal**)

8112 Melrose Avenue; West Los Angeles; (213) 653-1464

A restaurant, café, and gourmet cookware shop. Special cof-
fees and cheeses and foods to go.

Fred Segal

8100 Melrose Avenue; West Los Angeles; (213) 651-4129

Trendy clothing for men and women plus fashion accessories
and gift items. A favorite among rock stars and their groupies.

Melon's

8739 Melrose Avenue; West Los Angeles; (213) 854-3474

Featuring both European and American clothes and shoes for women.

Pasadena Plaza

Green Street (near Civic Center); Pasadena; (213) 795-3280

This is a new shopping center that has a number of specialty shops and department stores. It's a nice place to spend an afternoon in this newly renovated area.

Plum's

6298 West Third Street; Los Angeles; (213) 938-3391

Elegant designer sportswear at low discount prices. Special features include private dressing rooms and big savings on designer pantyhose. Three other locations in Tarzana, Torrance, and Santa Ana.

Regine

8336 Melrose Avenue; West Los Angeles; (213) 653-4080

Mostly European and some American clothing for women only.

Repeat Performance

7264 Melrose Avenue; West Los Angeles; (213) 938-0609

Fine antique clothing for men and women is here. The women's clothing ranges from 1900–1950 and the men's from the 1940s and 1950s. Campy and fun.

Rodeo Drive

Beverly Hills

Situated between Santa Monica and Wilshire boulevards, Rodeo Drive symbolizes all the glitter, glamour, and wealth that was once associated with old Hollywood. The elegant stores lining the street cater to the landed Beverly Hills gentry and the curious foreign visitor. If you don't have the necessary cold cash for a shopping expedition, make the trip just to people-watch. You're sure to see an occasional celebrity or

Arab sheikh being whisked off in a limousine. After hours the displays on Rodeo Drive represent a fantasy world, and the atmosphere is ripe for romantic evening window shopping. Some of the most famous names on the drive include:

Carroll & Company
466 N. Rodeo Drive; Beverly Hills; (213) 273-9060

Clothing for men and women featuring many European designers, plus standard fashion accessories and various gift items. This is one of the area's oldest shops.

Emanuel Ungaro
413 N. Rodeo Drive; Beverly Hills; (213) 274-6294

French and Italian designer clothing for men and women plus belts, bags, scarves, and other accessories.

Fendi
441 N. Rodeo Drive; Beverly Hills; (213) 271-0600

Exclusive Italian designer fashions for men and women plus leather purses, bags, belts and wallets.

Gianni Versace
421 N. Rodeo Drive; Beverly Hills; (213) 276-6799

Versace's own famous Italian designer wear for women and men is here plus shoes, ties, bags, accessories, and perfume.

Giorgio's
273 N. Rodeo Drive; Beverly Hills; (213) 278-7312

Giorgio's number-one seller is a new cologne that is definitely worth a sample. Also try on the trendy clothing for men and women with logos galore.

Gucci
347 N. Rodeo Drive; Beverly Hills; (213) 278-3451

Prestigious and expensive clothing, boots, shoes, gifts, and jewelry for men and women.

Jerry Magnin
323 N. Rodeo Drive; Beverly Hills; (213) 273-5910

A rich supply of men's wear, including formal and sportswear and featuring the Ralph Lauren "Polo" line.

Louis Vuitton
433 N. Rodeo Drive; Beverly Hills; (213) 859-0457

Stop here for the famous designer logo purses and luggage for men and women.

Nina Ricci
431 N. Rodeo Drive; Beverly Hills; (213) 858-8081

French designer dresses, sportswear, and accessories for women.

Nino Cerruti
421 N. Rodeo Drive; Beverly Hills; (213) 859-8558

Featuring imported Italian designer clothing for men and women.

The Rodeo Collection
421 N. Rodeo Drive; Beverly Hills; (213) 276-9600

This elegant and cosmopolitan shopping center lays the riches of Beverly Hills at your feet. The three-level building houses many famous European designer names from Versace to Yves St.-Laurent. Parking is also convenient in the adjacent private lot. This is really the crème de la crème of shopping atmosphere and the top of the price line. Please note that several Rodeo Collection stores have separate locations also in Beverly Hills. Among the Collection stores are:

Theodore Mann
451 N. Rodeo Drive; Beverly Hills; (213) 274-8029

Mann features European designers only with a range of dress and sportswear for men and women.

Theodore's
453 N. Rodeo Drive; Beverly Hills; (213) 276-9691

Women's formal and casual wear plus jewelry.

Yves St.-Laurent
417. N. Rodeo Drive; Beverly Hills; (213) 274-4483

Here you'll find the prestigious French designer's clothing and accessories for men and women—plus that well-known perfume.

Also Recommended:

Santa Monica Place
Colorado Avenue and 2nd St.;
315 Broadway; Santa Monica; (213) 394-5451

Over 150 stores, all types and sizes, are located in the Santa Monica Place, including Robinson's and Broadway. There are also restaurants and concessions. You'll find everything you need at this mall.

South Coast Plaza
3333 Bristol Street; Costa Mesa; (714) 546-6682

One of the finest collections of better stores in Southern California. You will find I. Magnin, Bullock's, Jaeger, Nordstrom's, and lots of top-notch boutiques like Courrèges and Krön Chocolatier in the big and beautiful mall. And across the street is the Noguchi Sculpture Garden at the Town Center.

Tower Records
8801 Sunset Boulevard; West Hollywood; (213) 657-7300

The "largest record store in the known world," this place is a continual wonder. People come and go, mill about and listen to the heavy strains of the latest group pulsate over the PA system. You will find simply anything you want at Tower Records, which is open every day (including Christmas!) until midnight. The classical-music section is located in its own annexed building across the street.

Westwood Village
Between Wilshire Boulevard and LeConte Avenue; Gayley
and Tiverton

The place where Hollywood likes to test their movies, and for
a reason: kids, kids, kids! It's located just south of UCLA (but,
to be fair, USC students enjoy the village just as much!), and
you'll find high-school, college, junior-high-school, and post-
school-age folk enjoying the shops and sights of Westwood.
Fight through the movie lines, and you'll find all types of small
shops, plus a large number of bookstores and confectionary-
type offerings. The big department store of the area is Bullock's.

Woodland Hills Promenade
Oxnard and Erwin Street on Topanga Canyon; Woodland
Hills; (213) 884-6750

A beautiful indoor mall that has attracted some of the finest
stores in the area, including Saks Fifth Avenue, Bullock's
Wilshire, Ann Taylor. Beautiful landscaping adds to the ambience.

Health and Beauty Spots

Aida Grey
9549 Wilshire Boulevard; Beverly Hills; (213) 276-2376

All kinds of beauty treatments are offered here: from manicures and pedicures to body massages and leg waxing plus a full-service hair salon. Miss Grey's famous "Day of Beauty" includes skin care, makeup tips, plus hairstyling.

Aida Thibiant
449 North Canon Drive; Beverly Hills; (213) 278-7565

The full range of skin and body care is available here, but the most popular services are Aida Thibiant's own inventions. One is "the European body facial" and the other is the sophisticated "panthermal" steam cabinet desired to rid the body of toxins.

Ambassador Tennis and Health Club
3400 Wilshire Boulevard; Mid-Wilshire; (213) 387-7011

For members and guests of the hotel, this is a full health club that includes a number of tennis courts.

The Ashram
2025 McKain Street; Calabasas, California; (213) 888-0232

A full-blown health spa, the Ashram offers a week of fitness, diet, and spiritual renewal.

Christine Valmy Skin Care Salon
9675 Wilshire Boulevard; Beverly Hills; (213) 273-3723

Lots of unique services here including a seven-day cosmetic skin peel with dramatic results. The "ultra treatment" and "the vegetal peel" are favorite facials. The three lines of Valmy skin-care products are pure and natural, and one is custom-blended in the lab for individual skin types. Call for a complimentary consultation.

Elizabeth Arden
434 North Rodeo Drive; Beverly Hills; (213) 273-9980

Elizabeth Arden is famous for its beauty treatments, which pamper the customer. All areas of the beauty treatment are offered. "Red Door Beauty Labs" and "Advanced Red Door Beauty Workshops" teach beginners and pros all the newest glamour techniques.

Florence Brossier Inc.
203½ South Beverly Drive; Beverly Hills; (213) 858-8511

The unique service is the full-body "balneotherapy," Ms. Brossier's own invention to combat cellulite and weight trouble. The treatment combines a bath, French seaweed wrap, and a vibro massage. Facials, makeup artistry, and Florence Brossier's exclusive line of collagen/elastin creams are available.

Georgette Klinger
312 North Rodeo Drive; Beverly Hills; (213) 274-6347

A complete skin-care and hair salon favored by many celebrities including Valerie Perrine, Cindy Williams, and the "Dallas" TV cast. Makeovers and full-body massages for women are popular. Ms. Klinger has her own New York labs, where she produces the skin care of makeup products for her salons. Full- or half-day treatments for men and women include lunch.

The Golden Door
777 Deer Springs Rd.; San Marcos; (619) 744-5777

This is truly a spectacular, ultra-deluxe health and beauty spa. During the week-long stay, you'll be pampered while you exercise and diet. It's a very special place.

Holiday Health Club
Various locations; (213) 469-6307 (Hollywood)

The Holiday Health Spas offer the full range of equipment (Nautilus and Universal), plus pools, Jacuzzis, steam rooms, and the ever-popular aerobics classes.

Jack La Lanne's European Health Spa
Various locations; (213) 938-3851 (Los Angeles)

Jack La Lanne's offers full health-club facilities, including weight machines, pools, saunas, and aerobics classes.

Jessica's Nail Clinic
8627 Sunset Boulevard; Los Angeles; (213) 659-9292

The specialty here is a fabulous nail-conditioning treatment that takes about one hour. Pedicures and waxing are also offered.

La Costa Hotel and Spa
Rancho La Costa; Carlsbad; (619) 438-9111

There isn't a set program at La Costa, but health and beauty facilities are available to anyone who wishes to partake. Tennis courts, golf, swimming, and fitness classes are available, as are beauty treatments.

Los Angeles Department of Recreation and Parks
For general information; call (213) 485-5515

Public swimming pools, golf courses, and tennis courts are available, most for a small fee.

Le Hot Tub Club
8054 W. Third Street; Los Angeles; (213) 653-4410

Purely for the purposes of relaxation, Le Hot Tub Club is just that: a building with nothing but small rooms, each equipped with a warm and bubbly hot tub, shower, and lounging area. Music is piped in on eight different channels to add to the atmosphere.

Nautilus Plus
Various locations; (213) 629-4336 (Los Angeles)

Nautilus Plus, naturally, offers full Nautilus equipment, plus aerobics and fitness classes.

Ole Henriksen of Denmark Skin Care
8601 West Sunset; Los Angeles; (213) 854-7700

An all-natural Scandinavian approach to skin care featuring facials, full-body waxing, makeup lessons, and manicuring.

Shirle's Fitness Center
Various locations; (213) 394-6782 (Santa Monica)

For women only, this health club offers lots and lots of aerobic and fitness classes. They also have saunas and steam rooms.

Sports Connection
Various locations; (213) 450-4464 (Santa Monica)

A full-range health club, the Sports Connection offers classes all day in aerobics, slimnastics, yoga, plus separate facilities for men and women. A lap pool, saunas, and steam rooms are available, as are full-body massages and tanning salons.

Suzanne's Clinique de Beauté
9424 Dayton Way, Suite 209; Beverly Hills; (213) 271-5850

A salon providing all kinds of facials for all skin types and ages. Correctional treatments are for faces only—no body work. Brow waxing is also offered.

Services

Food/Catering

Ambrosia
218 Pier Avenue; Santa Monica; (213) 392-8547

Epicurean catering for all social occasions. Ambrosia will handle all arrangements for parties of all sizes. Don't miss the chocolate truffles, delivered from San Francisco.

Charmer's Market, Bar and Restaurant
175 Marine Street; Santa Monica; (213) 399-9160

You'll have to do it yourself here going from counter to counter, gathering up all the freshly made items offered. Esoteric beer drinkers love the collection, and a moderately good wine selection is also available. Fresh pasta is available and a stop at the pastry counter overwhelms the senses. Counter displays are artistically done. Don't miss the clever spoof of "the Hollywood Walk of Fame" under your feet. And the best for last, the mousse and all the pastries are superb.

Greenblatt's
8017 W. Sunset Boulevard; West Hollywood;
(213) 656-0606

At Greenblatt's, a full deli is at your disposal. Freshly made cold salads can be side dishes to the full array of deli meats (including barbecued chicken). Fresh pastries are delightful, and the complete liquor store is an added bonus. Party platters prepared on request.

Junior's
2379 Westwood Boulevard; West Los Angeles;
(213) 475-5771

Junior's is a huge deli-bakery-restaurant. It's always crowded and the service can be slow. But the deli items, including the fresh-baked goodies, make you forget the difficult moments.

Jurgensen's
Various locations

Jurgensen's is one of the finest market chains in the city. It also has a small deli counter, where fresh salads and cooked meats are available. The bakery section offers freshly baked pastries. Picnic dinners and lunches are packed to go.

Michel Richard
310 South Robertson Boulevard; Beverly Hills;
(213) 275-5707; other location: 12321 Ventura Boulevard;
(213) 508-9977

Noted for sumptuous pastries, Michel Richard also offers food. But it's the cakes and tarts that are the specialties. If it's a special occasion, come here for your special dessert.

Pasta Pasta Pasta
8161 W. Third Street; Los Angeles; (213) 653-2051

A "one-stop shop for Northern Italian food," the service is always pleasant and the food is wonderful. Picnic baskets are also prepared.

Pioneer Boulangeries and Restaurant
2102 Main Street; Santa Monica; (213) 399-1405

A wonderful combination of deli, wine shop, and bakery surrounded by an indoor Basque restaurant and an outdoor cafeteria-style café. Shop from counter to counter to take out or eat in. Strong selections of wines, breads, cheeses, and pâtés. Breakfast, lunch, and dinner served.

Via Dolce Confectioners
215 E. Rose Avenue; Santa Monica; (213) 399-1774

The true definition of decadence. Liqueurs are blended with all kinds of homemade Venetian ice creams and gourmet chocolate candies. Ice-cream tasting is provided for first-timers. The award-winning Via Dolce also exports its goodies to Macy's, Robinson's, Sakowitz, and Buffums.

Weby's Delicatessen and Bakery
12131 Ventura Boulevard; Studio City; (213) 761-9391

A full-service deli and bakery under one roof. Sumptuous party platters can be ordered, including a variety of quiches. Also don't miss the tasty array of breads and cakes.

X-Rated Cakes
9029 Santa Monica Boulevard; West Hollywood;
(213) 276-9207

Anything you want is painted on a sheet cake, and the job is fabulous. Erotic, novelty, and specialty cakes and candies for any occasion are available. True works of art.

Yorkshire Grill
610 West 6th Street; Los Angeles; (213) 629-3020

A great place to get hot or cold sandwiches to go.

Flowers

Arturo's Flowers
1261 N. La Brea Avenue; Hollywood; (corner La Brea and Fountain); (213) 876-6482

All the usual florist services for all occasions, including citywide delivery, but the *real* feature is the Hollywood atmosphere. Campy window displays related to popular films are a must stop. Inside, you'll be surprised by a piano man singing nostalgic tunes.

Broadway Florist
218 W. 5th Street; Downtown Los Angeles; (213) 626-5511

With branch offices in Beverly Hills, San Marino.

Conroy's Florist
374 S. La Cienega; West Hollywood; (corner La Cienega and 4th) (various other locations); (213) 659–6616

Excellent quality fresh-cut flowers, plants, and decorative accessories. Great sales—especially on roses. This small chain features worldwide delivery. One of L.A's original, quality flower shops.

Crossley's Flowers
7819 Beverly Boulevard; Los Angeles; (213) 938-7172

With other offices in the Beverly Wilshire Hotel and the Beverly Hills Hotel.

La Cienega Flower Shop
8101 Melrose Avenue; West Hollywood; (213) 653-5444

With other stores in Beverly Hills and Mid-Wilshire areas.

Posie Peddler
4917 Melrose Avenue; Hollywood; (213) 465-2151

The best place to go for unusual floral arrangements and made-to-order designs. Very, very special.

University Florist
3203 S. Hoover Street; across from USC campus;
(213) 747-2234

Another shop is now in the University Hilton Hotel. The closest florist to the Olympic Games.

Balloons

Balloon Affair
10825 Washington Boulevard
Culver City
(213) 838-1889

Balloon Express
9062 W. Pico Boulevard
Los Angeles
(213) 272-8787

Balloon Bouquets
311 North Kings Road
Los Angeles
(213) 653-4062

Balloon Factory
8600 West Third St.
Los Angeles
(213) 275-0007

Kites

Colors of the Wind
2900 Main Street
Santa Monica
(213) 399-8044

Let's Fly a Kite
13755 Fiji Way
Marina del Rey
(213) 822-2561

Personal

Ambulance
(For Los Angeles City, call
[213] 384-3131)

Fire Station
(For Los Angeles City, call
[213] 384-3131)

Paramedics
(For Los Angeles City, call
[213] 384-3131)

Police or Sheriff
(or Highway Patrol)
Police or Sheriff: (for Los

Angeles City): (213) 485-2121;
(213) 625-3311
Highway Patrol: for emergency
in all localities, dial "O" and
ask for Zenith 1-2000.

**Los Angeles Olympic
Organizing Committee**
Olympic Information
(213) 209-4026
Employment (213) 209-4135
Ticket Information
(213) 520-1984
Arts Festival (213) 305-8444

Pharmacies

Horton and Converse
(Various locations throughout
the Southland)
For Los Angeles:
8631 W. 3rd Street
Los Angeles
(213) 659-6111

Rexall Discount Drugs
(Various locations)
For Los Angeles:
Rexall Square Drugs
8490 Beverly Boulevard
Los Angeles
(213) 653-4616

Sav-on Discount Drugs
(Various locations)
Downtown Los Angeles:
201 N. Los Angeles Street
Los Angeles
(213) 620-1494

**Thrifty Drug and Discount
Stores**
(Various locations)
For general information:
(213) 293-5111

Cleaners

Hollyway Cleaners
8359 Santa Monica Boulevard
West Hollywood
(213) 654-1271
1159 Echo Park Avenue
Echo Park
(213) 250-3961

Norge Laundry and Cleaning Village Stores
(Various locations)
7152 Melrose Avenue
Hollywood
(213) 939-7722
3824 Crenshaw Boulevard
Los Angeles
(213) 295-4811
1029 W. El Segundo Boulevard
Gardena (213) 777-9135

Rocket Cleaners
3650 Crenshaw Boulevard
Los Angeles
(213) 298-8721
1247 W. Washington Boulevard
Los Angeles
(213) 745-8390
2518 Daly; Los Angeles
(213) 225-6456

Sloan's Dry Cleaners & Laundry
Call main office for location
nearest you: (213) 225-1303

Churches

Archdiocese of Los Angeles Catholic Information Center
809 South Flower Street
Los Angeles
(213) 627-4861

Armenian Catholic Church Queen of Martyrs
Sunday service 10 & 11 A.M.
1 block east of Macy and
Mission
1339 Pleasant Avenue
(213) 261-9898

Chinese Congregational
734 9th Place
Los Angeles
(213) 688-0973

Church of Jesus Christ of the Latter-day Saints
Los Angeles Temple
10777 Santa Monica Blvd.
Los Angeles
(213) 272-8726

First Congregational Church
540 South Commonwealth Ave.
Los Angeles
(213) 385-1341

German United Methodist First Church
449 South Olive
Los Angeles
(213) 628-3813

The nave of St. Vincent de Paul's Church between the Coliseum and downtown Los Angeles.

Good Shepherd Catholic Church
505 North Bedford Drive
Beverly Hills
(213) 276-3139

Korean First Presbyterian Church
213 South Hobart Blvd.
Los Angeles
(213) 388-7101

Koyasan Buddhist Temple
342 East 1st Street
Los Angeles
(213) 624-1267

Newman Center-USC (Our Savior's)
(213) 749-5321

Nishi Hongwanji Buddhist Temple
815 East 1st Street
Los Angeles
(213) 680-9130

St. Basil's Catholic Church
637 South Kingsley Drive
(213) 381-6191

Saint Vincent de Paul Roman Catholic Church
621 West Adams Blvd.
Los Angeles
(213) 749-8950

Temple Beth Am
1039 La Cienega
West Los Angeles
(213) 652-7353

University Synagogue
11960 Sunset Blvd.
West Los Angeles
(213) 472-1255

Westwood United Methodist Church
10497 Wilshire Blvd.
Westwood
(213) 879-0281

Wilshire United Methodist Church
4350 Wilshire Blvd.
Los Angeles
(213) 931-1085

The Desert Has Bloomed:
Arts and Culture in Los Angeles
by Charles Champlin, Arts Editor

No city in which the Three Stooges filmed their finest hours, *The Drunkard* ran nightly for twenty-six years, and Tarzan had a suburb named for him can fairly be called a cultural desert.

But Los Angeles used to be so called, with a grain of cruel truth, despite the existence of a symphony orchestra, theaters, art collections, and a remarkable population of authors, composers, artists, directors, and distinguished actors and actresses.

Desert or oasis, Los Angeles has undergone a dramatic cultural greening in the last quarter-century. It is not to be compared with New York, London, or Paris for either the antiquity or the depth of its offerings, but its museums, galleries, theaters, and arenas have an unstaid freshness, verve, and openness that are unique and beguiling.

The post–World War II growth in the Los Angeles cultural scene has echoed the general vitality of the city. There has been an upsurge in population (a doubling since 1940, from 1.5 million to 3 million), and a great expansion in institutions of higher education, reflecting the national cultural optimism. New and enlarged public campuses like the University of California, Los Angeles (UCLA), and private institutions like the University of Southern California (USC) became and have remained lively and important centers for appearances by both local and visiting creators. (The Center Theater Group, now based at the Mark Taper Forum of the Music Center in downtown Los Angeles, had its origins in the late 1950s on the

UCLA campus under John Houseman, the late Robert Ryan, and others.)

The earliest civic embellishments of the 1960s cultural renewal were the Music Center complex atop Bunker Hill in downtown Los Angeles, and the Los Angeles County Museum of Art, just now completing a major expansion. Both have been functioning since 1964.

The city now has an uncommon richness of museums of many kinds, including what can be called the Exposition Park assemblage: the museums of Science and Industry, Natural History, Space, and others, the newest of which will be a Museum of Afro-American Art, now under way.

A surprise to many visitors may well be the extent and diversity of the city's public art collections, commencing at the handsome County Art Museum, with its eclectic and admirable offerings, from classical to ethnic to current California. But there are as well the Norton Simon Museum (formerly the Pasadena Art Museum, rescued by the financier partly as a home for his own matchless acquisitions), the small and charming Getty Museum founded by the late billionaire J. Paul Getty at the ocean in Malibu, and most recently, the brashly unorthodox Temporary Contemporary, constructed in the former Police Department garage near Little Tokyo in downtown Los Angeles, serving as the impermanent home of the Museum of Contemporary Art being built near the Music Center on Bunker Hill.

A stretch of La Cienega Boulevard running south from Santa Monica in West Hollywood is the Madison Avenue/57th Street or the Cork Street/Bond Street of Los Angeles; the number of commercial galleries, and the aspirations of the artists on view in many of them, hint at the extent to which Los Angeles has become a center for artists and collectors.

In the 1960s, West Coast artists such as Sam Francis, Frank Stella, Ed Kienholz, and Ken Price were making artworld news. And while no second wave of comparable prominence (or price) has yet emerged, the vitality on view is exciting and promising.

Given the presence of films and television and a large attendant, or expectant, colony of actors, it is not surprising that there has always been a good deal of theatrical activity in Los

The Getty Museum in Malibu. This graceful colonnaded walkway faces onto the central courtyard. *Julius Shulman*

Angeles, not all of it commercial and conspicuous. There has probably been an off-Sunset for as long as there has been an off-Broadway—cellar, attic, and storefront stages designed mostly to give actors the chance to practice their craft.

Today Los Angeles has an extraordinary number of little theaters, often built around acting workshops, with ninety-nine or fewer seats (by contract), presenting experimental work and obscure revivals as well as standard repertory, frequently featuring faces you might recognize from the TV screen. The plays are reviewed and listed (even if few can afford to advertise) and have become a nourishing ingredient in the local cultural diet well worth seeking out.

If two decades ago the Biltmore, now defunct, was the last theater large enough to accommodate a musical, and the Huntington Hartford, a gem of a smaller theater, was virtually the only surviving Class A house, the scene has changed dramatically.

The Music Center gave the city three new stages: the Dorothy Chandler Pavilion, permanent base for the Los Angeles Philharmonic under the soon-to-retire Carlo-Maria Giulini; the Mark Taper Forum, a smaller thrust-stage arena presenting innovative and sometimes controversial work; and the Ahmanson, a more traditional theater offering starry commercial dramas and musicals.

The Music Center was followed in Century City by the new Shubert Theater, which specializes in long-running Broadway imports, and by the reconstituted Pantages, an ornate early Hollywood cinema, now turned to legitimate stage. At least two other cinemas have converted to living performance and there have been several long-running hits at smaller theaters in Hollywood. Once dangerously near extinction, commercial theater has made a vigorous comeback.

Los Angeles has probably become the most important center for rock- and pop-music recording in the country, and accordingly has an abundance of rock-oriented clubs plus a heavy calendar of concerts at the Forum, the Universal Amphitheater, and other arenas.

The Philharmonic gained new attention under Zubin Mehta and new prestige internationally under Giulini. Opera here has suffered, as elsewhere, from rising costs and limited revenues; but the dance picture has been improved by the arrival of the semipermanent company, the Joffrey Ballet, dividing its year between Los Angeles and New York. The Bella Lewitsky Dance Company and the valiant and surviving Los Angeles Ballet under John Clifford make the dance offerings more varied than they have been in years.

Hollywood, through its films and now its television production, continues to exert a heavy hold on the world's imagination. Not surprisingly, the studios—what can be seen of them—and tickets for television tapings are priority items for visitors. The footprints left by departed giants in the forecourt of Mann's (formerly Grauman's) Chinese Theater on Hollywood Boulevard are still studied and photographed by thousands.

The Universal Studio Tour, relatively expensive and more entertaining than informative, has been a roaring success and is now the center of a still-expanding complex that includes a five-thousand-seat enclosed amphitheater, two hotels, and several restaurants; jostled by all the new construction but busy and hugely prosperous is the studio itself, dating from 1915, once a bean ranch and citrus grove.

By now the cultural desert has bloomed; visitors who can tear themselves away from sand, sea, sport, and surprisingly splendid food face a formidable but pleasing set of choices, including those unmusty museums and, of course, those footprints in the forecourt.

A Guide to Museums, Architecture, and Historic Sites

Avila Adobe
10 Olvera Street; Downtown Los Angeles; (213) 628-1274

Reportedly the oldest existing residence in Los Angeles. It serves as a museum of California life during the 1840s. Built by Don Francisco Avila.

Bonnie Brae Street
800 and 1000 blocks of South Bonnie Brae Street

Along these streets are some of the city's finest Victorian houses. They have been restored and are well maintained.

Bradbury Building
Broadway and Third Street; 304 South Broadway;
(213) 489-1411

This elegant and spacious structure was built in 1893 complete with skylighted atrium, open-cage elevators, and wrought-iron staircases. It is an excellent example of early commercial architecture.

Bullock's Wilshire
3050 Wilshire Boulevard; (213) 382-6161

A beautiful monument to Art Deco, this structure serves as a department store. Built in 1929, it had much influence on the westward expansion of Los Angeles.

Carroll Avenue
1300 Block of Carroll Avenue; (213) 624-5657

A Hollywood landmark since 1927, Mann's Chinese Theatre was conceived by the showman Sid Grauman. The famed entry courtyard contains the hand- and footprints of many stars.

This is one of the first suburban areas of the city. A number of Victorian homes remain and have been kept up and restored. The Carroll Avenue Foundation encourages preservation and offers annual tours of the homes.

Casino (Catalina)

This Spanish-Moderne structure is the primary landmark on the island of Catalina. Built in 1929 on the northwest end of Crescent Bay, it houses an art gallery, museum, motion-picture theater, and a ballroom.

Cliff May Office
13151 Sunset Boulevard; (213) 472-9576

Cliff May is the architect who popularized the California ranch-house style of architecture. This is the office in which he worked. Some of his other works can be seen in the area.

Coca-Cola Building
1334 South Central Avenue; (213) 746-2653

Five industrial buildings have been transformed by architect Robert V. Derrah into what looks like a giant ocean liner, complete with flying bridge.

Doheny Mansion/Chester Place

Chester Place near Adams Boulevard and the Harbor Freeway is part of a fifteen-acre residential park built around the turn of the century. Located here is the Doheny Mansion, considered one of the finest examples of French Gothic Château architecture in Los Angeles.

Gamble House
4 Westmoreland Place; Pasadena; (213) 793-3334

Charles and Henry Greene designed this masterpiece for David Gamble in 1908. Innovative in use of space and detailing, it was considered radical by many at the time of its construction. Gamble deeded this timeless structure to the City of Pasadena and the University of California.

General Phineas Banning Residence Museum
401 East M Street; Wilmington; (213) 548-7777

Greek-revival clapboard home built by the father of the Los Angeles Harbor, General Phineas Banning. It is located in Banning Park. Tour only. Admission free. Open Wednesday, Saturday, and Sunday.

Herald Examiner Building
1111 South Broadway; (213) 744-8000

Designed by Julia Morgan for William Randolph Hearst in 1903, it features the Spanish Mission Revival design and was inspired by the California Building at the 1893 Chicago World's Fair.

Heritage Square
3800 North Homer Street; Highland Park; (213) 222-3150

This square contains a collection of Victorian homes and a railroad station, all of which the Cultural Heritage Foundation relocated just off the Pasadena Freeway at Avenue Forty-three.

Hollyhock House
4800 Hollywood Boulevard at Vermont Avenue; Hollywood;
(213) 662-7272

This Frank Lloyd Wright house, now a cultural center, has
been restored by the city. It sits in Barnsdall Park on what was
once an olive grove.

Huntington Library and Gardens
1151 Oxford Drive; San Marino; (213) 792-6141

Formerly the residence of Henry E. Huntington, railroad tycoon, this 207-acre estate now houses a library, art gallery,
and botanical gardens. Among the famous works displayed in
the museum are Gainsborough's *Blue Boy* and Lawrence's
Pinkie. The library contains a Gutenberg bible, a first folio of
Shakespeare plays, and Ben Franklin's autobiography in manuscript.

J. Paul Getty Museum
17985 Pacific Coast Highway; Malibu; (213) 454-6541

This was built by oil billionaire J. Paul Getty as a replica of
a Roman seaside villa. It features Greek and Roman antiquities,
as well as European paintings from the Renaissance through
Baroque period. Open mid-June to mid-September. Parking
reservations are required.

Los Angeles Central Library
Fifth and Hope streets; 630 West Fifth Street;
(213) 626-7461

This impressive structure is a combination of various exotic
styles popular in the 1920s. The interior murals are by Dean
Cornwall and exemplify the period of pre-WPA American mu-
ral painting.

Los Angeles County Museum of Art
5905 Wilshire Boulevard; (213) 937-2590

Designed by William Pereira and Associates and opened in
1964, the museum complex is divided into three separate structures. The Ahmanson gallery houses the permanent collection,

the Hammer gallery exhibits temporary shows, and the Leo S. Bing Theater is used for regularly scheduled film series.

Los Angeles Mall

Main Street between First and north of Temple Street

Designed in 1975 by architects Stanton and Stockwell, the multilevel Mall contains shops, restaurants, and underground parking.

Los Angeles Times
202 West First Street; (213) 972-5000

Designed of beige limestone by Gordon Kaufman in 1935, it blends well with the steel and glass Times Mirror building recently done by William Pereira and Associates.

Mann's Chinese Theater
6925 Hollywood Boulevard; (213) 464-8111

The theater is most famous for its courtyard of footprints, handprints, and signatures of more than 160 stars. The design is also dramatic, an exotic interpretation of a Chinese temple with turned-up dragontail edges.

Mission San Fernando Rey de España
15151 San Fernando Mission Boulevard; (213) 361-0186

This mission was founded in 1797, but had to be rebuilt twice because of natural disasters. Still the richness of the adobe construction remains.

Mission San Gabriel Archangel
537 West Mission Drive; San Gabriel; (213) 282-5191

Built about 1812 by the Franciscan fathers, these mission buildings have been rebuilt and restored after years of neglect and natural disasters.

Mission San Juan Capistrano
Camino Capistrano and Ortega Highway; (714) 493-1111

Founded in 1776 by Father Junípero Serra, this simple adobe structure is considered one of the oldest churches in California.

The return of the swallows to Capistrano is celebrated each year on March 19, St. Joseph's Day. The birds nest in the ruins of the church.

Los Angeles Music Center
135 North Grand Avenue; Downtown

A lofty colonnade joins the Mark Taper Forum and the Ahmanson Theatre. There is a Jacques Lipchitz sculpture in the mall pool opening up to a view of the Dorothy Chandler Pavilion. All three structures offer plays and symphonies in varying degrees of size.

Neutra House
2300 East Silverlake Boulevard; Los Angeles

Built in 1932 out of experimental materials, this was architect Richard Neutra's home. Rebuilt after a fire in 1963, it is still considered a landmark in modern architecture.

Oviatt Building
617 South Olive Street; Los Angeles; (213) 623-5050

Designer René Lalique utilized etched-glass panel ceilings, mailboxes, and doors to fashion the most prestigious downtown men's store in 1927. Currently it functions as an office building, with an elegant Italian restaurant, The Rex, on the ground floor.

Pacific Design Center
8687 Melrose Avenue; (213) 657-0800

Nicknamed the "Blue Whale," this immense glass structure was designed in 1975 by Cesar Pelli. It houses interior-design businesses and dominates the surrounding area.

Pellissier Building
Southeast Corner of Wilshire and Western;
3780 Wilshire Boulevard

An interesting example of pre-Depression Art Deco architecture when buildings were extravagant, glittering, and decorative. 1930.

Pico House
430 North Main Street; Los Angeles

Built in 1868 by Don Pedro Pico, the last Mexican governor of California. The Pico House was the first three-story masonry building constructed in Los Angeles. It has recently been restored.

St. Basil's Catholic Church
637 South Kingsley Drive (at Wilshire Boulevard);
(213) 381-6191

This large church contains the Stations of the Cross by Franco Asseto done in huge plaster castings.

St. Vincent de Paul Roman Catholic Church
612 West Adams Boulevard; (213) 749-8950

A fine example of Churrigueresque architecture, named after Baroque architect José Churriguera. Its walls are decorated with huge intricate panels of meta-Baroque ornament.

Union Station
800 North Alameda Street; (213) 624-0171

The last great railroad passenger terminal built in the United States. Lofty wood-beamed ceilings and marble floors highlight this Spanish Mission design.

Watts Towers
1765 East 107th Street; (213) 623-2697

A series of spires created by Simon Rodia out of salvaged metal and cement, taking over thirty years to complete. Disfigured by vandals, this work of art was finally saved by citizens and is currently undergoing renovation.

Wayfarer's Chapel
5755 Palos Verdes Drive South; Rancho Palos Verdes; (213) 377-4458

Designed in 1946 by Lloyd Wright as a monument to Emanuel Swedenborg, the chapel blends into the hillside environment. Built out of glass and redwood, it is practically transparent as it overlooks the ocean and the South Bay coastline.

Additional Reading

"No one reads in Los Angeles." Maybe not, but for some weird L.A. reason there is much in print on Los Angeles, and by publishers from such literary meccas as London, San Francisco, and New York.

For the record, there are ninety newspapers, including fourteen dailies. The major metropolitan dailies (the *Los Angeles Times*, the *Herald Examiner*, the *Daily News*, etc.), and *California Magazine* and *Los Angeles Magazine*; and the alternative weeklies: *The Reader* and *LA Weekly*. And don't forget the daily *Hollywood Reporter*.

For books, a few among the many:

1. *California Coastal Access Guide* (University of California Press).

2. *Hiking Trails in the Santa Monica Mountains* (Canyon Publishing).

3. *LA/Access*, a general and useful guidebook to Los Angeles (Access Press).

4. *Trails of the Angeles: 100 Hikes in the San Gabriels* (Wilderness Press).

5. *Glad Rags II*, a delightful shopping and bargain-hunters guide (Chronicle Books, San Francisco).

6. *The Flavor of Los Angeles*, a very useful guide to ethnic restaurants including African, Armenian, and Argentinian (Chronicle Books, San Francisco).

7. Lois Dwan's *The Los Angeles Times Guide to Dining Out in L.A.* (NAL, New York).

8. *Southern California County*, by Carey McWilliams (1946), the classic writer on Southern California.

9. *Los Angeles, An Illustrated History*. Not flashy, but terrific pictorial glimpses of the past. (Alfred Knopf, New York).

10. *The Big Orange*, by Jack Smith (1976). Mr. Smith is the most popular present-day commentator; his daily columns in the *Los Angeles Times* are followed as avidly as the Dodgers and the Lakers.

11. *Los Angeles, the Architecture of Four Ecologues*, by Reyner Banham (1971, London). The classic analysis of the city of the future.

12. *The Best of Los Angeles*: *A Discriminating Guide* (Rosebud Books, 1980). This book is out of date as a guide, but it is one of the best overall introductions to Southern California, a "reader" to be sampled in order to understand the diversity of local lifestyles and their richness.

13. *The Architecture of Los Angeles* (Rosebud Books, 1981). A large-format hardcover, the best overall presentation of diverse and rich architectural styles of Los Angeles. Published in collaboration with Los Angeles Conservancy.

Index

SIGNET Books for Your Reference Shelf

Other SIGNET Books You'll Enjoy

(0451)

☐ **ENCYCLOPEDIA OF AMAZING BUT TRUE FACTS by Doug Stover.** Fantastic events, fascinating people, unusual animals—all gathered together in an around-the-world collection that ranges from the bizarre to the miraculous. Complete with over 200 incredible photos. (115597—$3.50)*

☐ **HOW TO KNOW THE BIRDS by Roger Tory Peterson.** Here is an authoritative, on-the-spot guide to help you recognize instantly most American birds on sight. Includes a 24-page color supplement. (129393—$4.50)*

☐ **HOW TO KNOW THE AMERICAN MARINE SHELLS by R. Tucker Abbott. Revised edition.** A definitive guide to the shells of our Atlantic and Pacific coasts—featuring a digest of shell-fishery laws, a list of shells by location, full-color photographs, and black and white drawings. (06528X—$1.50)

☐ **THE AMATEUR MAGICIAN'S HANDBOOK by Henry Hay.** Fourth revised edition. A professional magician teaches you hundreds of the tricks of his trade in this unsurpassed, illustrated guide. (122569—$3.95)

*Price is slightly higher in Canada

Buy them at your local

bookstore or use coupon

on next page for ordering.

SIGNET Reference Books